Praise for the Second Edition of
HELPING TEENS STOP VIOLENCE, BUILD COMMUNITY AND STAND FOR JUSTICE

"Remember when we were young people and we vowed to make the world a better place? This book provides insight, skills, and inspiration for creating youth–adult alliances that facilitate youth leadership and the creation of just, safe, and healed communities."

— Sharon Turner, Regional Director,
STAND! for Families Free of Violence

"This is essential reading for anyone working to prevent violence, from policy makers to parents and youth. I commend the book's emphasis on fostering environments that promote safety. The authors have in-depth knowledge and personal experience about what it takes to transform communities, and they have effectively translated this critical knowledge for a wide audience."

— Larry Cohen, Executive Director, Prevention Institute

"This book is a must-read for adults helping youth eliminate divisions based on race, gender, and sexual orientation; understand how to be allies to each other; and learn how to become leaders for social justice. *Helping Teens Stop Violence* should be required reading for any adult working with young people."

— Hugh Vasquez, social justice educator and
Senior Associate, National Equity Project

"*Helping Teens Stop Violence* offers practical and comprehensive insight and is a highly useful resource and set of tools that prepares educators, youth, and those of us concerned with the prevention of violence to better discuss, organize, and take action in the face of injustice."

— Ramesh Kathanadhi, domestic violence
prevention trainer and educator

Helping Teens Stop Violence, Build Community and Stand for Justice
is part of the **MAKING THE PEACE** program, which includes:

Making the Peace
A 15-Session Violence Prevention Curriculum for Young People (High School)

Making Allies, Making Friends
A Curriculum for Making the Peace in Middle School

Days of Respect
Organizing a School-Wide Violence Prevention Program

and four 22" × 32" classroom posters

Ordering
Trade bookstores in the U.S. and Canada please contact:

Publishers Group West
1700 Fourth Street, Berkeley CA 94710
Phone: (800) 788-3123   Fax: (800) 351-5073

Hunter House books are available at bulk discounts for textbook course adoptions;
to qualifying community, health-care, and government organizations;
and for special promotions and fund-raising. For details please contact:

Special Sales Department
Hunter House Inc., PO Box 2914, Alameda CA 94501-0914
Phone: (510) 865-5282   Fax: (510) 865-4295
E-mail: ordering@hunterhouse.com

Individuals can order our books from most bookstores,
by calling **(800) 266-5592**, or from our website at **www.hunterhouse.com**

HELPING TEENS STOP VIOLENCE, BUILD COMMUNITY AND STAND FOR JUSTICE

Twentieth Anniversary

SECOND EDITION

ALLAN CREIGHTON AND PAUL KIVEL

Hunter House PUBLISHERS

Hunter House Inc., Publishers
PO Box 2914
Alameda CA 94501-0914

Interior photos © Kathy Sloane. Used with permission.

Library of Congress Cataloging-in-Publication Data
Creighton, Allan.
Helping teens stop violence, build community and stand for justice /
Allan Creighton and Paul Kivel.
p.   cm.
Rev. ed. of: Helping teens stop violence : a practical guide for counselors, educators, and parents / by Allan Creighton with Paul Kivel. 1st ed. c1992.
Includes bibliographical references.
ISBN 978-0-89793-568-5 (pbk.) — ISBN 978-0-89793-569-2 (spiral)
1. Social work with teenagers — United States.   2. Teenagers — Abuse of —
United States — Prevention.   I. Kivel, Paul.   II. Creighton, Allan.
Helping teens stop violence.   III. Title.
HV1431.C74 2011
362.76'8083 — dc22   2011003663

Project Credits

Cover Design: Brian Dittmar Design	Editorial Intern: Kelsey Comes
Book Production: John McKercher	Senior Marketing Associate: Reina Santana
Photographer: Kathy Sloane	Publicity Coordinator: Sean Harvey
Developmental Editor: Jude Berman	Rights Coordinator: Candace Groskreutz
Copy Editor: Heather Wilcox	Customer Service Manager: Christina Sverdrup
Proofreader: John David Marion	Order Fulfillment: Washul Lakdhon
Managing Editor: Alexandra Mummery	Administrator: Theresa Nelson
Acquisitions Assistant: Elizabeth Kracht	Computer Support: Peter Eichelberger
Publisher: Kiran S. Rana	

Printed and bound by Bang Printing, Brainerd, Minnesota
Manufactured in the United States of America

9 8 7 6 5 4 3 2 1   Second Edition   11 12 13 14 15

Contents

List of Exercises, Role-Plays, and Agreements

Acknowledgments

For this substantially revised and expanded edition of *Helping Teens Stop Violence*, we are grateful for the dense network of social justice activists, families, and friends who jointly developed and practiced the book's concepts, exercises, program directions, and spirit. They represent the several generations of facilitators and educators who carry on, develop, and improve the work. Prominent among them are our colleagues who directly reviewed the material: Jen Angel, Andrea del Moral, Ramesh Kathanadhi, Dana Kivel, Alberto Ledesma, Ariel Luckey, Nell Myhand, Hugh Vasquez, and Shirley Yee. Beyond this immediate circle are the founding generation of activists: Robert Allen, Nefer Ra Amen, Amy Bingamon, Isoke Femi, Linda Gonzalez, Lakota Harden, Cesar Lagleva, David Lee, Victor Lewis, and Yeshi Neumann, as well as Hugh, Nell, and Shirley. The inspiring next generation includes Jakada Amani, Amani Carey-Simms, Jeff Issenberg, and Sam and Ryan Luckey, as well as Ariel and Ramesh. Other fellow travelers are Ralph Cantor, Katiana Carey-Simms, Lisa Carey-Simms, Laura Head, Francie Kendall, Micki Luckey, Carrie McCluer, Sandra McGee, Julie Nesnansky, Amanda Salzman, Helen Schneider, Jackie Schonerd, Allan Shore, and our wonderful publisher, Kiran Rana. These and many others are among the members of the Oakland Men's Project (OMP) and STAND! (referenced below), as well as the former TODOS Alliance-Building Institute, the three primary locales and workplaces where these ideas and their applications first flourished.

Special thanks to the University of California Berkeley's Immigrant Student Issues Coalition, Summer Bridge project, Gender Equity Resource Center, and Sarah Gamble and the Health Promotion unit, where the latest versions of many of these exercises have been practiced. Thanks also to the trainers and facilitators of the Dismantling Oppression Working Group of the California Coalition Against Sexual Assault: Alena Donovan, Jacquie Marroquin, Lita Mercado, and Tiombe Preston.

Special thanks to David Ludlow for permission to revise and use "Facilitating Social Justice" and "Access Now" from Creighton and Vasquez's on-line curriculum *Building Social Justice*.

The original version of this book was produced through years of education and counseling for adolescent youth provided by STAND! For Families Free of Violence (originally named Battered Women's Alternatives) and the OMP. STAND!

is the authority on domestic and dating violence in Contra Costa County, California, operating since 1977 to provide counseling, shelter, legal support, life-skills training, and job placement for battered women and their children. OMP operated from 1979 to 1998 as a multiracial community-based violence prevention program dedicated to eliminating male violence and promoting cross-gender and cross-racial alliance.

For the original version, special thanks for thinking and direction to Kristy Brodeur, Tracy Cuneo, Isoke Femi, Rebecca Isaacs, Dana Kivel, Katie Krichbaum, Jenny Mish, Toni Taylor, Hugh Vasquez, and Steven Wisbaum. The Office of Criminal Justice Planning, the State of California, and the San Francisco Foundation provided funding for the original version.

We fondly remember and honor Erica Sherover-Marcuse and Harrison Simms, each of whom authored and inspired this vision and community, and Martin Cano, who created the foundational original of the "Class Race" exercise outlined in Section 3.

Finally, we acknowledge the essential role that thousands of young people have played in inspiring us and shaping this material to be relevant to their needs, hopes, and desires.

IMPORTANT NOTE

The material in this book is intended to provide a review of information regarding violence prevention and social-justice education. Every effort has been made to provide accurate and dependable information. The contents of this book have been compiled through professional research and in consultation with professionals in the fields of violence prevention and social-justice education. However, professionals have differing opinions, and some of the information may become outdated.

Therefore, the publisher, authors, and editors, as well as the professionals quoted in the book, cannot be held responsible for any error, omission, or dated material. The authors and publisher assume no responsibility for any outcome of applying the information in this book. If you have questions about the application of the information described in this book, consult a qualified professional.

Note for Parents

It is not easy being a parent, even in the best of times and circumstances. Today, in the face of massive cutbacks in jobs, benefits, education, child care, and other family support, it is even more difficult. Those of us who are single parents, step-parents, or lesbian or gay parents or who live in interfaith or multiracial families face even further difficulties. On top of all this is the reality of family and community violence we must prepare our children to face.

How do we support young people making choices and resolving conflicts using alternatives to violence? How do we give them the information they need, the benefits of our experience, and the access to resources without either overprotecting them or controlling them?

This manual identifies the violence that young people face in their daily lives. The best way to address these issues is through experiences you have in common with your children. Events and relationships within the neighborhood and family, the news, movies, and music all provide countless opportunities to discuss violence. Present family dynamics and past experiences of abuse, sibling relationships, falling in love, money, child-raising practices, social media and networking, cultural background, and jobs are also topics useful for raising issues of abuse and injustice with young people. Young people are often eager to talk if they feel respected, listened to, and not threatened, so if your family has a history of emotional, sexual, or physical abuse, this trauma must be addressed and healed first. If you have perpetuated a history of silence, denial of problems, or avoidance of difficult issues, it will take time for young people to believe that you honestly want to change those patterns. Trust builds slowly. After all, there are often few, if any, places that allow young people to feel safe from adult power. Be patient and honest. Don't promise more than you can provide.

Despite our best efforts, some young people will still take risks, including life-threatening ones. We can help them see the choices they have. Beyond that, sometimes the only thing we can do is let them know that we will be there when they need help or want to talk.

Our focus in this manual is on how we, as adults, can be more powerful allies for young people. Make a commitment to being a strong ally for young people and think realistically about what this will require of you.

Beyond this commitment, we must identify what we as adults carry with us from our own experiences of adolescence so these issues do not influence our interactions with young people today. You can use the exercises on pages 6–7, "I Remember When I Was Young" and "Adult–Youth Questions for Facilitators," to begin. Next we suggest you continue reading through the articles in Sections 1–3. If you have a partner or friends who are parents of adolescents, you might want to talk with them about the material in the articles. Supporting young people means supporting ourselves and each other as well.

Section 4, on education, may be useful in understanding what young people face in most school settings. It closes with outlines of our school-based curricula that we use in the classroom. Consulting these sections will help you learn how violence is learned and passed on. You may want to help organize a local team to do these presentations with young people or help set up support groups. Be creative. You probably influence young people other than your own children. They all could use your help supporting their safety, healing, and liberation. This manual will enhance your efforts to do so.

Introduction

Welcome to the twentieth-anniversary edition of what was originally titled *Helping Teens Stop Violence*. Our first book presented our work with young people in classes and support groups, addressing violence in families and relationships, particularly as it expressed larger societal and institutional oppressions based on gender, race, sexual orientation, economic background, and age. Since that first publication we have published curricula and books that expand and apply the ideas of *Helping Teens Stop Violence* to more detailed work with youth in middle and high schools as well as to in-depth examinations of several forms of oppression directly. Tie-ins to these works are outlined in Section 4.

But beyond the original setting for *Helping Teens Stop Violence*, how does violence fit into young people's lives, twenty years later? We have taken the occasion of rewriting this book to look at what young people are facing now in the United States at the end of the first decade of the twenty-first century.

In the United States today, millions of young people live in poverty; lack health care; experience physical, emotional, and sexual abuse from adults; and experience inadequate educational opportunities and a lack of living-wage job opportunities. Young people lack political representation, and many live in toxic environments. Adults and adult-centered institutions routinely belittle, interrupt, or criminalize young people's efforts to survive, sustain their relationships, nurture their opportunities, work for justice, and express their creativity.

At the same time, whole populations of young people are labeled as problems needing to be fixed: immature, irresponsible, dangerous threats to the safety and stability of our society who need to be monitored, controlled, isolated, and punished. Despite the significant decline of youth violence over the years, young people continue to be accused of being the main perpetrators of violence when, in fact, adults are much more violent than young people and young people are much more likely to experience violence at the hands of adults than from each other.

Young people are often blamed for societal evils that adults actually perpetrate to a greater extent. The headlines blame youth for using guns. In fact, adults are much more likely to use guns, including wielding them against young people. Adults and adult-run corporations manufacture guns, make guns available in our communities, resist gun control, and profit from the sale of guns. Young people are often blamed for using drugs. Yet adults use drugs at much higher rates than young people, with much more destructive results, and youth drug use has dropped consistently over the years to an all-time low. Young people are often blamed for having sex: Young men are blamed for getting young women pregnant, and young women are blamed for being pregnant and having babies. But it is adults who deny young people information about sex and sexuality, sexual health and healthy relationships, contraception, sexual orientation, and sexual identity. Because of this withholding, young people don't have adequate information to make healthy choices.

Young people do bear some responsibility for the choices they make—and they pay dearly for the consequences of bad choices. But most make smart choices, and the dangers attributed to their decisions are often greatly exaggerated. It is the assumption of our work that *young people are not the problem—they are part of the solution*. Adults are responsible for creating the conditions in which young people make choices and are also responsible for public policy that either provides or denies youth safety, support, information, and youth-defined ways to become involved in the community. Youth are not only our future but our present, and we will not solve any pressing social problems without their active, creative participation and leadership.

Whether you are a teacher, youth worker, parent, community educator, or activist, you have most likely been granted access to young people in an institution that itself reflects and may perpetuate certain forms of injustice. You may be charged with focusing on a particular area of youth behavior that adults have identified—or diagnosed—as a problem. Some of the most commonly identified problems include drug abuse, gangs, bullying, family violence, teen-dating violence and sexual assault, sexuality, media impact on youth, and the umbrella term "youth violence." Any of these issues can serve as a lens to facilitate social-justice education. But if the focus is on fixing young people and returning them, thus fixed, to institutional environments that are oppressive to them without giving them the information and skills they need to work together to address that oppression, then the work would be better labeled "youth management" than "social justice."

Our country currently (in 2011) faces major social, political, economic, and cultural challenges. We are at war in several countries in the Middle East and live in an increasingly militarized society. We have military bases around the world and produce and sell as much military equipment and arms as the entire rest of the world combined. The use of force is extolled by our highest political leaders, condoned in our families, and glamorized in the media. We face a widespread financial depression in which millions have lost their jobs, their homes, and their life savings. Mounting environmental destruction, global warming, and an increasingly toxic environment present daily threats to our health and well-being, including the air we breathe, the food we eat, and the water we drink.

In this environment, how do we prepare young people not just to stay safe and out of trouble but also to become active family and community members, critically thinking citizens who can participate in solving our collective problems and shaping our collective future? How are young people turned into adults who accept hierarchy, exploitation, and the larger-scale violence in our society? We explore this process that we call *adultism*, which is the daily systematic and institutionalized oppression that young people face at the hands of adults, in Sections 1–3. Educating adults and young people about adultism helps them understand this process. At the same time, an introduction to adultism gives people a sense of our common ground in taking responsibility for fighting oppression and building community.

As the result of years of research, we now know that training in adultism and the other "isms" starts between ages two and five.[1] At these early ages, children are already internalizing lies and misinformation about themselves and each other; about such differences as skin color, gender, language, national origin, and class; and about the workings of hierarchies based on these differences. During these preschool years, they are already constructing identities and acting out interpersonal relationships based on feelings of superiority, entitlement, vulnerability, and defense of their personal integrity. In our decades of experience as educators and activists, we have found that before people are able to look at the systems of oppression that divide us, such as racism and sexism, they must understand the common conditioning we all endure and the common ground we share.

Part of our common ground is the violence that adultism itself causes. This violence includes internalizing the messages of adultism and looking to harm the less powerful or directing the pain inward and hurting ourselves. This tendency to pass on abuse is also part of our common ground. Most of us were not only the bullied but also the bully, not only the teased but the teaser, not only the one who was put down but the one who put down others. At the same time, we share common concerns, needs, loving natures, and an unstoppable pursuit of connection, inclusion, and participation in safe and healthy communities. Our need and desire for community is the basis for common ground upon which we can build in our work for social justice.

We have found two questions useful in doing this work. The first is a question that we often ask ourselves and the young people in our lives: "What do you stand for?" It is a question about values. "Are you a person worthy of respect?" "Are you trustworthy?" "Do you live with integrity?" "What kind of moral values do you act out in your everyday life?" This question is important; it is one we need to continue to ask ourselves and each other to keep us true to the ideals that we hold.

Another question that we ask less often is equally important. "Who do you stand with?" "Do you stand with those who are being abused, excluded, bullied, harassed, and exploited?" We can stand for many wonderful values, but unless we stand with others, those we know and those we don't, we are not working for social justice. Standing with others challenges us to get involved, to act as *allies*. Working for social justice means, above all, standing together to uproot the tree of violence and to nurture and sustain the tree of life.

A person might be against bullying. They might stand for respect for all. But what does it mean for that person to stand with the bullied? First of all, we must be clear that standing with the bullied does not mean standing against, beating up, or otherwise punishing the bully. Bullying occurs in a school or other environment in which it is supported and allowed to occur. Eliminating one or two bullies will not eliminate the act of bullying, and, more importantly, it will not equip young people to take care of each other and to create an environment where no one feels the need to bully. Someone who stands with the bullied looks for the roots of the problem — the systematic ways that violence and inequality is maintained.

Of course, an immediate intervention might be needed to stop the abuse. But an ally will not just intervene; they will work with others to address the ways that the institutional environment, the adults in the community, and the young people themselves contribute to the perpetuation of abusive behavior and the maintenance of oppressive social systems.

Young people are neither victims *nor* perpetrators, participants *nor* bystanders. Often various forms of violence-prevention work are framed as processes of either eliminating the perpetrators or protecting the victims. But young people play complex and ever-shifting roles: They form living communities in schools, afterschool programs, residential programs, and neighborhoods. In fact, it is often when they become locked into specific roles that they are most unable to work together as allies. Facilitating social justice means acknowledging and valuing the community that a group of young people create and helping strengthen and expand that community so its members can act as allies to each other and to others outside their immediate circles.

The articles and exercises contained in this book serve as a framework for working with youth. They provide the tools and understanding to help us step up as powerful allies to young people. This book is also designed to serve as a guide and preparation for using our curricula *Making the Peace* and *Making Allies, Making Friends*. The book can serve to train youth workers, parents, and teachers as well as youth themselves. It can also enhance a *Days of Respect* program or group work using our *Young Men's Work* and *Young Women's Lives* curricula.

A tool is only effective when it is used. We encourage you to take our work, built on the work of so many others, and adapt it, add to it, drop the parts that don't work, and share it with others, particularly with young people. Some of the young people you are working with have already stepped out into the community to make a difference. For others, this may be the first time they have been offered an invitation to step up as allies. You are inviting them to join the growing efforts of people, young people and adults together, to transform our families, our relationships, our communities, and our societies. These multigenerational struggles are happening in the villages in Chiapas and Oaxaca, the streets of Venezuela, the towns in Kerala, the shop floors in South Korea, and the villages in the Niger Delta. Your opportunity is to provide young people with the inspiration, understanding, tools, and practices that will enable them to take active roles in the global struggle for collective liberation. We wish you much learning, connection, joy, and success in your efforts.

Preparing to Work with Youth

This section addresses important questions for adults who work with young people: What was life like for you as a young person? How is your experience likely to affect your exchanges with young people now? We begin with two questionnaires, "I Remember When I Was Young" and "Adult–Youth Questions for Facilitators." Work through these exercises before you read the article "Working with Youth." The section ends with a larger exploration of the issues for you to consider in facilitating social justice.

I REMEMBER WHEN I WAS YOUNG

Please briefly answer the following questions:

1. My favorite kind of music was _____

2. My favorite radio stations were _____

3. My favorite D.J. was _____

4. The clothes I wore the most were _____

5. My best friend was _____

6. The biggest crush I had was on _____

7. My worst teacher was _____

8. My worst subject was _____

9. I had too much / too little body hair (circle one)

10. What scared me most about sex was _____

11. My main source of information about sex was _____

12. What scared me most about people of the same gender was _____

13. I could tell my secrets to _____

14. The secret I never told anyone was _____

15. The adult I most trusted or who "understood" was _____

16. My most disgusting habit was _____

17. My most embarrassing moment was _____

18. My most powerful moment was _____

19. I was different from everyone else because _____

20. The thing I most wanted to change about myself was _____

21. I most wanted to be _____

22. One thing I've almost forgotten about those years is _____

23. One thing I'll never forget is _____

ADULT–YOUTH QUESTIONS FOR FACILITATORS

In preparation for working with youth, talk through the questions in Part I with co-leaders or other parents, co-workers, or friends. Then try the exercises in Part II as a group.

Part I

1. What is one thing about young people that drives you up the wall? Or, think of a young person you don't like—what specifically about that person don't you like?

2. Think of any way this person reminds you of your own youth; for example, consider ways you acted or things you didn't like about yourself or something someone else disapproved of in you. What from your own memories seems to make it difficult to be with this young person now?

3. For a moment, interpret the young person's characteristics or behavior as a survival mechanism. Can you make a good justification for why the person is acting this way?

4. When you were young, which adults came through for you? What did they do to help or encourage you? How could you tell they were on your side?

5. In your work with youth now, what kind of support from other adults around you would be the most helpful? What might prevent you from asking for this support?

Part II

1. What is the most difficult, most feared, or most embarrassing situation you expect when you encounter young people in a classroom?

2. With other facilitators playing youth and adults, act out this scene, exaggerating everything, and do the most outrageously wrong thing you can think of to deal with the situation as a facilitator. Blow it completely and hilariously. Notice your feelings.

3. Process those feelings, and then brainstorm responses that turn this potentially difficult situation into a learning process for the whole class.

WORKING WITH YOUTH

As adults (and youth) who work with and support young people, we can use some help and direction in how to do this work well. We are part of a group that, both in fact and in young people's perception, sometimes has discriminated against and abused power over youth. It may also be hard for us to think clearly about young people, because we were once young and perhaps retain our own unresolved conflicts from those earlier years. After all, adults sometimes exercised power abusively over us when we were young, too.

Abuse and violence have intimately touched all young people. If we define *abuse* as restricting, putting down, controlling, humiliating, or hurting another, it is clear that abuse is a daily experience for most young people. As mentioned previously, we have a word for this system of abuse: *adultism*.

Obvious examples of adultism are all around us: physical and sexual abuse, extreme forms of "discipline," fights, the corporal "toughening up" process for boys, and the instillation of fear in girls. The still-pervasive teaching of male and female roles—that women are dependent victims and men are abusive monsters—is a disaster for young people. But beyond this, emotional, verbal, financial, sexual, social, and political forms of abuse exist. Perhaps the most pervasive form of this abuse is our educational process itself, carried on in schools, families, religious and cultural institutions, and the public media. This process, despite its best intentions, continually invalidates or trivializes young people's intelligence, denies them access to important information (for example, about birth control), and then faults them for not having it. The process arbitrarily subjects them to either control or dependence and denies them life resources—money, transportation, and the chance to speak for and represent themselves. Perhaps most crucially, it continually passes on adults' resignation to the fact that what people can do and what the world will allow have limits—in other words, we teach them our own hopelessness.

In young people we find powerful resistance to such teachings and, at the same time, internalization of them. Youth fight the roles *and* inhabit them, and in that confusion they abuse one another and themselves.

How can we be allies of young people in these circumstances? The first step is to affirm that we are indeed allies. We care, and we are in a great position to support youth. We all have memories of an adult or two who was there for us, and we all have some immediate information about what we can do for youth in our lives. But more basically, our youth have become accustomed to mistreatment by adults, and we completely contradict that principle by becoming an adult who cares and is willing to do something to express that care. We can do a lot more. The following suggestions are meant for those of us who work with youth in educational settings. In general, in our work we are participating in adult-constructed institutions, such as schools, detention centers, residential programs, and recreational and cultural programs, that contribute to the power inequality between adults and youth and that represent that inequality to many young people. Awareness of the power dynamics in these settings as well as the barriers already set in place by the adult abuse of youth outside these institutions is a prerequisite to being an effective ally. This also means being aware of the existence of other power differences (such as racial and class inequities) that may separate adult presenters from youths in the classroom. However, "being aware" does not mean "being paralyzed by" or "being helpless about"! It means considering where our own confusion about these differences lies, recognizing where confusion and misinformation may exist for young people, and being prepared to talk honestly about these issues.

As adults, the best thing we can do with youth, right from the start, is to contradict directly, in our actions, the traditional adult behaviors youth often encounter.

For example, where youth are traditionally denied information, we provide it, answering all questions and not faulting the asker for lacking the facts. No question is trivial. Similarly, young people and children hear in hundreds of ways that they are stupid or not smart enough. In contrast, we start with the assumption that they *are* smart and are doing everything they can to live creative and nonabusive lives. We assume that the only deterrents to their success are institutional barriers and the abuses that happen and have happened to them.

Youth often have incorrect information or misinformation about, for example, the ways boys and girls should act, or behave, or about each gender's "natural" or biological qualities. This confusion exists in addition to the misinformation that adults have passed on to them about race, class, and sexual orientation. We do not necessarily blame young people for believing these things, because it makes sense for them to believe stereotypes about African Americans, Jews, or people with disabilities when an entire culture teaches and reinforces these images. We can only explore such seemingly inherent beliefs by allowing them to surface, keeping the discussion open, and letting young people work out the issues with each other.

This work is in large part about making information — and thereby power — accessible. And it is also, in part, about acknowledging feelings stemming from the abuse that people have already experienced. To carry on this work we must make what we say simple and direct, structured around a few basic goals. We must be clear and use real-life language. In particular, we can avoid the jargon we have all learned to use that distances us from what we are trying to convey. Such words as "perpetrator," "instigate," "continuum," and even "violence" can be walls to real experience. Even the words adults use to categorize young people — "youth," "teen," and "adolescent," terms found in the text and title of this book — can serve to pigeonhole young people, holding them at a distance. This work is also about how we as adults can learn from young people. In thinking about the traditional roles of young people, we begin to think about the traditional roles of adults. Roles emerge that we are supposed to have mastered — knowing how much work is appropriate; making our way in a world alive with violence and unequal power distribution; feeling we have to know everything; and assuming responsibility for the support, maintenance, safety, and physical and mental health, twenty-four hours a day, of young people as well as ourselves. We notice how we have all learned what consequences can follow from making mistakes. We think about the lies we have ingested from counselors, educators, and child-care experts that result in the feelings all adults experience: "I've been trying so hard and this isn't easy, so I must not be good enough." By sharing power with young people in the classroom, we can let down the adult "guard" we've learned and experience a refreshing relief from these oppressive roles. By trusting the expertise of young people, by finding out what they think and what their lives are like, we lighten this load of adult responsibility. Giving up the role of omniscient teacher with all the answers gives us a chance to learn ourselves.

Adults in cultures across the world often have turned to young people for inspiration. The younger generations' hope that the world can be different, their outright insistence on justice and fair treatment (sometimes mislabeled "rebelliousness"), their insight, and their irreverence are essential to our own freedom. Acknowledging this fact to ourselves is a crucial step forward in our work with young people.

Adults do not routinely show respect to youth or treat them as having equal rights. Here again we can turn the situation around by being personal and direct, speaking informally for ourselves and from our own experiences with honesty, respect, and humor.

Beyond adultism's stipulated roles, young people carry misinformation about themselves that is always appropriate for us to correct. A boy who has learned that men are, on a basic level, monsters needs interaction with adults who clearly believe that men have learned violence but are not naturally abusive. This boy will also benefit from being exposed to adults who support the many ways men resist abuse — crying when they are hurt, walking away from fights, seeking nontraditional careers, and fighting for the rights of women and children. A girl who has learned that women survive based upon how they look and how they relate to men needs an adult ally who supports her efforts to move beyond these limited conceptions.

Another part of the disaster of adultism is the teaching of other oppressions to young people, especially those of race, class, and sexual orientation. Here, too, our supportive corrections are crucial (and, of course, not easy to make). A racist or homophobic remark or abusive act that goes unchallenged hurts everyone, including the perpetrator. It lowers the youthful community's hopes that these oppressions can be overcome and eliminated from the world. It passes on, directly, the abuse that keeps youth separated from each other in the first place.

Young people do form a community; they have learned together, and they have collectively experienced control by adults. Calling upon them to resist abuse as a community is a genuine act of alliance. It means supporting them by recognizing their strengths and the ways they have resisted abuse. Further, it means expecting them to be powerful and to handle their problems by reaching out to each other, with our help and confidence backing them up.

Finally, we do this work for ourselves and to keep alive our own hopes for a nonabusive world. We do this work not "for" young people but "with" them, knowing that we are engaged in our collective liberation.

We should not hunt for or expect gratitude from young people. We can just enjoy being with them, teaching and learning together. We can get support for our good work by finding other adults to talk with, especially when hopelessness, exhaustion, or our own unresolved teen issues creep back into our lives. We must support each other, make loads of mistakes, fix them, and continue with our work.

FACILITATING SOCIAL JUSTICE[2]

One of the tasks of the educational system is to prepare young people to live and prosper in the world. In a school system, this task is undertaken in large part by daily instruction of groups of students roughly the same age. These groups of students may be composed of people of the same gender, race, first language, religious belief, or economic background; they might be slightly diverse or fully diverse. One thing common to all students, regardless of likenesses or differences, is their participation in this learning community. How this community is structured and facilitated, how students are positioned to relate to each other, what and how they are taught — these are all lessons, whether explicit or hidden, about how they are to live with and act toward each other and others in the world. How people live together, after all, reflects how they define and practice justice and is itself a part of what constitutes justice.

The topic of social justice draws attention to students' relationships to each other as well as to the larger world. What are these relationships? How do people "get along" with each other? Does differential treatment exist? Is inequality of resources, opportunity, or access a concern? What differences are represented in, or made invisible in, the classroom? How do students' experiences of the larger world enter the classroom with them and manifest in who speaks most and who is silent? What does the institutional setup do to lessen or heighten these differences? And what are students *really* learning from the process about how to be with each other, regardless of whether these lessons are consciously instructed?

However "social justice" is to be defined, the term applies to the classroom itself: Young people learn together the factors that separate and unite them as well as how their learning community operates. To teach social justice is to *facilitate* — to enable youth to function as a cooperative community, becoming visible to and learning from each other and themselves, examining their differences and commonalities. It is a process by which students come to consciousness about who they are, about the unjust institutions of power that they live within, and about how people can come together to build community and to establish justice. In other words, teaching social justice goes beyond the individual or group; students are taught to become conscious of the institutions in our society and how these institutions affect our lives. The purpose of the process is emancipatory, enhancing young people's ability to think critically and to engage in the profoundly multicultural challenges of the twenty-first century with a commitment to social justice.

Some kinds of multicultural education propose that the goal of this education is simply to develop awareness of each other's "cultures," as if in accomplishing this task we would then all have equal places in the playing field and would in fact be "equal." Awareness here is not enough; stating that we are "all the same" would not only be false but ingenuous. Even if the same resources within a classroom could be provided equally to all students, students come to a classroom already separated in their abilities to use those resources. What may ultimately be hardest to face in any classroom, however, is the recognition of *stratification*—the fact that some students are part of groups that are elevated and others are part of groups that are diminished. In addition, when young people in the United States are compared to young people across the globe, young people in the United States are elevated in privilege and resources far above the majority of youth worldwide. There should be not simply equal access but equal success under a suppler and wider definition of what counts as success. The goal of social justice education is to facilitate students to face and work together across their separations and to engage in critical thinking about the history of those separations in order to become effective allies for justice.

How does facilitation work? Obviously it involves the students, the facilitator, and the process itself. We address each of these in turn, closing with how to prepare for implementing the curriculum and building a learning environment in the classroom.

Some Assumptions about Unlearning the "Isms" with Young People

Here is your class: a gathering of young people of differing or uniform gender, racial background, economic background, religious culture, age, sexual orientation, body size, abilities, and first language. Left to themselves, they would probably form smaller groups, the ubiquitous "cliques," filling the room with jokes, loud or continual conversation, and pockets of silence. The room may hold students with personal friendships, intimate relationships, indifferent contact, and momentary or longer-term dislikes, even enmities. They likely form a society with one another and experience themselves as a community by generation, more or less separate from you, the facilitator. They have each had profound experiences of being treated unequally, and each holds strong opinions about fair play and respect. They may not, or not yet, experience the class itself as a group, much less a "learning community." Before the first session even begins, what do they already know about differences?

"Isms" in the Lives of Young People

We make the following very broad assumptions about the young people you engage:

▸ Young people come into the world with common physical and emotional needs, curious, eager to learn, expecting care, and not hesitant to proclaim needs and display feelings. They are ready to engage with one another and with adults around them.

▸ Existing disparities in wealth, privilege, and power among peoples identified by race, gender, and many other differences, as well as the conflicts these disparities generate, structure the world young people come into. These are the "*isms*" — racism, sexism, classism, and others. The "isms" appear most obviously as prejudicial attitudes that may be used to justify disparities, but even the disparities themselves result from injustice.

▸ Young people are made part of the world in a *conditioning* process: Children are taught, but they are also shaped. They learn not only by programmed instruction but also by how they are treated and by witnessing how others are treated.

▸ Many of the ways in which children are conditioned are hurtful. Hurt comes systematically in a society where disparities exist, so all young people experience mistreatment simply because they are young people in a world defined by adults. They may also further experience mistreatment directly, as members of a less powerful group, or they may experience indirect misinformation when they are taught that others are different or less than themselves — for instance, that they are superior and therefore more entitled to society's benefits.

▸ The measure of children's resilience is their ability to deal powerfully with hurt. One obvious way to cope is to adapt to the conditioning. Another is to resist mistreatment directly and to make alliances with others who are being mistreated.

▸ A major negative end effect of the day-to-day "lessons" of hurt is the conditioning of young people to accede to and to continue structural inequality, generation by generation. Outright prejudice against less powerful groups is one way people sustain inequality. This prejudice can be exposed and "unlearned" in a classroom in a relatively direct manner. Institutions that cover up inequality, making it appear normal, inevitable, and beyond transformation, also sustain inequality in a more serious and intransigent way.

- Major positive end effects of the day-to-day experience of curiosity, hunger to learn, engagement with the world, and resilience to hurt reflect young people's ongoing enthusiastic engagements with the world and each other, as well as their ongoing commitment to fair play.

- As a result, in any classroom, young people already have powerful stories to tell about their own curiosity and intelligence, mistreatment of and misinformation about themselves and others, and acts of resistance and alliance.

- Given a chance to share stories, to unlearn their socialization, and to practice supporting one another, young people will readily act as allies to one another across the lines that separate them, building equity and justice.

Working on social justice requires students to pay attention to their own and to each other's stories and the institutional frameworks within which these stories are generated. Some stories involve pain or ignorance and may be hard to express and difficult to listen to. A general criticism that has been applied to "diversity work" of various kinds, especially that of the women's and civil rights movements, is that it focuses participants on their experiences of victimization, rendering them helpless or setting them up to blame their own shortcomings on others. But it is crucial to note that inequality *is* painful to those victimized by it, and awareness of it brings discomfort to people who may be unaware of how they benefit from it. Because developing skills to overcome inequality is a central concern of this work, expressing difficult feelings when inequality is unearthed is also part of the work. Facing it and working through it together is not a renewed experience of victimization but of overcoming it. In the end, you will call upon and celebrate the most powerful strengths of your students…and yourself.

In the Classroom

How do these assumptions apply to your group? The first thing to notice is that students come to the discussion of "social justice" with misinformation or outright falsehoods, experiences of mistreatment or outright hurt, and some expertise in each of the areas you address. The process of taking on the "isms" invariably, at one point or another, touches upon difficult occurrences from students' lives outside the classroom as well as current separations, visible and not, among youth right in the room. And it also calls upon students' equally powerful experiences of taking stands against unequal treatment and having others take stands with them.

Moreover, the classroom — and the educational system it represents — is one of the basic institutions of society. Expect to see the disparities of our larger society mirrored in the differential treatment students witness and receive. The disparities and differential treatment are alive in the ways students treat each other, see each other, and see and treat you, and they are further mirrored by the relationship of your institution to other institutions serving other youth populations.

At the very least, every student in the educational system at one time or another has had their intelligence questioned or invalidated by an adult, even in the seemingly objective process of grading. Doubts about one's own thinking count as some of the most profound barriers young people (and we as former young people) have to deal with and are a basic pillar of adultism, the mistreatment of young people. Often the doubts are instilled or enhanced right in the classroom.

At the same time, the educational system can be and historically has been an arena of emancipation in which students can learn, together and across differences, to recognize inequality and to organize against it — actual democracy in action. To this emancipation, you can add the great strengths and ingenuities students have adopted to survive mistreatment, their curiosity about and interest in each other, and the ideals of fair play and equity in young people's cultures.

Your Place as Facilitator

To prepare for facilitation first requires taking some time to think through your own experiences of injustice and how they will affect the discussions about to come up in your classroom. Then, turning to your role as an adult, ask yourself: What does an adult, acting as an ally, do to support young people? In the following sections, you are invited to take some time to prepare. Discussions about hurt, separation, conflict, and privilege — and resilience, resistance, and alliance — among young people can become very personal; it is essential for you to examine ahead of time how particular issues might affect you or even get in your way.

As a successful adult survivor of childhood conditioning, you are modeling how adults successfully take on and address the "isms." The assumptions we make about young people (for example, in "The Heart Exercise") apply to you as well. Like them, you came into the world curious, intelligent, and vulnerable. Like them, you have negotiated your way through mistreatment, misinformation or no information, resistance, and alliance. And now you are an adult, with a specific relationship to young people as an adult ally.

Looking at Your Heart

Review the following multipart exercise from our curricula, answering the discussion questions using your own experiences. The exercise brings out some of the issues that may arise for you in the course of organizing and alliance building.

THE HEART EXERCISE

a. Imagine you are holding a newborn child. Sit for a few moments and think as you gaze into the baby's face. What words or phrases pop into your head to describe the child?

b. Write responses in a column or bunch, converting more obviously negative words, such as "selfish," into more positive ones, such as "powerful," "assertive," or "not hesitant."

c. Draw a heart shape around the words. We all come here as "hearts"—beautiful, smart, strong, expecting to be loved, and so forth—but we "bruise" or "scar" easily.

d. Think of words that adults say to infants, toddlers, and young children that may not be so great to hear. For each word or phrase, draw a slash—"a scar"—across the heart. You might go on to write answers to the following questions: What hurtful things might be said to you as a child born with a big body? As a child in the United States speaking a language other than that very narrow dialect, "basic English"? As someone whose skin color is darker than white people's? What hurtful things might be said to you about people with darker skin if you are a white child? What about if your parents don't have a lot of money? If you are a Jewish child? A Muslim child? What gets said to girls? To boys? What gets said if you are a child with a physical or mental disability? For each of the words or phrases, draw a slash.

e. What do you notice about the heart? Obviously, the scars—so many that it is hard or impossible to read the words—cover up the qualities written within the heart. This illustration demonstrates how everyone undergoes hurt.

f. Hearts are strong, powerful muscles, for we have always resisted this abuse. But one of the ways we cope with abuse is to build up *shields*, ways of coping and protecting ourselves. For example, what might someone learn to do to cope when they are being called stupid? (Learn to withdraw, to act stupid, to drop out, to be mad.) What might someone learn

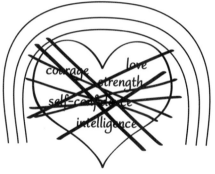

to do when they are called ugly? When they are told they are not good enough? When they are called weak? For each response, draw a semicircle over the top of the heart to represent a shield.

g. You now have a heart encumbered with many scars and many shields, making it very difficult for two hearts, when they are in the same vicinity, to communicate with each other. When someone speaks to me, their words must negotiate through all their scars and shields, and then through mine. Anything I say back has the same difficult journey. So our challenge in building trust with each other is to learn how to slowly and carefully lower our shields and reach through the scars to find each other. Work through the questions below about *your* heart.

Your Experience as a Young Person

▸ What has been your experience of your own qualities?

▸ What limits or hurts were placed upon you?

▸ What qualities are still strong within you (for example, curiosity, openness)?

▸ What "shields" have you developed to deal with the hurts you have experienced?

▸ In what ways have you resisted, fought back against, or just said no to these hurts?

▸ Who are some allies who stood up for you?

▸ How do the negative, limiting experiences and shields still affect you, and how might they surface in your work with young people now?

▸ What qualities, strengths of resistance, and experiences of alliance can you bring to your work with young people now?

A Model of Power

Notice that many or most "scars" mentioned in this exercise come to us systematically, based upon our membership within various groups — the categories of race, gender, sexual orientation, economic status, and the rest under which we live. That is to say, we inhabit a social structure in which people become categorized and separated into groups that are allowed either more or fewer social resources, such as wealth, housing, sustenance, education, civil rights, leisure, or political representation. The allotment of social resources is based upon existing inequalities — differences in power. Some groups are targeted for institutionalized degradation, exploitation, and violence: They are targets of oppression. What happens to people who are targeted?

- They experience *oppression* — exploitation and violence in routine, day-to-day, institutionalized, and systematic ways. One form of oppression is the continual dissemination of misinformation or outright lies about the targeted people's character, making them and their concerns invisible or discredited in larger society.

- One harsh effect of oppression is *internalized oppression* — the targeted people come to believe in the lies or misinformation about themselves or other members of their group.

- The contradiction to oppression and internalized oppression lies in the fact that people in target groups have always put up *resistance* — fighting back against both.

The corresponding groups on the other side of each issue are not targeted; they are *nontarget* groups. What happens to people who are nontargets?

- Nontarget people receive the same misinformation or lies about target groups that members of target groups receive about themselves. Often this misinformation comes from people the nontarget child or young person trusts — parents, siblings, friends at school, and teachers — in a situation called *conditioning*. Sometimes conditioning also includes misinformation or hurtful expectations about the experience of being a nontarget (for example, training a boy to "act like a man" even though that training includes shutting down feelings and enduring physical mistreatment). Experiencing conditioning is not the same as experiencing oppression, but it is also hurtful and scarring.

- The understanding that nontarget people receive unearned benefits in society simply by being members of that group is difficult for them to face. For people with wealth and power particularly, these benefits amount to *privilege*. What can make this condition especially hard to recognize is that benefits may be invisible to or taken for granted by the people who have them, even if they are not invisible to the targeted people who lack them. What can make this recognition even more difficult is that the concept of privileges, perhaps from race or gender, doesn't resonate with a lot of people who lack privilege elsewhere in their lives, such as those who are poor or working-class.

- Finally, it is also true that some people in nontarget groups have found ways, however local and limited, to act as allies to people in target groups, assisting them in intervening against oppression and internalized oppression — for example, by using their privilege or benefits on behalf of target groups or to make room for leadership from members of target groups.

Your Heart and Power

Take a few moments to think about groups to which you belong or with whom you are identified, in a loose and general way. (See the "Power Chart" exercise in Section 2 for a list of some target and nontarget groups.) You will probably notice that you have experiences in both targeted and nontargeted groups. Use the following questions to explore thoughts and feelings that may arise for you in the process of facilitating social justice.

Your Experience as a Person on the Downside—The Target Groups

Pick one or several target groups to which you belong (some examples: women, children, people of color, elders, poor or low-income people), including those that you were part of as a child, are part of now, and will be part of in the future.

▸ What experiences do you have as part of each group of being discriminated against, mistreated, exploited or violated directly, or learning that your group was "less than" the corresponding nontarget group?

▸ Think of any ways this mistreatment was "internalized"—ways you were made to feel less intelligent or less valuable as an individual and ways you were made to separate yourself from other people in your group.

▸ What experiences of overcoming oppression have you had?

▸ What experiences of overcoming internalized oppression have you had?

▸ Think of allies you have had in this area, such as people from nontarget groups who stood in the way of the mistreatment, even if only once. Who are they, and what did they do?

▸ Which of these categories that you belong to is most likely to bring up personal feelings for you while facilitating the curriculum? What kind of support or preparation will you need to handle these feelings?

Your Experience as a Person on the Upside—The Nontarget Groups

Turning to the nontarget groups to which you may belong (adults, white people, men, able-bodied people, heterosexuals), pick one that stands out for you and think about your experience using the following questions:

▸ As a member of this group, what are the earliest experiences you have of being told that people in the opposite, "downside" category were different or less than you?

▸ How might these early experiences still affect you?

- What are your earliest experiences of learning about how people in your category are supposed to act?

- How might these experiences still affect you? What might they cost you?

- As thoroughly as possible, list the benefits that come to you relative to the other group—what benefits you have as a member of each of your particular nontarget groups, even if sometimes these don't feel like privileges.

- Think of a time when you felt anger or resentment toward a person or people in a target group. As best as you can, think about what parts of those feelings might have been motivated not by the target of your anger but by misinformation or prejudice.

- Think of a time when you felt anger or resentment toward a person (or people) in a target group when that person was also a nontarget group member in relation to you. For example, you are an adult female teacher and find yourself angry at a young male student for his sexist remarks. Do you use your privilege as a member of the nontarget group to suppress, limit, or punish the person from the target group rather than confront him directly about his oppressive actions?

- Think of a time when you felt guilt toward a person or people in a target group. How did the guilt affect you? What about this guilt might have been useful, and how might it have hindered you or kept you from acting?

- What are your earliest experiences of challenging or refusing the mistreatment of members in a target group?

- Which of your nontarget categories is likely to bring up the most personal feelings for you while facilitating? What kind of support or preparation will you need to handle these feelings?

Your Experience of Upside and Downside Positions

Now consider any target/nontarget pairs in which you may find it difficult to decide whether you are on the target or nontarget side—for example, social class, if you feel you are neither rich nor poor; age, where you may be an adult but are still young (for example, between ages eighteen and twenty-five) or are approaching "elder" status (for example, over age fifty); or disabled, but the disability is hidden or "not that bad."

- What pressures have you experienced in your life to connect with the target group or to associate with the nontarget group?

- In what ways do you experience mistreatment or "less-than" status from people clearly in the nontarget group?

- In what ways do you have privileges or benefits denied to people more clearly in the target group?
- Which of these categories are likely to bring up the most personal feelings—or confusion—for you in working with young people? What kind of information, support, or preparation will you need to handle these feelings?

Your Role as an Ally: Your Freedom Is My Freedom

We employ the word *ally*, for the most part, to represent the person from a nontarget, "upside" group who takes a stand against the mistreatment of the target group. More loosely, it can mean people in target groups who stand up for each other within the group or stand up for members of other target groups. This kind of alliance is called *solidarity*, and it has a powerful, longstanding, and inspiring history from political movements across the world. An ally challenges the operation of a system of oppression by interrupting mistreatment or internalized mistreatment — not by rescuing, taking care of, or taking over from, but by standing shoulder to shoulder with. As you worked through the questions in the previous exercise, you may have pictured people who have acted as your allies when you were young, and you may have thought of your own experiences of acting as an ally to targeted people. Finally, as an adult, you are already in the position of being an ally to young people.

In the work of building justice, you are inviting young people to acknowledge and to make a commitment to each other across lines that separate them. In particular, you are asking for their commitment to be allies — to see violence or discrimination against target groups that are not their own as injuries to themselves. In seeing someone else's freedom as their own, they can pledge to join together as allies against the mistreatment. What does this commitment mean for you?

You will encounter barriers to being an ally. Some of the most prominent are already in place from the conditioning you have received:

- *The oppression itself.* Systems of oppression produce segregation, misinformation, and lies about history and current reality so that much of what you have been told about other groups is false and limits your awareness.
- *Privilege.* Your benefits or comforts, many of which are invisible to you, limit your sensitivity to those who are subordinated and lack them.
- *Your own target experiences.* Mistreatment you have received on the downside of other "isms" makes your hurt prominent and hinders your capacity to recognize others' pain.

- *Internalized oppression from your target experiences.* Internalizing the negative messages about your target group and believing that what the nontarget group says about you and those in your group is true compromise your empathy and compassion.

- *Guilt/resentment.* Guilt about your own past actions or those of members of your nontarget group puts you in the position of feeling hopeless or, alternatively, trying to prove your innocence to target group members. Resentment is the feeling that you have already done too much, spent too much time "bending over backward," and should not have to do any more.

Other barriers arise when you take a stand:

- *Sanctions.* Taking a stand against injustice exposes you to backlash and may expose you to even greater enmity from members of your own group — friends, colleagues, and relatives included — who see you as someone who interrupts or embarrasses or perceive you to be a traitor. For example, white people who supported the struggle of African Americans during the civil rights movement were labeled "race traitors," and some suffered other kinds of backlash and violence.

- *Anger of a target group.* Making yourself available as an ally sometimes means committing yourself to hearing the anger about oppression that target groups feel. In fact, it may be a mark of genuine alliance when target-group members trust you to be able to listen to their anger.

Against these barriers, you have rewards:

- *Learning your own strength.* Taking action as an ally calls upon your strength to contradict limits or negative messages that conditioning may have imposed on you.

- *Stepping out of internalized oppression.* Being an ally compels you to refuse the negative messages you may have received about people (and yourself) in the target groups that you are part of (for example, as an adult white woman acting as an ally to young people or people of color, you are silencing every voice that ever told you, as a woman, "You can't do that" or "Girls can't do that").

- *Your community.* To engage in alliance is to build and sustain community that, in turn, sustains you.

- *Gaining understanding of reality.* To the extent that existing institutions hide or mystify inequality, acting as an ally enables you to recognize and to bring reality into the room: the real conditions of inequality as well as the rich and untold history of alliances, individual and organized, that are part of our daily lives.

- *Witnessing transformation.* Social justice education and action transforms people. Witnessing that transformation in people and their formation of alliances is one of the greatest experiences of inspiration for those who organize.

- *Hope.* With inspiration comes hope that social justice and peace can be sustained. Especially for adults, the renewal of hope against ongoing conditioning is crucial, and hope is certainly important for us to pass on to young people.

So consider your role as an ally to young people or as an ally to people in other targeted groups: What does an ally do?

1. *Take action.* Before everything else, the mark of an ally is taking action, however small or large, against inequality or mistreatment.

2. *Listen/learn.* A gift of alliance is finding out, from the target-group experience, how someone whose life is different from yours perceives and experiences the world, providing information that has been withheld from you by the conditioning you received. A first act of alliance is to make space for target groups, with unconditioned support from you, to define the issues with which they grapple and the structure of the "ism" from their own experience. A companion act of alliance is to research and to discover in detail how the relevant "ism" works by uncovering statistics, facts, and history you can pass on to others.

3. *Use your privilege.* As an ally, identify the resources you have and use your resources on behalf of the target group, gaining them access and opportunity.

4. *Support the target person's leadership.* True alliance means getting out of the way of target-group members, supporting them in taking charge of their lives and making their own decisions about what must be done. To rescue or to take over removes their power once again. Conversely, to step out of the way without offering support, resources, or tactful guidance if requested is to abandon the group.

5. *Challenge and mobilize other nontarget members.* Target-group members, engaged in their own work, need you to intervene with and to educate other members of your group. Moreover, your intervention must come from the standpoint of support, not differentiating yourself as better than the others of your group. To the extent you reject or push the members of your nontarget group away, you are pushing away part of yourself.

6. *Take a chance, and make mistakes.* Expect to make mistakes and agree to fix them when you do. Alliance work is built upon trying things, making mistakes, and moving forward.

7. *Take care of yourself.* Alliance is a lifelong activity. It can't be sustained unless you are rested, replenished, and hopeful. So in light of that:

8. *Get support.* Rally friends, family, colleagues, people you can trust, and like-minded members of the groups to which you belong. Talk with them about the challenges you experience, the areas where you get stuck, and your success stories. Discuss strategies for social justice education and how to establish ongoing networks of support. Alliance works best when you are not alone but rather are a member of a community of people dedicated to being allies and dedicated to you.

Liberation Theory and Practice

As adults who want to work effectively in community with young people we need a shared framework and vocabulary for understanding and talking about power and violence in our society. We also need practical tools for connecting this framework to our everyday lived experience so we can develop strategies for community building and justice.

INTRODUCTION

This section describes the philosophy underlying our social justice work with young people. "It's about Power" analyzes social power relations in the United States through a series of exercises that demonstrate how power differences affect us by creating conditions conducive to violence. Violence, in turn, sustains and enforces systems of exploitation that benefit the governing elites — interlocking networks of owners, directors, and the heads of business and state enterprises across the world — who create those conditions in their day-to-day practices and decisions. The exercises also demonstrate how we can overcome our differences to establish alliances and to challenge the exploitation and the violence. "Some Notes on Using the Power Chart" examines more closely the complexities of power relations, and "The Culture of Power" details the actual function of those relations in day-to-day life.

The articles in Section 3 apply the basic theory presented in "It's about Power" to specific systems of oppression — sexism, racism, adultism, and others. We have highlighted these particular issues because of their immediate relevance to young people. It is important and useful to young people to understand these imbalances of power in relation to economic and environmental exploitation, war, and interpersonal violence. Young people actively organize to confront these issues across the country, so having a power analysis helps frame their work in broader discussions of social justice. The theory easily extends to an analysis of other systems of oppression alluded to in the Power Chart. It also is useful in looking at how we may, consciously or not, participate in maintaining power imbalances, securing some provisional safety and small-scale benefits in exchange for targeting others around us.

This section and the following include many of the key exercises we use in workshops, which we go on to refer to throughout the book. In a book, as in a classroom, theory is hard to digest and takes time. Use this section as a reference to read and to refer back to as you employ the curricula and agendas that follow.

It's about Power

In the classroom with young people, and in workshops among adults, differences exist — differences in gender, racial and ethnic heritage, age, physical ability, economic class, sexual orientation, and many others. Some differences are visible, some we look for automatically, and some we may pretend not to see. But what is true about these differences is that governing elites have used them to separate people along lines of power. This power takes the form of access to resources, work, housing, education, physical security, protection by law, and representation in government. And although some groups are designated and socially sanctioned to be powerful, their accumulation of disproportionate power comes at the expense of other groups and is promoted for the benefit of those governing elites.

The social perspective from which we operate is that the primary roots of violence in the United States are the systematic, institutionalized, and day-to-day imbalances of power that governing elites exploit to consolidate and to maintain control over all sources of power and wealth. Social groups that have less social, economic, and political power — women, children, people of color, workers, recent immigrants, and others — have less control over their lives and are targets of physical and sexual violence, discrimination, harassment, and exploitation by those with more power at home, in the workplace, and in the wider community. This pattern of power imbalances is continually renewed through the training of each generation of young people. When children in this country are abused by adults, and lies, jokes, stereotypes, rewritten history, and biased research teach them misinformation about groups of people different from themselves, they are being trained to justify, to enforce, and to continue the power differences at the institutional, interpersonal, and internalized levels. They are promised safety and economic and social success if they comply, and they may be threatened with violence if they resist.

All systems of social inequality have been created to reinforce one another. It is clear that violence against women and children will not be stopped unless violence against people of color, gays, lesbians, Muslims, Jews, people with disabilities, working-class people, elders, and the rest is also eliminated. So, for example, we cannot effectively support young people in "unlearning" the lies of sexism unless we are prepared to assist them and ourselves in unlearning the other "isms."

Differences between individuals and between groups of people are not the problem but rather the source of the variety, richness, and strengths of human cultures. Nor is prejudice the problem. Power differentials based on differences, created by governing elites to consolidate their power, are the root of injustice. Prejudice is, rather, the effect of training in justifying and maintaining these governing systems of oppression. To take an example, when white and black indentured servants rose up together in Bacon's rebellion in 1676, the landed elite in Virginia quickly realized that such solidarity posed a threat to their wealth. They enacted a series of laws that gave distinct privileges to working-class white people while at the same time taking away opportunities from African American people, creating a system of racialized power imbalance that benefitted elites. Out of this intentionally created system of oppression, "white people," now marked as a group separate from and superior to "black people," developed stereotypes and ultimately prejudices that served to justify further oppression.

As we explore issues of power more closely, we notice that language itself is an instrument of power and is often used to define the world and to control the way people think. Throughout this book we use the terms "sexism," "racism," "anti-Jewish oppression and anti-Muslim oppression," "heterosexism," and "adultism" as terms describing different systems of oppression. We are aware that although these words are in common usage, they are more or less inadequate and even misleading. For instance, "adultism" as a term for the oppression of young people defines the oppression in terms of the oppressive group, not the targeted group. "Heterosexism" does the same thing, and although it is slightly less clumsy than "the oppression of gays, lesbians, and bisexuals," it usually only means heterosexual prejudice, not full-blown oppression. It is also often incorrectly used to reference discrimination against transgendered people (which is better referred to as "gender-identity oppression," or oppression based on a binary-gender system). We do not generally use the word "anti-Semitism,"[3] because, although it is normally used as a synonym for the oppression of Jews, it hides the fact that non-Jewish Semitic (Arab) people are oppressed in ways different from Jews. Also, current uses of the word are being contested within the Jewish community.

Names for target groups are always problematic, because the corresponding nontarget groups that have power almost always assign them. "Teen," for example, is a word that adults often use to trivialize, to judge, or to diminish young people. (And, of course, we use it in the title of this book: *Helping Teens Stop Violence.*) At the same time, terminology is always contested by those affected by it. African Americans, gays, lesbians, and other groups have claimed or reclaimed names and linguistic practices in which they take pride and that counter negative connotations. One such example is the feminist and transgender rejection of the male and binary-gender bias implicit in the use of "man" and "he" as stand-ins for "human" in English composition; a well-known linguistic practice we adapt in this book is the use of the gender-neutral "they" and "them" when referring to individuals not otherwise identified by gender.

Part of all unlearning is continuing to question our terminology. Even the choice of terms to designate groups of people of varying degrees of power is not neutral. As noted below, people denied power are not "powerless" victims, and those with privilege may not recognize that they have privilege, recoiling at the idea that they are colluding with powerful groups to oppress others. But it is verifiably true that some groups are more powerful — they have more social, economic, political, and cultural power — and other groups are less powerful and are more vulnerable to violence. By using the compromise terms of "target" and "nontarget," we attempt to address these significant differences. We explore these power differences through the following exercise.

THE POWER SHUFFLE[4]

(The facilitator must determine in advance how to include any participants with limited mobility in the following exercise, which involves slow-paced movement back and forth across the room.) Everyone gathers at one end of the room, after moving desks, chairs, and other obstacles aside; participants are standing or in wheelchairs, and so forth. The facilitator stands to the front and side of the group and states that they will be giving the group a series of instructions. Participants are asked to follow the instructions silently, paying attention to who is with them and who is separated from them and recognizing feelings that come up while performing this exercise. Silence enables participants to show respect for each other's experiences and to pay attention to their own feelings as the exercise proceeds.

The facilitator states that people do not have to identify themselves as members of a group that is called out if they don't wish to (they have "the right to pass"), but they should notice any feelings that come up about not identifying themselves. If anyone is unsure about which group they belong to, they are to decide for themselves where it makes sense for them to go. It is important that no one feel pressure to come out in any category that may have negative repercussions for them. The facilitator should acknowledge in advance that it may not be completely safe for everyone to step across the room for all the groups of which they are members and that accordingly each person gets to decide, for each category, how much to participate.

With each instruction, the facilitator asks certain people to move across the room from the full group, turn, and look back. The two groups then stand still for a few seconds, observing each other and examining their own feelings. Then the facilitator brings them together again for the next "shuffle."

For each category, the facilitator says: "Please step to the other side of the room if you are [the category]. [Pause.] Notice who's with you. Notice who's not. [Pause.] Notice how you feel. [Pause.] Come back together."

Phrases in parentheses in this exercise are alternative statements we use, depending on the composition of the group.

The Categories

Please step or move to the other side of the room if...

1. you are a woman

2. you are of Arab-American, Arab, Persian, or Middle Eastern descent

3. you are of African-American, black, Afro-Caribbean, or African descent

4. you are of Asian, South Asian, East Asian, Southeast Asian, or Asian-American descent

5. you are of Latino/a, Chicano/a, mestizo/a, Puertorriqueño/a, Cubano/a, or Hispanic descent

6. you have Native American Indian lineage

7. you are a Native American Indian, or at least one of your parents or grandparents is a full-blooded Native American Indian and you were raised as a Native American Indian

8. you are Filipino/a or Pacific Islander

9. you are multiheritage—that is, your original parents are from different races

10. you are of Jewish heritage (additional categories: Muslim, Buddhist, Hindu, Sikh, other non-Christian religions)

11. you are forty-five or over

12. you are twenty-four or under (OR twenty-one or under; OR eighteen or under)

13. you were raised poor, or the people who raised you did not have a lot of money

14. your parent/s or the people who raised you did not go to college

15. your parent/s or the people who raised you were or are working class, performing manual labor, skilled, unskilled, or pink-collar clerical or service work to make a living

16. you were raised Catholic

17. you have a visible or hidden physical disability or impairment

18. you have ever been dangerously or continuously sick

19. you are an immigrant to this country

20. you are a refugee to this country

21. your native language is one other than English

22. you were raised in or are now part of a religious community other than Christian

23. someone in your family is lesbian, gay, bisexual, or transgender

24. you are lesbian, gay, or bisexual

25. you are transgender or intersex

26. you are a front-line worker on your job and do not supervise anyone

27. you are a veteran

28. you or a member of your family was ever labeled mentally ill or crazy

29. you have been incarcerated or been in the juvenile justice system for more than a misdemeanor

30. you have been publicly labeled fat (NOT: if you've ever felt fat)

31. you had an adult's needs put ahead of yours as a child

The preceding are direct target-group categories. The following represent other target groups or the effects of being in a target group. They can be added according to the makeup of the group.

1. you were raised by a single parent or currently are a single parent

2. you were raised in a farming community

3. you were raised in the South (what is known as the "Deep South" in the United States)

4. you never completed high school

5. you were ever held back, failed or flunked a grade, or were tracked for noncollege courses in junior or senior high school

6. you come from a family where alcohol or drugs were or are a problem

7. you are currently unemployed, not by choice

8. you have ever received public assistance

9. you have ever been homeless

10. you have ever had an eating disorder

11. you have had or have a learning disability

12. you have ever been or currently are a student

13. you grew up with foster parent/s

14. you grew up with violence in your household

15. you have ever lost a family member or close friend to violence in your community

16. you have ever attempted (OR: seriously considered) suicide

Other categories may be added as appropriate, and some of these can be deleted, depending upon the composition of the group, the issues to be covered, safety and boundaries for the participants, and the amount of time available.

The facilitator then has participants walk or move to the center of the room and, for a few moments, mingle silently, making eye contact and acknowledging each other as people present together in this group. Then participants form dyads to describe the feelings they had while doing this exercise. Finally, the group is brought back together, and people are asked to share responses to the exercise.

One alternative way to conduct this exercise is to give participants a choice about how far they walk across the room. For example, people of multiple heritages, people who are transgender or who only partly identify as one gender, or people with one parent raised working class and one raised wealthy might want to walk half-way or three-quarters of the way across the room for certain categories. This variation breaks down the somewhat inaccurate binary nature of the exercise and allows participants more choice in how to express their experiences. It can also lead to very rich discussions.[5]

Another alternative way to conduct this exercise is to mark categories of unearned power and privilege by having men, white people, and those who are able-bodied walk over to the other side. This separation sets the stage for a discussion about the culture of power and how these categories usually go unremarked upon. It could be labeled the "unearned benefit shuffle."[6]

THE POWER CHART

The Power Chart exercise allows participants to identify for themselves some of the inequities of power that exist in the United States. The exercise begins with a blank chart. The group is asked to provide examples of social groups in the United States that have power, people "not targeted" for violence, and their counterparts who are denied power, people "targeted" for violence. The result of this exercise should look something like the chart shown below, including these key groups (there are others, of course). If any key groups are missing, the facilitators can add them.[7]

The Power Chart

NONTARGET	TARGET
adults	youth
men	women
whites	people of color, multiracial people
rich or upper-middle income	poor, working, or middle class
adults	elders/seniors
heterosexuals	lesbians/gays/bisexuals
native English–speakers	first language other than English
traditionally defined male or female	transgender/intersex/transsexual
US citizens	refugees/immigrants
Christian	Muslim, Jewish, Buddhist, other religions
bosses	workers
teachers	students
college-educated	not college-educated
"normal"	labeled "mentally ill"
"normal" body size	labeled "fat"
able-bodied	living with physical, emotional, mental, learning disability, whether visible or hidden
from United States/Western Europe	from nations in the "global south"/majority world/rest of world

We use the chart to make the following six points, taking time for a group to question and to discuss each point.

1. *Nontarget/target:* We describe the difference between the two sides of the chart by noting that the right side consists of "target" groups and the left of "nontarget" groups. On each line, one group has more social, political, and economic power than the other group. This categorization does not mean that "target" groups are intrinsically powerless but that society creates conditions that give them less power than the corresponding groups on the left. If we look at positions of power in the United States — positions controlling wealth, resources, and decisions that affect our lives — we are more likely to see people from groups on the power side of the chart. These people, who run corporations, political parties, universities, the military, think tanks, and foundations, are more likely to make decisions that benefit people like themselves and that exploit people in less powerful groups.

   What are the consequences of this power differential? Looking at the chart, we see that members of the target groups are targeted for violence — in the narrowest and widest senses of that term — by members of the corresponding nontarget groups. It is also true that members of nontarget groups are relatively safer than comparable members of the target group (members who share the same class, race, gender, immigrant status, and so forth). Ask the group for examples of what types of violence are done to children by adults. To people of color by white people? To women by men?

2. *The violence is institutionalized — it is an "ism":* Target groups undergo systematic, pervasive, routine, day-to-day degradation, exploitation, and violence, in forms as basic as reduced access to jobs, food, and housing. As members of target groups, we frequently experience this violence as individuals and often experience it at the hands of other individuals, but it has its source in existing institutional inequality. The institutions of family, education, work, business, religion, housing, law, and government in which we are raised sustain this inequality. Inequality is made to look "normal" to those in powerful groups; it can even be made to look normal to those with less power, or it is made invisible or denied. But it is precisely because inequality is institutionalized that it is so thorough. Each inequality represents an "ism," some of which we have names for — racism, sexism, heterosexism, ableism, and so forth — and some of which we don't, such as discrimination against immigrants and transgender people.

3. *There is no reverse "ism":* Because the institutional imbalance favors one direction — nontarget over target — it is counterproductive to use concepts like "reverse racism," "reverse sexism," and so forth. Individuals in the target group can stereotype or have prejudices about people in the nontarget group. They can act aggressively or violently toward them. But the power imbalance

nonetheless remains. Members of less powerful groups do not have the social power and command of resources to limit the powerful or to protect themselves from system-wide violence.

4. *Our differences do not cause the power imbalance:* This statement cannot be emphasized too strongly: Our differences do not cause the institutional power imbalances. They are used to justify already existing imbalances. People do not earn mistreatment because they are Latino or female or have disabilities. Nothing natural or biological about these differences causes oppression. Rather, the imbalance of power is already there, in existing social relationships, brought about through immediate and long-term struggles to obtain control over the basic resources of human life. At any given moment, the social structure crystallizes ongoing, dynamic processes in which people from particular social groupings attempt to achieve and to maintain power while people from other groups resist. This is the set of conditions we inherit and to which we are exposed as children, learning lies about target groups (and corresponding assumptions about the "normalness" and outright superiority of nontarget groups) often long before we actually meet any of these individuals.

5. *We live on both sides (and sometimes in the middle):* What do you notice about where you live on this chart? The first thing to see is that each of us has places on both sides. Each of us knows what it is like to be in a position of power and what it is like to have someone wield power over us. Each of us, as a member of a target group (initially, as young people), has experienced mistreatment and learned lies about ourselves. Each of us, as a member of a nontarget group, has learned lies about the target group and about ourselves as nontarget-group members. We have been placed in a position of relative privilege over target-group members, and we have been socially sanctioned to discriminate against them.

   You may also notice that it is possible to experience being on both sides of some categories — and being in the middle over a lifetime. For example, all of us have been or are young people, all of us are or will become adults, many of us are or will become elders, and all of us have inhabited such "middle" positions as young adults. Other categories we are part of may be fixed over a lifetime, at least until this system of power and violence is overturned.

6. *Intersections:* We also inhabit multiple "slots" at the same time, target and nontarget: I can be male and a college graduate, but I can also be living with a disability, the child of immigrants from Puerto Rico or Korea, and gay or bisexual. None of these categories alone constitutes my full identity; even their gathering does not capture me completely, because there are always

other categories to add. These complexities mean that the categories are not simple or monolithic identities but positions of power or its limits that we live within. Each is defined by its relation to, and dependency upon, the others. The categories are real: They have real-life effects upon us, we define ourselves continually by struggling with and negotiating them, and we cannot simply claim not to be shaped by them. Nor can we simply reside comfortably in any one of them, whether a target or a nontarget, as a full reflection of who we are.

The intersections are more like a system of rivers and streams than of roads. Identities are not well defined or well contained like roads are. They spill out and flow into each other, some carrying more nutrients or debris than others. On the surface the water can look clear, untroubled, or clean, and yet below the surface complex currents and eddies may flow. And rivers receive various kinds of runoff and pollution from the land they flow past and from the streams they run into them. A whole systems approach is necessary to understand identities, the systems of oppressions that produce them, their intersections, and the larger system of power and wealth that they serve.[8]

The Cycle of Violence

How we handle these categories in our own lives amounts to a kind of calculus. We all learn in this society that "power" really means "power *over*" and that if we are targeted for violence in one area, the easiest way to deal with it is to find someone with less power so we can pass our pain, anger, and frustration on to them. If your boss yells at you at work, or if your dad yelled at and hit you as a child, then you are permitted to take it out on someone younger than you, on a woman if you are a man, on a person of color if you are white, on a gay person if you are heterosexual. The final upshot is to transfer the blame for the violence you suffered onto someone else rather than face the risk of confronting those who targeted you. This is what we call the *cycle of violence*. Each of us, every day, moves in and out of relationships in which we have more power or less power than those we are relating to. We therefore make decisions about whether to continue the cycle of violence by being abusive or to interrupt the pattern by refusing to abuse others and working with them to actually stop the cycle by addressing its roots.

We all start out in a target group: children. People we depend upon and whom we may love and trust pass on training in power differences at a time when it is difficult to evaluate what we are taught. Every instance of this passing on is painful and counts as violence. Where the "training" involves physical or sexual abuse, it is obviously violence, obviously producing injury and physical pain. But another effect of the conditioning process also has potentially damaging long-term consequences: emotional violence. *Emotional violence*—witnessing mistreatment, learning abusive stereotypes, experiencing putdowns or invalidations of our intelligence—brings about inner suffering and distress, often suppressed and often unconscious, that influence how we negotiate our relationships as we grow up. Based on hurtful experiences, our distress falsifies our sense of the world and inhibits us from thinking creatively about the present and future.

DISMANTLING INJUSTICE

In understanding and beginning to dismantle this unjust system, we use six essential concepts, three for target groups and three for nontarget groups. Have students try out these concepts by filling in a target table and a nontarget table. This exercise brings the points you explored for yourself in "Facilitating Social Justice" (see page 12) into a full classroom discussion.

For Target Groups

Turn to a category on the "target" side of the chart—one you inhabit now or used to inhabit—to see how the following concepts might apply.

1. Oppression

Pick an issue on which you are in the target group, and notice how people on your side of the line are mistreated by people on the other side. Think of physical, emotional, mental, verbal, economic, social, and political forms of this mistreatment. Look at three of the categories in the chart below to see some examples of oppression. Notice that many of the same hurts are inflicted upon people all up and down the target side.

How can people in power get away with or justify oppression? A key element is the dynamic of blame or *scapegoating*—fabricating through myths, stereotypes, or "scientific" research features about target-group members that make them responsible for what is done to them.

2. Internalized Oppression

Oppression that goes on long enough is internalized. If we grow up continually being taught lies about who we are, we come to believe them. Think about the same target group you picked in #1. What are you sometimes afraid is true about what they say regarding people in your group (even if you "know" rationally that it is not true)?

Internalized oppression is as pervasive as oppression, teaching members of a target group to attack, to give up on, and to separate themselves from each other as well as to attack, to compete with, and to separate themselves from other target groups. Even worse, it trains people to isolate and to blame themselves and one another.

3. Resistance/Insurgence

Targeted people have always resisted violence in one way or another, even if just by saying "no" to oppression internally. And members of targeted groups have always rebelled and fought against mistreatment. United States and world histories are actually histories of ongoing insurgence against and resistance to oppression. Going back to your target group, consider moments in history and in your own life when people from your group, and/or you, have resisted oppression.

We can fight back against external and internalized oppression by understanding that they exist and affect us and that we will not accept either one. In particular, this means being an ally to people in our own target groups. When women come together, when African American people organize, when workers unite, they break down the isolation and blame of internalized oppression and begin to resist oppression directly. When these groups in turn link their struggles with other groups up and down the target side, their strength increases exponentially.

Ultimately, this struggle means holding the people directly across the line on the nontarget side accountable for being complete allies for you and your group. This accountability means expecting that mistreatment is not inevitable — it can be ended. It means refusing to accept limitations of your power, remembering all the ways you and the people in your group have resisted mistreatment, and expecting that nontarget-group people do not "naturally" engage in mistreatment but want, more than anything, to work to end it.

Let's look at three of the "isms" for examples of these concepts.

The Target Table

"Ism"	Target Group	Oppression	Internalized Oppression	Resistance/ Insurgence
Adultism	Youth	Physical assault, sexual assault, neglect, exploitation, verbal abuse, withheld rights and choices	Bullying, putdowns, cliques, "other kids are losers," "they deserve what they get," "they are so immature," "some kids are just bad," "I'm not old enough," "I don't have anything important to say"	Youth popular culture, youth organizing, noncooperation, mutual support, breaking the rules

(cont'd.)

"Ism"	Target Group	Oppression	Internalized Oppression	Resistance/Insurgence
Sexism	Women	Rape, battering, harassment, economic discrimination, poverty, poor health care, unequal pay	Self-hate, depression, eating disorders and diets, competition with other women, "some other women are flighty," "some other women will use sex to get what they want," "maybe women *are* too emotional"	Women's movements for suffrage, stopping violence against women, reproductive freedom, and equal pay; challenging male authority
Racism	People of color	Physical assault, segregation, economic discrimination, poor health care, police brutality, withheld education, poverty, camp internments, immigration quotas, extermination of native peoples	"Some of my people really *are* lazy," "if they really wanted to, they could succeed," "some of them *are* stupid," "they'll never amount to anything"	Civil rights; black/Chicano power movements; organizing for economic justice and immigrants' rights; preservation of languages, cultures, and sovereignty

For Nontarget Groups

Now turn to a category on the "nontarget" side of the chart — one you inhabit now or used to inhabit — to see how the following concepts might apply.

1. Conditioning

What is done to nontarget groups to "train" them to dominate? What happens to a boy to cause him as a man to use violence against his intimate partner? What happens to a white child that prepares her, before she might actually meet people of color socially, to be afraid or wary of them? What is done to nontarget-group members to make them obey, to go along with, or to not even recognize oppression? We call this process *conditioning* — the explicit and implicit mental and physical processes that train young people, overtly and subtly, to accept the assumptions of the Power Chart. Conditioning is built into and accomplished by education, media, family, and other institutions young people grow up within. In that respect, its negative aspects are forms of adultism.

Thinking of your nontarget group, consider what early messages you might have received about who the corresponding target members are and how you were to relate to them. How did this information come to you, and how did it feel (if you felt anything at all) to receive it?

2. Privilege

Nontarget status confers privilege or benefits that accrue to each of us as a member of a nontarget group. These are goods that a member of the nontarget group does not earn and is often unaware that they possess, simply because these privileges are part of the assumed daily conditions of mainstream culture for the group. An obvious example of privilege for men is the differential pay that men and women receive for the same work; one for heterosexual people is the unquestioned right for heterosexual people to marry, with the tax and health benefits and legitimacy that this convention confers. What are benefits that have automatically come to you as a member of a nontarget group?

3. Alliance

Alliance is a term we use particularly to stand for actions nontarget groups take, in solidarity with people from target groups, to dismantle oppression and to interrupt internalized oppression. Each of us, in our nontarget roles, is in position to be an ally to target groups, refusing to accept misinformation about and mistreatment of them, and always intervening. This position means remembering all the ways that we, as members of nontarget groups, resist learning about mistreatment, take pride in our people, find and celebrate all the ways past members resisted learning the oppressor role, and refuse to accept that members of our groups want mistreatment to continue. It means refusing to give in to guilt or defensiveness and instead believing in our own good will, taking steps, making mistakes, fixing them, and becoming close and full allies for people across the line.

Reviewing the same three "isms," what are some examples of these concepts?

These concepts are integral to our work with young people. That work is liberation, and liberation only works when all of us choose to be free, to break out of the cycle of oppression and internalized oppression, and to be allies for each other's freedom. It is exciting, creative, and joyous work. Let's get on with it.

The Nontarget Table

"Ism"	Nontarget group	Conditioning	Privilege/Benefits	Alliance/ Solidarity
Adultism	Adults	Grow up; obtain education and a successful career; raise and support a family; do it yourself; be mature; live on your own; be responsible; "kids" are immature, lazy, and irresponsible	Voting; making the rules and educational guidelines for youth; financial independence; respect and attention from public officials, business people, and police; financial credit	Parenting, teaching, mentoring, and caring for youth; organizing against juvenile imprisonment; supporting youth voice and leadership in all aspects of youths' lives

(cont'd.)

"ISM"	NONTARGET GROUP	CONDITIONING	PRIVILEGE/BENEFITS	ALLIANCE/ SOLIDARITY
Sexism	Men	Toughen up, and stop crying; endure physical training and punishment; score with women; "be all you can be"; strive to succeed; "women are too emotional and not as smart as men"	Differential pay; funding for sports; access to higher positions in business, sciences, government, and most other professions; double standards for sexual behavior (e.g., "stud"/"slut")	Organizing for equal pay, reproductive rights, violence prevention, health care, and economic justice; supporting and promoting women's leadership in all social institutions
Racism	White people	"You can't play with them", "they're dangerous/stupid/ dirty", "slavery was over a long time ago so there is no racism now", "be careful to lock your doors", "they don't belong here"	Taken-for-granted respect and service from police and public and government officials; access to adequate housing, medical care, and education	Organizing and providing funding for voter and other civil rights, prison reform or abolition, economic justice, and antiwar efforts; supporting and promoting the leadership of people of color

SOME NOTES ON USING THE POWER CHART

The Power Chart is a widely used tool in workshops and trainings across the country. Sometimes used as an explicit exercise, more often implicit in the theory motivating our work, the Power Chart and the concepts on which it is built have become inlaid in much of the training on issues of family violence, sexual assault, racism, multiculturalism, homophobia, and gender.

It is a very useful tool, for it clears away some of the misunderstanding about where power lies and how it is used. It makes a direct connection between power and violence, and it provides a social and political framework for understanding more particular issues of interpersonal relationships. It illustrates the link between institutional, interpersonal, and internalized oppression in ways that few other models do.

However, like all models, it distorts and oversimplifies reality, and consequently it may contribute to furthering some of the oppression we are trying to eliminate. It may also confuse some key issues and relationships that keep our work from being more effective in promoting social justice. Any of the following complications can surface in classroom discussion.

1. Either/Or

Looking at the chart more closely and more critically, we immediately notice how neat and tidy it is. The categories are simple, and most people can decide quickly into which boxes they fall, where they can "locate" themselves on the chart. They see that they are oppressors or oppressed, privileged or not, targets of violence or not (depending on your language). The chart makes it appear too clear that the world is not only neat and tidy but binary and polarized. Of course, reality is not so tidy, nor, for that matter, is it neatly divided into two parts (either/or).

The first binary category, adult/child, is meant to convey the power relationships between adults and children, but certainly it oversimplifies. Into which category do adolescents fall? They are less powerful in relation to adult society but more powerful than younger people. At what point does someone become an adult? It varies widely, depending on the person's particular class, race, gender, physical ability, education level, and health. Turning to adult/elder, at what point does someone lose access to adult power? Women do so earlier than men, and some men do not lose access at all. Some people are never accorded full adult status; that is, they are treated like children all their lives. Because age is tied to appearance, which is tied to physical and cultural factors, the beginning of adult status is a very slippery one to define, and it remains slippery at the other end as well. At some highly variable age we each become older or senior. Whether this change enhances or decreases our status and power also varies. In general, older people are less fully powerful compared to middle-age adults. However, many of the most powerful people in our society, including those holding most economic and political power, are senior citizens.

If age categories don't work so well, how about race? Besides the obvious fact that race as a biological reality doesn't exist, the words "white" and "people of color" convey some kind of difference in power. Again, it is useful to describe our society this way, as long as we are aware of the limits of our language. What is "white" has been variously defined over time to include or exclude southern Europeans, eastern Europeans, European Jews, Irish, Asians, and Mexicans of Spanish origin. Some people say that it means the way you are responded to when you walk down the street. In other words, are you seen and responded to as "white"? It depends on what neighborhood you venture into and to whom you are being compared. But are people of color not easily recognizable? Perhaps not those who "pass" as white—and many do. Such a simple opposition doesn't account for the multitudes who are biracial or multiracial, a group that includes a sizable minority of Americans. The fact is that some people are the result of intermarriage or rape, and their very existence contradicts the simple distinctions of the chart.

In addition, race as a binary category doesn't work well, because no one group can be labeled "people of color." People called Asian American or Latino barely fit into definable groups, because each label condenses potentially hundreds of different cultures into one catch-all category. The specificities of people's cultures, countries of origin, resistance to racism, and identities are so important and diverse that such simple categorization begs more questions than it answers. Only by defining people against whiteness and therefore perpetuating their invisibility can we maintain such a polarity. But this polarity is exactly what we are trying to change.

Does the category of heterosexual/lesbian, gay, and bisexual work any better? What if we add "transgender"? Some of us add transgender without fully understanding what it means and who transgendered people are, and we do this because we mistakenly believe it is correct. But transgender is not a sexual orientation — an account of whom one chooses for a sexual partner — but a gender identity, an account of the gender someone identifies as. In any case, sexual orientation is a highly fluid quality. It is certainly not an "either/or" characteristic. The amount of sexual latitude that is tolerated in "heterosexuals" at any given time is changeable. Some people's sexual identities remain unchanged for a lifetime, but for many people, they do change. Many people have some attraction to people of both the same and the other gender and, depending upon complex factors, may act on one, the other, or both types of attraction over the course of their lives. Sexual orientation is more likely a continuum than a polarity, and a flexible, fluid one at that. Defining sexual orientation as a political position doesn't make it any easier, because political definitions change as well. Finally, tying sexual orientation to gender may not anchor it securely. Although controversial, mounting evidence shows that human biology is complex and even anatomy is not always as precise as we might like it to be. Not only do women pass as men and men as women, but we can now alter people's sexuality through medical means. Even at birth, many children are much less clearly male or female than we might want to admit.

Clearly, men have more political power, and women have less. However, the acceptance of that binary opposition may be the result of emphasizing biological difference more than political reality. If that is the case, we need to question how much we reinforce the opposition in our strategies of resistance. Human biological qualities of body size, genitalia, hairiness, and breast size are more overlapping than distinct, and human psychological qualities are not easily or usefully divided into "female" and "male" categories. Any such gendered categorizations are a binary projection onto people by patriarchal institutions. Therefore, we need to be careful to focus our attention on the political results of gender polarization without contributing to a widespread belief in some inherent biological or psychological differences between men and women that the chart appears to represent. Here, as in all the examples cited above, we find that every line on the chart is more complex, less binary, than it appears at first glance.

2. The Differences

Another weakness of the chart is that, because all these qualities are put into a parallel structure, they begin to look like parallel issues (for example, racism is just like sexism, which is just like classism). Although some structural similarities exist regarding how these issues work in our society, the differences are crucial. Racism is not like sexism. The differences are crucial because they dramatically affect our strategies for challenging each system of oppression.. It is very easy to mislead people into thinking that our society is very simple, and therefore our strategies for change can be simple as well. People may also believe that if we just attack injustice, inequality, or prejudice individually, we will eliminate them all. No evidence indicates that this is so.

3. Complexities, Intersections, and the Politics of Identity

Just as human qualities don't fall into tidy boxes, lines, and charts, neither do whole people. No one is simply a lesbian, able-bodied, male, or a boss without that trait automatically being mediated by class, race, gender, health, age, religion, and the rest. The chart doesn't speak to the complexity of human lives. Obviously we inhabit multiple categories; clearly our identities reflect intersections of categories.

In the past several decades, liberation movements for women, people of color, queer people, and other groups have practiced identity politics. To demand equality, parity, and autonomy for these and other heretofore marginalized groups in the name of their identities and unique histories was and is part of the crucial struggle for collective liberation.

But what has also ensued from those struggles was the highlighting and "essentializing" of those single identities, ignoring the reality that we each possess multiple intertwined subject positions. It might be even more accurate to say that we inhabit one constantly evolving subject position with multiple intertwined identities. Every line on the chart needs much more in-depth focus, discussion, and cross-fertilization with the other lines than we generally give them. In this sense, the chart is a good beginning for a discussion rather than the final word. Rather than simply convincing people of the validity of the chart, we use their discussion questions and responses to explore it more deeply. Even these discussions, however, need to occur in a larger understanding of why we use the chart and what is at stake in looking at the nature of power.

4. How Social Change Happens

Because the visual focus of attention is on the relationship between, for example, men and women, it can look like changing the power imbalance between men and women is a question of mediating the relationship between them. Many of us use concepts of becoming allies in working with the chart that perpetuate this misconception. We talk about men becoming allies of women, whites of people of color, and so forth. We are, in fact, proposing an intergroup (and interpersonal) model of social change.

Historically, this is not how change actually happens. Women's economic and political gains have come because women have organized themselves for change, built alliances, and mobilized for particular transformations in cultural norms, institutional structures, and relationships of power. Some men have supported them, but many have not. Most resisted change. Some men were allies in sympathy but inactive in the social struggle. Some male allies treated their female friends and partners better, and some did not. Few were on the front lines challenging sexism. Similarly, workers, people of color, lesbians and gays, the physically challenged — each group has organized itself for social change and not waited for allies to step forward.

Using the chart as we do may direct our attention away from the realities of social struggle and into the fuzzy dynamics of interpersonal relationships, away from the specifics of how people have historically organized themselves for social change and into the more popular arena of how men should treat women and what women should expect from men. This can leave men (or white people, or other groups) trying to change their attitudes and behavior toward particular women without deciding to act concretely for institutional change. It can also leave women once again focused on men (or people of color on white people) rather than on their common political situation and effective strategies for resistance. Unless we can also keep our attention on social policy issues and strategies, most people will continue to see social change as change in individual growth, awareness, and sensitivity.

5. The Economic Basis of Inequality

A further way that the chart may mislead us politically is in obscuring, rather than highlighting, the economic structure that frames our lives. (See "The Class Race" in Section 3.) The chart lends itself to talking about oppression rather than exploitation, downplaying the economic basis for many of the structural inequalities in our society. Further, because it can look as though we are all on both sides of the chart, sometimes as oppressors and sometimes as the oppressed, it can seem as though no one really wins big. We're all tied into a calculus of violence, moving into and out of different powerful and less powerful roles. In fact, the ruling class in the United States controls most of the wealth and political power in the country. This top 1 percent (or 10 percent, depending upon where you draw the line) is invisible to most of us most of the time. The true power wielders do not live, work, play, or go to school with the rest of us. The chart perpetuates their invisibility, because it focuses on the rest of us and our relationships.

Economics does not determine everything. But economic violence — exploitation — is a key element driving and driven by all the oppressions. Exploitation includes the appropriation of land, labor, reproduction, culture, and spiritual practices from people in targeted groups. Most real-life resistance to the "isms" comes from groups of people fighting instances of exploitation at work, at home, or in the neighborhood. Unless we help people analyze the forms this exploitation takes, we may be distracting them from understanding the workings of the institutional systems of power.

Global Perspective

Finally, we should note the last line in the Power Chart on page 33, given the preeminent role that the United States plays in the world economy. This line has the United States on the powerful side and most of the rest of the world on the other side (and we could discuss where Germany, Japan, or China might fit). However, we don't generally use such a line; in the space of a class, workshop, or training, we will likely focus only on power dynamics internal to the United States. How do we bring an international understanding to our work? How would it change our understanding of all the other categories if we regularly included an international line? How would it better reflect the transnational political, economic, and military realities of our times and thereby enable us to develop more appropriate organizing and solidarity strategies?

We must continue to use the Power Chart in our education and prevention work, because we need the social/political framework it provides. Such a framework is completely lacking in most of the training, education, counseling, and therapy taking place in this country. The Power Chart helps politicize people's understandings of their lives. However, we also have to analyze the nature of the politics it brings up and the kinds of strategies it leads people toward. It can be a tool for bringing up and questioning the structure and justification for power and violence in our society, or it can perpetuate and lock people into a more conservative, binary analysis that limits strategies for change. The choice of how to use it is up to us.

THE CULTURE OF POWER[9]

Although it can be relatively easy to identify individual incidents of the oppressive use of power — racist or sexist comments, acts of hate, violence, and the like — it can be harder to identify the deeper structures of power imbalance in our society: the culture of power. To call these structures a culture of power is to indicate that such a culture is established, in place, set up already to govern our relations with one another, and set up in the categories by which we are educated to make sense of our relationships. It comes off as "the way things are," the taken-for-granted, operating on a much more foundational level than the surface incidents mentioned above. Until challenged, the culture is what is embedded in us, in how we see each other and see ourselves.

You know what it is like to experience the culture of power if you are a woman and have ever walked into a men's meeting, or if you are a person of color who has walked into a white-dominated organization or a child who has walked into the principal's office or a Jew or Muslim who has entered a Christian space. In these instances, you entered a culture not of your making, a culture in which you were less likely to be fully heard or taken seriously, a culture in which you were more likely to be talked over or undervalued. You might have felt insecure, unsafe, disrespected, unseen, or marginalized. You knew you had to tread carefully.

Whenever one group of people accumulates more power than another group, this group almost inevitably creates an environment that places its members at the cultural center and other groups at the margins. As noted before, we use the terms "nontarget" for the former and "target" for the latter. In the target group, you may easily be able to see the benefits denied to you. People in the nontarget group (the "in group") are accepted as the norm, but if you are in that group, it can be very hard for you to recognize the benefits you receive, because you are inside the culture of power.

A man lives in a culture in which, by gender at least, men have more social, political, and economic power than women, so he may often not notice that women are treated differently than he is. He is inside a culture of power — he can expect, unless that culture has been critically addressed, to be more likely to be treated with respect, to be listened to, and to have his opinions valued (for instance, at a business meeting, in a government office, or at a car dealership) than a woman in the same position. He expects to be welcomed. He expects, without thinking about it, to see men in positions of authority. He expects to find books and newspapers that are written by men reflecting his perspective and that show men in central roles. He doesn't necessarily notice that the women around him are treated less respectfully, ignored, or silenced; that they are not visible in positions of authority or welcomed in certain spaces; that they are charged more for a variety of goods and services; and that they are not always safe in situations where he feels perfectly comfortable.

Being Young in an Adult Culture of Power

Remember when you were a young person entering a space that reflected an adult culture of power — a classroom, store, or office where adults were in charge? What let you know that you were on adult turf, that adults were at the center of power?

You might remember abundant signs that adults were in control and youth were not, from the shape, decoration, and furnishing of the rooms to the spatial locale of authority: the teacher in the front of the room, the principal in the central office. Adults made the decisions. They might be considerate enough to ask you what you thought, but they did not have to take your concerns into account. You could be dismissed or made to feel wrong, bad, "immature," or "just a kid" at any time, so you learned to be cautious. You could look around and see what was on the walls (even where posters showed youth who looked like you — designed and produced by adults who may have been marketing to you), what music was being played, what topics were being discussed, and, most important, who made those decisions, and you knew that you were in an adult culture of power. You may have felt you were under scrutiny, being evaluated or graded. You had to change your behavior — how you dressed ("pull up your pants," "tuck in your shirt," "you're not going to wear that to school"), how you spoke ("speak up," "don't mumble"), even your posture ("sit up, don't slouch," "look me in the eye when I'm talking to you") — so you would be accepted and heard. You could not appear as smart as you were, or you'd be considered at best a show-off and at worst a troublemaker. You had to learn the adults' code, to talk about what they wanted to talk about, and to find allies among them, adults who would speak up for your needs in your absence. And in many cases, your future depended on making it through the tests, standards, and gateways to the future that adults designed and monitored.

Sometimes you may have had to cover up your family background, religion, or first language (if any of these reflected target statuses) in order to be at less risk of receiving adult disapproval. And if any disagreement or problem developed between an adult and you, you probably had little credibility. The adult's word was almost always believed over yours.

The effects on young people of an adult culture of power are similar to the effects on people of color of a white culture of power, the effects on women of a male culture of power, and the effects on people living with disabilities in a culture structured for those people conventionally seen as "abled." As an adult, you may rarely notice that you are surrounded by an adult culture of power that often puts young people and their cultures at a severe disadvantage, as they are judged, valued, and given credibility (or not) by adults on adult terms. Similarly, if you are a white person, when you are driving on the freeway, you are unlikely to think about how your racial identity might decrease your chances of being pulled over by police and how much a person of color's racial identity might make them more likely to be pulled over. When you are in a store, you are unlikely to notice that sometimes people of color are being followed, not being served as well, or being charged more for the same items. You might assume that everyone can vote as easily as you can and that everyone's vote counts. You are never asked where you are from (and this would be true even if you had stepped off the boat from another country yesterday). In a society that proclaims equal opportunity, you may not even believe that other people are being paid less than you are for the same work or being turned away from jobs and housing because of the color of their skin. When you are in public spaces, the music played in the background, the art on the walls, the language spoken, the layout of the space, and the design of the buildings are all things you might not even notice, because, as a white person, you are so comfortable with them. If you did notice them, you would probably consider them to be bland, culturally neutral items. Most of the time, you would be so much inside the white culture of power, and it would be so invisible to you, that you would have to rely on people of color to point out to you what that culture really looks like, what it feels like, and what impact it has on them.

Toward a Culture of Inclusion

The problem with a culture of power is that it reinforces the prevailing hierarchy — it makes it normal. When we are inside a culture of power as its "normal" members, we expect to have things our way, the way with which we are most comfortable. We may go through life complacent in that "universal" normality, unaware of the limits of our perspectives, the gaps in our knowledge, the inadequacy of our understanding. We remain unaware of the superior status and opportunities we have simply because we're white, male, able-bodied, or heterosexual. Of course a culture of power also dramatically limits the ability of those on the margins to participate in an event, a situation, or an organization. They are only able to participate on unfavorable terms, at others' discretion — a situation that puts them at a big disadvantage. They often have to give up or hide much of who they are in order to participate in any way in the dominant culture. And if any problems emerge, it becomes very easy for those in power to identify the people on the margins as the source of those problems and to blame or attack them rather than the problem itself.

Every organization has work to do to become more inclusive. Often, when groups talk about diversity issues, they address those issues of race, gender, and sexual orientation that are most visible. But, for example, without an understanding of how economic class limits people's abilities to participate in organizations, a group may end up with a remarkably diverse group — of middle-class participants. Those who are homeless, poor, single parents, working two jobs, or poorly educated (and many people fall into more than one of these categories) are unable to attend meetings or events, because they cannot afford the time, the fees, the child care, or the energy. When they do make it, they may feel unwelcome, because they have not been as able to participate previously, because they do not speak the language (or the jargon) of the organizers, or because they are unfamiliar or uncomfortable with the middle-class values and styles of the group.

People with disabilities can be similarly excluded when meetings are held in rooms and buildings that are not wheelchair-accessible, when sign-language interpretation is not provided, when accessible public transportation is not available, or when the pace and organization of the meeting does not allow people with disabilities to participate. People for whom English is not their primary language may face comparable barriers to finding out about meeting schedules and locations, attending events, becoming part of the leadership of an organization, or simply participating as a member when interpretation is not provided, when non-English media and communication networks are not utilized, or, again, when the pace and style of the controlling group does not allow for the slower pace that a multilingual process calls for.

How does this work with groups that may be targeted on one issue while nontargeted on another, such as all-white youth groups (target youth/nontarget white), elder US citizens (target elders/nontarget US citizens), or able-bodied people who are queer (target queer/nontarget abled)? To take the latter, lesbian, gay, bisexual, or transgender people (target) in a "heteronormative" culture (nontarget) are often aware of ways that the dominant culture of organizations works to exclude them. But how does it work when members of this queer group all happen to be, or at least seem to be, able-bodied? When they get together with other queer people in a group, they can feel so relieved they are all queer that they fail to notice ways that some parts of the queer community — queer people living with disabilities — may have been excluded. Because the members are in the culture of power in terms of lacking any disability, they can unwittingly overlook that they scheduled an event in a place that is not accessible.

We each have ways in which we are in the culture of power and ways in which we are marginalized. Although we may be good at recognizing how we have been excluded, we are probably less adept at realizing how we exclude others. We have to look to people from marginalized groups to provide leadership for us.

ASSESSING THE CULTURE OF POWER

What does the culture of power look like in your organization? In your office or area where you work? In your school or classroom? In your living room or living space? In your congregation? Where you shop for clothes? In agencies whose services you use?

Identify Cultures of Power

The following questions can be used to identify cultures of power based on gender, class, sexual orientation, religion, age, race, language, physical ability, immigrant status, education, or any of the other classifications based on power imbalances.

1. Who is in authority?
2. Who has credibility (whose words and ideas are listened to with most attention and respect)?
3. Who is treated with full respect?
4. Whose experience is valued?
5. Whose voices are heard?
6. Who has access to or is given important information?
7. Who talks most at meetings?
8. Whose ideas are given importance?
9. Who is assigned to or expected to take on background roles?
10. How is the space designed? Who has physical access?
11. What is on the walls? Who is represented?
12. Which language(s) are used? Which are represented on the walls and in textbooks and communications, such as with parents? Which are acceptable?
13. What music and food is available? Who provides it?
14. How much are different people paid? How are wages and prices determined?
15. Who cleans up?
16. Who decides?
17. Who is expected to succeed and to fail?
18. Who sees people like themselves in positions of leadership and who sees people like themselves primarily in devalued positions?

Every person has the right to complete respect, equitable access, and full participation in public life, including young people. Anything less limits the effectiveness of an organization by denying it the contributions — the experiences, insights, and creative input — of those individuals and groups excluded or discriminated against. Because those excluded are often acutely sensitive to how they and others are being marginalized, leadership in efforts to eliminate the culture of power must come from those in excluded or marginalized groups. Unless they are in leadership positions, with sufficient respect, status, and authority, the organization's efforts to change will be token and insufficient, with limited effectiveness.

As they become better at identifying patterns of exclusion, people from within the culture of power can learn to take leadership in identifying marginalizing

practices so the organization doesn't have to rely as much on people at the margins of power to do this work. Although groups will always have to look to the insights of people at the margins to completely identify how systems of oppression are currently operating, those inside the culture of power have an important role in taking the initiative to be allies to those excluded. They can challenge the status quo and can educate other "insiders" who are resistant to change. It is precisely because they have more credibility, status, and access that people on the inside make good allies. They can do this best not by speaking for or representing those marginalized but by challenging the status quo and opening up opportunities for others to step forward and to speak for themselves.

Every youth-related organization and institution has a culture of power. And departments, classrooms, programs, and offices within any system may have their own subcultures of power. These may not be consistent or overlapping. To be in opposition to the prevailing culture of power does not preclude us from creating subcultures of power that, in turn, exclude others who are even more marginalized than we are.

We have a responsibility as nontarget allies within a culture of power to use our insider position to eliminate the barriers to those on the outside. For most of us, that means listening to those on the margins, acknowledging our insider status compared to some other groups, and acknowledging our access to power, our resources, and our privileges. Then we can work with others to use our power, resources, and privileges to open up the structures to those who continue to knock on the doors, pushing every group we are a part of to move from a culture of power to a culture of inclusion.

Benefits and Privilege

One issue that arises constantly in social justice education is how to engage young people who are endowed with privilege. Their privilege can protect them from understanding the impact of oppression, making them less likely to become effective allies for social justice. Young people who are economically well off, white, male, and heterosexual not only are often ill-informed about oppression facing others but often have attitudes of superiority, entitlement, charitable patronization and service, scapegoating, or blame that have been reinforced by parents, teachers, peers, and the media. They also may feel knowledgeable, entitled to voice their opinions even when those opinions are based on misinformation and self-serving truths. These dynamics are particularly present in well-off schools and communities that are economically or racially segregated — as most are in the United States.

Living within the culture of power in any category blinds one to the experience of those who are outside it and protects one from the impact of oppression. But nobody lives completely within cultures of power. We all share the experience of growing up as young people who experience adultism, and most of us have other categories as well in which we are targeted for oppression. This shared experience can be an entry point for talking about privilege. For white women or men of color, for example, one can use analogies between sexism and racism to build compassion, understanding, and solidarity within a group.

To begin to understand the degree of one's privilege is to learn more about how the world actually is. It can make sense of one's previous tacit, uncertain feeling that something is wrong or out of balance. Privilege is not something to feel guilty about; most privileges we have come to us without our choosing. Privilege is not something one can disclaim or deny, even when it is easily seen by those without privilege, nor is it something one can easily sacrifice or give away. But it can be *used*; one can respond to the discovery of one's privilege by taking it up and using it as an ally, opening doors and confronting power in places inaccessible to those who are targeted.

Pointing out examples of how those in powerful groups have stepped out as allies in historical struggles for social justice also challenges privileged people to think about the choices they have and the obligation to take their actions seriously. White people who supported the civil rights movement, men who supported the women's liberation movement, able-bodied people who supported the struggle for disability rights — these examples show that individuals can and do choose their relationship to systems of oppression, regardless of their degree of privilege.

Finally, specific exercises and activities (see Section 3) help people with privilege understand how they benefit and how those benefits are directly connected to the exploitation of others. When white people learn that their clothes; their cell phones and computers; the coffee, tea, bananas, and chocolate they enjoy; and the gasoline in their cars are benefits based on the low wages, dangerous work, short life spans, and polluted communities of others, they often become more able to recognize that they are part of an interconnected human family that has obligations to all of its members.

Speak-Outs

What does alliance look like? One tool we use in our social justice trainings with youth and adults is the *speak-out* — a group exercise in which, on a given target/nontarget issue, members of the target group speak to members of the nontarget group about what they expect from those who intend to act as allies, and the latter repeat back, as carefully as possible, what has been said. In the normal functioning of oppression, those who experience the oppression are silenced or made invisible, while the voices, opinions, and activities of those on the upside prevail. In a carefully structured speak-out, both groups practice changing this pattern, making room for the targeted group to detail their experiences and for the nontargeted group to learn about them. They can then take a public stand as allies. From that exchange, the next steps of a shared alliance can proceed.

It takes time and several steps to increase group safety and to prepare a group for a speak-out. What follows is a stage-by-stage process for setting up a successful speak-out.

THE SPEAK-OUT PROCESS

1. Preconditions

Participants should (a) have learned and had a chance to practice using the agreements (see page 170 in Section 4), (b) understand the target/nontarget model of power and the Power Chart, and (c) have explored and understood the target/nontarget structure of the oppression being addressed by this speak-out. Finally, the exercise assumes that more than a token number of members of the relevant target and nontarget groups are present (for example, more than two to three women and more than two to three men if the speak-out is about sexism).

2. The Caucuses

After the facilitator outlines the purpose and structure of the speak-out process, participants are invited to divide into target and nontarget *caucuses*—facilitated discussion/affinity groups set up to prepare for the speak-out. Preferably, each caucus is facilitated by someone sharing the identity of caucus members, with target facilitators for target caucuses and nontargets for nontargets.

Allow for some time, confusion or uncertainty, and a few questions about where they "belong" for students choosing caucuses to attend. If the topic is racism, for example, biracial (person of color/white) youth may feel conflicts about whether to join the people of color or the white caucus. In general, we support multiracial youth joining the person-of-color caucus or, if a number of multiracial students are present, to form a (facilitated) multiracial caucus. If the topic is heterosexism, enough queer students may be present to further break into (facilitated) lesbian, gay, and bi- groups or queer male and queer female groups. For a speak-out on sexism, the facilitator may acknowledge that not everyone identifies as male or female and encourage those who don't to choose the group where they feel most comfortable or, if enough people iden-tify as transgender, to form a separate caucus.

The caucuses require separate meeting spaces. At a minimum, the target caucus stays in the current room while the nontarget caucus leaves to meet elsewhere. The following describes recommended questions for each caucus to address.

a. Target Caucus

Target groups are those groups in the United States that are objects of institutional discrimination, systematic mistreatment, or denial of resources and treatment equal to those of corresponding nontarget groups. Individual target group members can and do "get ahead," but this success is almost always by being or becoming members of other nontarget groups (for example, a person of color or woman who is born into or achieves wealth). Members of target groups experience oppression, internalized oppression, and resistance. Here are the topics that could be addressed in dyads (stu-dents paired off to talk to each other) or triads (three students) in a larger caucus or in the full caucus if time and space allow everyone the chance to speak:

▶ How does it feel to be in this group right now?

▶ Talk about your earliest experience of being mistreated or hearing/witnessing that people in your group were "less than" people in the group across the line, and how that experience still might affect you.

▶ What are examples of oppression, internalized oppression, or resistance to op-pression that you have experienced?

▶ In preparation for the speak-out, discuss:
  • What do you want nontarget people to know about your group?
  • What is one thing you never want to see/hear/have happen to your group again?
  • How can nontarget group members act as allies to you?

b. Nontarget Caucus

Nontarget groups are those that do not experience institutional mistreatment, discrimination, or denial of resources based on their identities and that gain benefits denied to target group members. Individual nontarget group members may experience discrimination, stereotyping, or mistreatment from particular target group members, but nonetheless they have more resources as a group than members of the target group. Furthermore, situations where they are targeted most likely stem from their membership in other target groups (such as a white person who is also poor or low-income). Nontarget people get conditioned hurtfully as children, receive privileges or unearned benefits (often without realizing it), and may feel guilt or resentment. But nontarget people have acted in the past and will continue to act as allies to target groups. Here are the topics that could be addressed in the caucus:

▸ How does it feel to be in this group right now?

▸ Talk about your earliest experience of conditioning, learning that people on the other side of the chart were "less than" people on your side—what happened? Did you receive other messages that reinforced that information? How did these experiences affect you then, and do they still affect you now?

▸ Did you resist the misinformation or act as an ally in any way?

▸ As members of a nontarget group, brainstorm and write up a list of privileges or benefits you can think of, however slight, that you suspect people in your group have in US daily life that target group people do not enjoy simply because they are members of their target groups.

▸ In preparation for the speak-out, discuss:
  • What does an ally do?
  • What does an ally not do?
  • What might be hard for you to hear when listening to the other group?
  • How can you be present as an ally (and support each other to be allies) to the target group in the speak-out?

3. The Speak-Out

After the caucuses, participants take a short break (while honoring such agreements as confidentiality) and then return to the main meeting space. Members of the target group caucus are invited to stand (if able) and come to the front of the room to face the nontarget caucus, whose members sit in chairs facing them. Explain that you are asking target group members to stand as an act of power and of speaking out. If several target groups are present (for example, different groups of people of color and multiple-heritage people), you may have to decide in advance whether to hold several consecutive speak-outs, one for each target group.

Briefly explain the speak-out and report-back process to the entire group. Then turn to the target group to explain that members of the group may speak to any of the following three statements "popcorn" style (anyone can speak whenever they are ready), making the statement and completing it as they wish (trying to be relatively concise so that hearers can remember and repeat what was said). The statements are either announced or written up on a poster or board so everyone can see them.

- ▶ What I want you to know about us is…
- ▶ What I never want to see/hear/have happen to us again is…
- ▶ What I expect from you as my ally is…

(In repeating the third statement, you may specify that students are not asking what they need or what they want but, more powerfully, what they expect from people who are allies.)

The speaker makes one statement and stops, another speaks, and so forth. Speakers can speak again, offering different statements or different versions of the same statement, as long as they make room for others to speak. Moments of silence are fine. Finally, note that the group has ten minutes and that you will let them know when they have one minute left. The speak-out is timed this way and with this duration to provide a clear beginning-and-end structure for the participants and to enable listeners to be able to remember and to report back what they have heard relatively soon after the speakers make their statements.

Remind the nontarget group of its role of alliance, and encourage its members to support the target group through active, respectful listening as well as maintaining confidentiality for the target-group members.

4. Ally Report-Back

At the close of the speak-out, spend a few moments in silence (no applause). Then instruct members of the ally (nontarget) group to take turns, also popcorn style, standing up and repeating back one statement they heard, as much as possible word-for-word, without responding to, adding to, or commenting on the statement they heard, and then sitting down. This is a time simply to ensure that they have heard clearly what was said. Duplications are fine. Explain that they will have five minutes to do this and that you will also let them know when they have one minute left.

5. The Closing

a. Dyad/Process

When the report-back closes, invite target-group members to say good-bye to each other in any way they wish. Then break the entire group into dyads, targets with targets and nontargets with nontargets, to process how this exercise felt. Then convene for appreciations and commitments (see below).

A question from members of either group may arise about whether and when the nontarget group gets to speak out. Review the purpose of the speak-out: The exercise is intended to help students try on the process of challenging the fact that nontarget perspectives are much more likely to get attention in day-to-day practice. Invite students to consider this situation and to think about what it means to make this challenge—what it means for the target group to be heard and what it means for the nontarget group to get a chance to listen. Then turn to the final exercise.

b. Appreciations/Commitments

The entire group reconvenes, standing and moving around to form a full circle, target groups and nontarget groups mingled. Take a few moments to have people silently look around the group to observe one another. Remind them that the agreements, particularly confidentiality, are still in place. Then have participants volunteer to offer a personal appreciation of someone in the group or to state a specific commitment they are making to resist the oppression at issue or to act as an ally against it. Alternatively, pass out sticky notes and writing instruments, have participants write down their commitments anonymously, and then post them on a prearranged poster hanging on a nearby wall or lying on the floor in the center of the circle. Begin with your appreciation of the entire group.

This section includes effective tools for building bridges across privilege and isolation; it is also useful to address issues of privilege more directly. In situations where few people from oppressed groups are present, this is even more essential. People within cultures of power can be powerful allies to those who are marginalized and excluded. It is going to take people within and outside systems of power and privilege working together to dismantle systems of injustice.

SECTION 3

Overview of the "Isms"

INTRODUCTION

The following articles apply the theory presented in "It's about Power" (see page 27) to the specific power imbalances of sexism, racism, heterosexism and transgender oppression, classism, ableism, religious oppression, and environmental destruction, beginning with adultism. We highlight these particular issues because of their immediate relevance to young people, but the theory can easily be extended to other social inequalities. This section also includes many of the key exercises we use in workshops as well as particular directions for working with youth on dealing with privilege. These exercises are referred to throughout the book.

ADULTISM

Why do young people do poorly in school? Why do young people use drugs, hang out on street corners, get pregnant, or use guns? A common answer to these questions when we first wrote this book was that many young people suffer from low *self-esteem*, generally defined as a poor sense of one's worth or ability — a lack of confidence. Professional literature about adolescents, social-service priorities, and funding trends all emphasized programs that built self-esteem. This concept still enjoys wide credibility and is often believed to be the root of young people's problems. Many youth workers convey to young people that if they just had higher self-esteem, they could overcome any obstacle and succeed at anything they set out to do. So is the problem low self-esteem or delinquency, or any other adult-assigned pathology?

When you think back to your years as a young person, you probably recall how much you wanted to do and how little power you had to do it. You wanted to go places you couldn't, and you wanted to try to do things you weren't supposed to. You wanted to affect and change your school, your community, or your neighborhood, and you weren't able to. You most likely did not have the money, transportation, friends, influence, or credibility to make a difference. And over a quarter of you went to bed hungry each year or survived on unhealthy fast food as your main meal.

Adults made lots of promises. If you studied hard, worked hard, stayed out of fights, stayed safe, didn't have sex, didn't drink or smoke, and didn't mess up, adults promised you a life filled with power and privileges. But the promise of power ten or twenty years in the future was not inviting or convincing. In the meantime, probably few adults listened to you, allowed you to participate, trusted you, or even really noticed you and your fellow young people.

Of course, when adults systematically don't listen to you or allow you to participate in making meaningful decisions, your sense of self-worth deteriorates. When they grade you continually on something like your academic performance, your concept of your own value can hinge on that opinion, too. If, on top of this, they belittle, randomly punish, or molest you, your self-esteem can plummet and your level of delinquency might soar.

Finally, when you are face to face with globally lower expectations for quality of life, economic breakdown, widespread defunding of education at all levels, and horrendous ecological destruction, despite the hype that you are living in a glamorous youth culture, you might feel alienated or pushed toward doing whatever you need to survive.

Oppression: The Issue Is Power

Our problem as young people was not based on low self-esteem or any of the other psychologically defined problems. Rather, we had no real power over our lives. Without power to protect ourselves, we were constantly restricted, disrespected, and abused by adults. Everywhere we went, adults had the authority to decide how we should dress, where we could be, and who we could be with. They decided our future through daily decisions including discipline, records, diagnoses, arrests, report cards, evaluations, and allowances or just by ignoring, interrupting, or neglecting us.

Young people today face the same lack of power. Adults may believe that adolescence is a time of promise, of open futures, of the possibility of meaningful education, fully compensated work, and healthy relationships. The reality is a broken promise and an epidemic of violence in its many forms.

In the United States today, tens of millions of young people live in poverty; lack health care; experience physical, emotional, and sexual abuse from adults; and experience inadequate educational opportunities and a lack of job opportunities. Many live in toxic environments. Young people lack political representation. Adults routinely belittle and sabotage their efforts to survive, to sustain their relationships, to nurture their opportunities, to work for justice, and to express their creativity. Young people are being socialized into adults, in effect, to inhabit and to replicate a society — the culture of power described in previous sections — with hierarchies of race, gender and other identities, exploitation, and violence.

We use the term "adultism" to stand for the everyday, systematic, and institutionalized oppression that young people face at the hands of adults. Some obvious features of adultism are the abuses cited above as well as unequal pay for work; induction into low-paid jobs and the military; rising incarceration, including sentencing of youth as adults; denial of information and resources regarding reproductive health; impoverishment; and denial of most forms of control over their lives. But the most destructive effect of adultism may be the wholesale adult conditioning of generations of young people to enter an adult world built on systems of oppression. "The Heart Exercise" on page 17 outlines the process by which our society teaches babies and young children that the way to survive in the world is to put up shields of protection around their loving, spontaneous, curious, connected, and creative selves and, in self-defense, to pass on their pain, anger, and frustration in abuse toward themselves and other people. Children are trained to think of themselves as separate, isolated, and in competition with others and to believe that this separation is natural and inevitable. As a result, young people learn to accept exploitation and violence in our society and to participate in work, family, and community roles that maintain the status quo of wealth and power.

In our years of experience as educators and activists, we have found that before people are able to look at systems of oppression that divide us, they need to understand the common socialization that we all endure and the common ground we share. Part of our common ground is the socialization that adultism produces and the recognition of our common concerns, needs, capacities to care, desires for connection, and inclusion in safe and healthy communities.

We also share the hurtful messages we received from adults or other children that say we are wrong and bad. Because the conditioning happens systematically yet personally, child by child, each child can come to feel that something is wrong with themself or with the other "kids." They may feel that they are to blame for being teased, harassed, bullied, marginalized, excluded, put down, abused, or otherwise attacked and that it is acceptable to do the same to others. Most of us were not only bullied but also the bully, not only the teased but the teaser, not only the one who was put down but the one who put down others.

The messages are found in the labels adults place upon youth: troublemaking, irresponsible, immature, apathetic, spoiled, lazy, dishonest, troubled, underachieving, attention deficient, addicted, hormone crazed, or just plain stupid. The basic message is that you have something wrong with your body, your feelings, your attitude, your ideas, your clothes, your hair, or your skin color. Parents, teachers, peers, and the media reinforce the message.

Most young people, even with adult support, find it difficult to resist these messages. All forms of youth violence, including the youth-to-youth abuse that happens in gangs, in couples, or from the school bully; the self-abuse from drugs or alcohol; cutting/self-mutilation; eating disorders; unwanted pregnancy; suicide; sexual assault; and homicide can be seen as forms of learned helplessness and hopelessness in youth. Youth violence is how the internalized oppression of adultism manifests in young people's lives.

To make clear the impact of adultism on young people, we sometimes use the following visualization and exercise.

ADULTISM VISUALIZATION

Group participants, regardless of age, think of themselves as young people, close their eyes, and pay attention to their feelings as the facilitator, playing an "adult," throws out the following statements in an increasingly angry and abusive tone:

- ▶ Not now. I don't have time.
- ▶ You're too young to understand.
- ▶ We'll talk about it later.
- ▶ Go to your room.
- ▶ Not until you finish your homework.
- ▶ Clean your plate.

- ▶ I work my fingers to the bone for you.
- ▶ Wait until you have children.
- ▶ Wait until your father gets home.
- ▶ When I was your age, I had it a lot harder.
- ▶ Do what I say.
- ▶ Not in my house, you don't.
- ▶ Because I said so.
- ▶ Sit up. Sit up straight.
- ▶ Don't you talk back to me.
- ▶ Is that the best you can do?
- ▶ You're just a kid.
- ▶ Pay attention when I'm talking to you.
- ▶ You're stupid.
- ▶ Shut up.
- ▶ You show me some respect.
- ▶ This hurts me more than it hurts you.
- ▶ Don't tell your mother about this; it's just our secret.
- ▶ You get back upstairs and change into something decent.
- ▶ Turn off the goddamned TV.
- ▶ Get the hell out of here.
- ▶ All right, now you're gonna get what's coming to you.
- ▶ I brought you into this world—I can take you out.

At the close of this exercise, the facilitator has participants open their eyes and take part in the following activity.

LEARNING ADULTISM

The facilitator reads the following statements to the group. For each statement, participants stand silently if the statement applies to them as young people, notice who else is standing, and notice their feelings, whether standing or sitting. Again, make sure any mixed-age group includes enough young people for them to feel safe. (If you are facilitating this exercise for adults who work with young people, ask them to think back to when they were sixteen and younger to respond to these statements.) If you have participants with limited mobility, ask them to indicate their participation by raising their hands if they are able ("Please stand up or raise your hand if…").

Please stand up silently if you have ever...

1. been called a name by an older person
2. had your dress or appearance criticized by an adult
3. had an adult refuse to hold, hug, or show you affection when you wanted them to
4. been called "stupid" or been made to feel less intelligent by an adult
5. been unfavorably compared with other children by an adult
6. been humiliated (for example, joked about, put down, yelled at, or punished) in public by an adult
7. been ignored, served last, or watched suspiciously in a store by an adult
8. been told you were too young to understand
9. had your personal privacy invaded in any way by an adult
10. been told to stop crying by an adult
11. been left for a long period of time, left alone when you didn't want to be, or abandoned by an adult
12. unwillingly and over a long period of time had to perform an adult task (such as having to parent younger siblings for an ongoing period), because no other adults were able to be there
13. been lied to by an adult
14. been cheated out of money by an adult
15. had to take a job before the legal age to support your household
16. been paid less than an adult for doing equal work
17. lived in a community that didn't offer any or enough youth-friendly facilities or alternatives with things for youth to do that didn't cost a lot of money
18. attended a school where there weren't enough textbooks or where facilities were substandard
19. been bullied, beaten, or robbed by other youth
20. been stopped by the police on the street
22. been arrested or made part of the juvenile justice system
23. been made to enter counseling or therapy without informed consent
24. been prescribed or given medication to alter or control your emotions or behavior
25. been manhandled, physically restrained, trapped, or put on restriction by an adult
26. been yelled at by an adult

27. had an adult physically threaten you

28. become drunk or taken drugs, undereaten, overeaten, or done something dangerous or unsafe to cover your feelings or hide pain

The following categories are sometimes added in groups where youth have developed long-lasting, trusting relationships with each other:

Please stand up if you know a youth who...

1. was held or touched by an adult in a sexual way when they didn't want to be

2. witnessed an adult in their immediate family or household emotionally brutalize,
hit, or beat another adult in the family

3. has a cut or mark or scar on their body purposefully inflicted by someone else or
by themselves

4. has ever felt like blowing themselves away

5. has been hit by an adult

6. has ever been beaten regularly or terrorized by an adult

7. has ever been sexually molested by an adult

At the close of the exercise, ask participants to form dyads to discuss what emotions and reactions they experienced during the exercise. Then conduct a group discussion on the same question.

We Have Failed Them

The two exercises just described predictably bring up many experiences and feelings for young people. When we use them with adult groups, the same intense responses occur. Clearly adultism is part of the daily experience of all young people.
In reality, we have failed them. We discriminate against youth, keeping them unemployed, vulnerable to abuse, exposed to violence and drugs, and uninformed
about health and reproductive issues. Then we blame them if they get strung out on
drugs. We blame them if they get pregnant or get someone else pregnant. We blame
them if they drop out of school or get picked up for hanging out.

And beyond young people's powerlessness, actual abuse keeps them from succeeding. Current national estimates indicate that one out of four girls and one out
of six boys is sexually abused by adults or people who are at least six years older. The
rates of physical, sexual, and emotional abuse and neglect toward young people
are alarming. Violence against children — which can range from emotional and
physical abuse to throwing an object to using a weapon to sexual assault — happens
to one in five children of US families every year.[10] Past experiences of personal

violence drastically limit a young person's ability to succeed in the future, because they foster self-doubt, mistrust, withdrawal, and self-destructive behavior.

Young people also correctly perceive that if they are a person of color; a woman; lesbian, gay, bisexual, or transgender; have a disability; or come from a poorer family, their opportunities to achieve are severely limited. For example, girls face lower expectations and sexual harassment. Black and Latino males face higher rates of institutional discipline, suspensions, and arrests. Lesbian, gay, bisexual, and transgender youth have to deal with physical and verbal attacks and intimidation. Youth learn to blame themselves for this abuse as well.

When we only help them develop higher self-esteem without addressing larger issues of oppression and internalized oppression, we lie to young people. We lead them to believe that they individually are the problem and they individually are to blame. We mislead them into thinking that personal virtue, effort, perseverance, and skill can completely change their lives. The reality is that many will fail. Their chances of surviving and succeeding are increased when they know what they are up against. Then they can work together, with us as allies, to change the odds.

It is the fundamental assumption of our work that young people are not the problem. They are part of the solution. We desperately need their courage, insight, experience, creativity, sense of humor, resilience, loyalty, voice, and sense of fairness and justice. It is our challenge as adult allies to figure out how to support their coming together to be part of efforts to build a healthy, sustainable, and just community.

How Adults Can Stop Adultism

If, as an adult, you are first encountering the concept or the term "adultism," you may find yourself resisting its implications or even its existence. After all, adults — parents, relatives, teachers, coaches, mentors, child-care providers, older siblings, and many others — have had and do take responsibility for caring for and raising the entire next generation of young people, a monumental task. We are already in the position of being allies to youth. And most of this work is underpaid or unpaid and certainly unheralded, confined to single-family households and overburdened youth workers. The daily stresses of this task may keep us from adequately recognizing the realities of adultism, much less giving us the time or inclination to reflect upon our own younger selves and our likely painful and unresolved experiences of adultism.

How can we persevere as the allies we actually are, looking at adultism openly and taking steps to back young people up? We have found the following tactics to be helpful:

- *Be an ally.* Young people need to see us as strong, reliable, and completely on their side, knowing that we trust them, respect them, and will tell them the truth.

- *Tell the truth about power.* Young people need us to tell them about how power is used and abused in this society. We need to be informed, clear, and firm about how racism, sexism, adultism, and the other "isms" work. We must be ready to share that information openly and in clear, direct language that does not fault them for lacking it.

- *Tell the truth about violence.* We also must help them identify the social violence directed at them because they are women, people of color; lesbian, gay, bisexual, and transgender; poor; and young. Confirming this reality can help them take power to stop the violence.

- *Support healing.* We need to let them know that it is not their fault that they have been demeaned, assaulted, or discriminated against and that these abuses happen to many of us. We need to pass on skills to them for avoiding further violence in their lives.

- *Interrupt adultism.* It is always appropriate to intervene supportively where adults are denying young people's rights or due respect.

- *Interrupt internalized adultism.* It is always appropriate to intervene supportively when youth put down or devalue one another or themselves.

- *Promote youth history.* Young people need information about their struggles and achievements as young people and the leading roles young people have taken in most struggles for social justice so they can take pride in and build upon this history. This information directs them to think of themselves as a community responsible for one another's well-being.

- *Share power.* Young people need us to be willing to share the power and work with them.

- *Make mistakes openly and without self-deprecation.* Adults, of course, are never supposed to make mistakes. This expectation can mean we never take the chance to reach that young person who is hardest to reach. Go ahead. Try anyway. And when you make a mistake, it is okay. Just fix it, and try again.

- *Don't do it alone.* Work with other adult allies so you have support when your own issues come up, when you feel you have made a mistake, and so forth. Adult support helps decrease your possibility of taking out your hurt on young people or trying to enlist support from them when they shouldn't have to be in a position to give it.

- *Trust youth to be powerful.* This is about to be their world. They are strong and have convictions and experience about what is right and wrong. Support them to make their own decisions. Nothing will change until they do.

- *Celebrate their successes.* Every day, young people make dozens of choices to value their own thinking, relationships, and desires. Every young person finds ways to get attention and to communicate that the oppression is hurting them. And every youth finds ways to express love, even to those adults passing on the oppression. These are all victories. They deserve adult allies who point out these acts of self-determination and celebrate them.

We can be strong and powerful adult allies to young people if we shift our emphasis from raising their self-esteem to increasing their power. Adults in youth-serving agencies can assess the operation of adultism within their organization and build their capacity at the individual and organizational level to effectively support young people. That, in turn, will allow the exuberance, insight, and creativity of young people to contribute to the betterment of all our lives.

CLASSISM

As adults who work with youth in a class-based society, our relationships are complicated by the fact that we belong to a group charged with preparing young people to take their economic places in society, even if we are inviting them to change it. Regardless of our personal intentions, the larger institutions we work within operate as gatekeepers (as later described in the "The Buffer Zone," in the follow-up to "The Class Race" exercise). Even in the work of preventing violence, we are in the position of training youth in how to get ahead and get by, an effort that maintains, or even strengthens, social inequality. Can we be educators who not only help young people get ahead individually but also help them get together for social change?

To approach these challenges—and class inequality itself—from a social justice perspective, it helps to reflect upon our own experiences of economic inequality in a class-based system. We are taught that if we are obedient, religious, and focused, we will achieve our goals. Many of us and many of the youth in our lives are promised a level playing field in pursuing life goals, but our real experiences show a different reality. The following exercise enables youth and adult participants to notice exactly how we don't actually begin with equal opportunity. It was created as, in effect, the next step of "The Power Shuffle" exercise (see page 29 in Section 2) and as an introduction to understanding the class structure of our society.

THE CLASS RACE[11]

This exercise begins at the starting line of a race with everyone apparently having equal opportunity and starting positions, representing the "level playing field." Guided by the statements, participants rearrange themselves based on their actual experiences of advantages and disadvantages to better reflect actual opportunity structures in our society. The exercise helps people understand the impact of race, class, and other differences on economic opportunity in the United States and, through the paired and whole-group discussions following the exercise, think about the implications of differentiated opportunity in their own lives and in those around them. The exercise also prepares them for talking about the economic pyramid.

Carefully review the list of categories ahead of time to select between twenty and thirty that may be most relevant to your group, keeping some balance between the "steps forward" and "steps back" (note that forty categories are a *lot*, especially for a large group, and may make the exercise last too long for participants to remain engaged). Make sure to include categories that in your estimation will give every participant at least one experience of stepping forward and at least one experience of stepping back.

Opening Instructions

1. Have everyone stand and come toward the middle of the room, moving all chairs and items on the floor completely out of the way. (This exercise can also be conducted in an open outside area.)

2. Invite participants to form a shoulder-to-shoulder line in the middle of the room, facing one wall. If not everyone can fit into a single line, have them form several lines, one behind the other. Ask those who have limited physical mobility to decide whether they can participate and, if so, what accommodation is appropriate. If they cannot participate, invite them (and the group) to notice how that feels, and explain that the group will address this obvious exclusion in what follows. An alternative is to position participants with disabilities who cannot be accommodated in the back of the room right from the start, as an indication of the exclusions people living with disabilities face. Then have everyone silently notice how this feels and what it means for those who can't participate in the race and for those included in the race.

3. Have everyone reach out to either side (in their own line, if this applies) and hold hands with the people on both sides. Ask the group to accommodate those who are physically unable to do this.

4. Explain that this is a version of "the level playing field." All of us deserve (and are promised by our democratic institutions) the same chances and opportunities for education, meaningful work, health and shelter, spiritual support, and emotional care as everyone else. They are standing on the starting line for a race to get some well-paying jobs, which they need to take care of their families. Before the race starts, people's starting positions will be adjusted somewhat via the exercise. To the extent that the exercise is like the (un)level playing field, it is also not set up to accommodate those with physical and mental disabilities.

5. Say that this exercise is about noticing some of the ways we become separated from each other and ways that "equal opportunity" may be more imagined than real. We may begin by noticing how some people with disabilities might already be separated because of a lack of accommodation to their needs.

6. Explain that you will call out a category and instruct people who fit that category (and are willing to acknowledge that they do) to step forward or backward as you direct, as much as possible keeping steps the same size throughout the exercise. Participants in wheelchairs may roll their chairs about a step forward or backward as directed by the statements.

7. As they do the exercise, participants are to continue looking forward to the front wall without turning around to see where everyone is behind them.

8. Explain:
   - Everyone has the right to pass, so they don't have to acknowledge membership in the category if they don't wish to, except that you will ask everyone to notice, silently, their own feelings and thoughts.
   - Everyone has to decide for themselves whether the category fits—you will repeat the category if someone didn't hear it, but you won't explain it, and if someone isn't sure, they can simply stay still.
   - The exercise is done in silence. Remind people not to talk, joke, or laugh but to notice any feelings, memories, or thoughts that come up.
   - As the exercise proceeds, participants will begin to be pulled away from each other. Invite them to release handholds when these become uncomfortable and to notice any feelings that come up when they do.
   - Whether people take steps or don't is confidential, so if you want to discuss with someone what they did, you must ask (and receive) their permission to bring it up.

9. Take a few moments to have everyone get ready. Invite them to take a breath.

Instructions for Conducting the Exercise

1. Begin the exercise, calling out categories clearly and allowing people time to move and, once they've moved, to notice what they feel. The exercise should move somewhat like a ritual, with a certain rhythm:
   - Call out the category.
   - Allow time to move.
   - Say "notice how you feel" or "notice thoughts/feelings."
   - Call out the next category.

2. You will probably have to remind people gently, several times, to remain silent, to notice feelings, and to keep looking forward.

3. When you have four to five categories left, let the group know.

4. At the close, continue with the meditation "Noticing Where You Are."

Categories: If...

1. you grew up with both your parents, take one step FORWARD

2. you grew up in a single parent household, take one step BACK

3. you or your parent/s own their own home, take one step FORWARD

4. you or members of your family are or have been day laborers, sweatshop workers, or migrant workers, take one step BACK

5. you or members of your family are documented or undocumented immigrants or refugees to this country, take one step BACK

6. your ancestors were forced to come to this country or forced to relocate from where they were living, either temporarily or permanently, or restricted from living in certain areas, take one step BACK

7. you were taken to art galleries, museums, or plays by your parents, take one step FORWARD

8. one of your parents was ever laid off, unemployed, or underemployed not by choice, take one step BACK

9. you ever attended a private school or summer camp, take one step FORWARD

10. you were ever discouraged or prevented from pursuing academic or work goals, or tracked into a lower level because of your race, class, or ethnicity, take one step BACK

11. you grew up in a household with more than fifty books, take one step FORWARD

12. you ever skipped a meal or went away from a meal hungry because there wasn't enough money to buy food in your family, take one step BACK

13. you or your family ever had to move because there wasn't enough money to pay the rent, take one step BACK

14. your ancestors came to this country voluntarily and legally and have never had to relocate unwillingly once they were here, take a step FORWARD

15. you or immediate family members ever received public assistance or welfare, or if you or your siblings were ever removed from your parents' care by social-service workers, take a step BACK

16. you have immediate family members who are doctors, lawyers, or other professionals, take one step FORWARD

17. you or other family members ever inherited money or property, take one step FORWARD

18. any women in your family (including yourself, if you are female) were ever physically or sexually assaulted in any way by men in your family, take one step BACK

19. you have parents or grandparents from two different racial groups, take a step BACK

20. in your family, as a child, you were the intermediary between your parent/s and store clerks or public officials (social workers, school officials, and so forth) because of language or other differences, take a step BACK

21. you grew up with people of color or working-class people who were servants, maids, gardeners, or babysitters in your house, take one step FORWARD

22. prior to your eighteenth birthday you took a vacation outside your home state, take one step FORWARD

23. you were ever embarrassed or ashamed of your clothes, your house, or your family car when growing up, take one step BACK

24. you feel that your primary ethnic identity is "American," take one step FORWARD

25. you are, or someone in your family is, lesbian, gay, bisexual, or transgender, take one step BACK

26. you are a man, take one step FORWARD; a woman, take one step BACK

27. you were raised in a household whose religious practice was Muslim, Jewish, Buddhist, Hindu, Native American, or other non-Christian religion, take one step BACK

28. you are under age twenty-four [OR: age twenty-one; OR: age eighteen], take one step BACK

29. you are over age fifty-nine, take one step BACK

30. you were ever publicly labeled "fat," take one step BACK

31. you are able-bodied, take one step FORWARD; live with a hidden or visible physical, emotional, psychological, or learning disability, take one step BACK

32. you routinely don't and don't have to think at all about your gender identity or sexual orientation in approaching a new social situation, such as applying for a job or going to a party, take one step FORWARD

33. you were ever called names or ridiculed because of your race, ethnicity, gender, sexual orientation, physical or mental abilities, or class background, take one step BACK

34. you ever tried to change your physical appearance, mannerisms, language, or behavior to avoid being judged or ridiculed, take one step BACK

35. you have ever been enrolled in gifted and talented classes, or your school had more than five Advanced Placement courses, take one step FORWARD

36. you are the first in your family to go to college, take one step BACK

37. it was easy to find and study the history and culture of your ethnic ancestors in elementary and secondary school, take one step FORWARD

38. you started school speaking a language other than English, take one step BACK

39. you were ever given less support than the boys in your family for going to college or pursuing work goals because of your gender, take one step BACK.

40. you went to schools with all or almost all white students, take one step FORWARD

41. you got called on regularly in class in school or college, take one step FORWARD

42. you don't (or didn't) need a job to support yourself or your family if you are (were) in school, take one step FORWARD

43. you were told by your parents that you were beautiful, smart, and capable of achieving your dreams, take two steps FORWARD

44. you can *very easily* find many people of your racial background in positions of leadership in government, business, the academic world, the entertainment industry, and so forth, take one step FORWARD

45. you commonly see people of your race or ethnicity on television or in the movies in roles that you consider to be degrading, take one step BACK

46. you grew up or lived in a community where residents were subject to gun, street, youth, or police violence or where drugs, gambling, pimping, sex work, or other illegal activities were a major occupational alternative in the community, take one step BACK

47. you have been stopped by the police, followed by security, or denied service because of your ethnicity, class, or age, take a step BACK

48. you worked or work in a job where people of color made less for doing comparable work or did more menial jobs, take a step FORWARD

49. your religious or cultural holidays were not recognized on your job or at your school, and, for example, meetings and work time were scheduled during those periods, take a step BACK

50. you or close friends or family members were ever victims of violence because of your race or ethnicity, sexual orientation, physical appearance, religion, or gender, take one step BACK

Meditation: Noticing Where You Are

After the last statement, everyone is asked to freeze in place and to look *forward* and from side to side (but not back) to notice where they and those they can see are. Invite people not to speak but just to think of answers to the questions you are going to pose. What do they notice so far about where they are and what/who they see?

Instruct people toward the front of the room to think about where they are, how it feels to be there, and how it feels not to be able to see who's behind them but to know they're there. How might they come to feel about people behind them? Around them?

Instruct those toward the middle to notice those in front of them and how it feels to see backs turned toward them while feeling the presence of more people behind them. How might they come to feel about the people in front of them? The people behind? The people around them?

Instruct those in the back of the room to notice how it feels to have no one behind them and everyone in front of them with backs turned. How might they feel about the people in front of them? About each other?

Then ask participants to look around and notice briefly where they are and where everyone else is. What feelings do they have, and what patterns do they notice?

The Media

Ask people to imagine that the front wall represents the locus of power and wealth. The view of the group from this vantage point is the perspective by which the corporately controlled media portray everyone in the room. Invite everyone to think about who has access to and the ability to control their images in the media. Whose lives and whose viewpoints are most likely to be represented in the media and by whom? How will the people nearest the vantage point of wealth be portrayed? The people farthest from this vantage point?

The Race

Then explain that the participants are in a race to the front wall for well-paying, good jobs—to get a piece of the "American Dream." They are to consider themselves now on the starting lines, and, if they are physically able, they are to run toward the wall as fast as they can. The first few to the front wall will get those jobs. Quickly say, "Ready, set, go!" to start the race (and get out of the way!).

OR: Give the instruction (without telling them whether to participate): "Ready, set, go!"

After participants have moved (or refused to move), have them take a few moments to notice where they are.

Closing Instructions

End the exercise by having participants form dyads and talk for a few minutes about whatever feelings came up during the exercise. Reconvene the group to share reflections.

This exercise works well as a follow-up to the Power Chart to make concrete what the differences in power mean. It introduces class and how it is intertwined with race. It raises issues of individual achievement, "level playing field," affirmative action, and the different reactions people have to an unequal system. (For instance, given where they ended up in the room, how did that affect how hard they ran toward the front wall? Did they bother to run at all?) The exercise is also a good setup for the discussion of the economic pyramid exercise and the economic system.

After the exercise, it is important to point out that some groups are unable to or are excluded from participating in the race at all; some are actually excluded from being in the room presently. Obviously, people with disabilities face barriers to participation. But other groups—undocumented immigrants, people who are homeless, poor people, mothers of young children, and other caregivers—might be excluded as well. We all learn to think that those of us who are in the race deserve to win. What does this assumption mean about those who are systematically excluded but whose work and presence are important to our society? How does it feel to be excluded? How does it feel to know that others are excluded?

Finally, note that the race actually takes place in a stadium. The winners of the race were declared before the race started. The ruling class is sitting in the stands watching the whole event with amusement. They don't have to race, because they've been awarded the very best, highest-paying jobs before the race began. Because their own futures are secure and they have plenty of money, they've been betting on who would run for jobs the fastest. How does this added information affect people's commitment to the race? To how hard they might run? To their sense of justice?

The Economic Pyramid

Our current political/economic structure looks like the pyramid below (see Figure 3.1). In the United States, 1 percent of the population controls about 43 percent of the net financial wealth,[12] and the next 19 percent of the population controls another 50 percent. That leaves 80 percent of the population struggling to gain a share of just under 7 percent of what is left. The result is that large numbers of people in the United States spend most of their time trying to get enough money to feed, to house, to clothe, and to otherwise support themselves and their families. Regardless of how hard they work, many end up without adequate housing, food, health care, work, or educational opportunities.

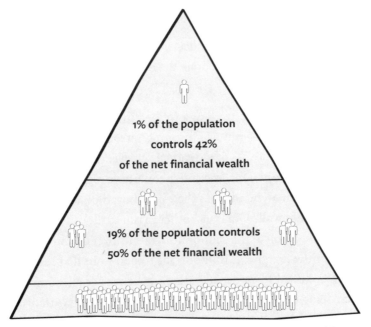

1% of the population
controls 42%
of the net financial wealth

19% of the population controls
50% of the net financial wealth

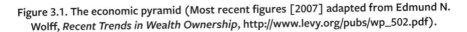

80% of the population controls 8% of the net financial wealth

Figure 3.1. The economic pyramid (Most recent figures [2007] adapted from Edmund N. Wolff, *Recent Trends in Wealth Ownership*, http://www.levy.org/pubs/wp_502.pdf).

The economic pyramid is only a rough instrument for measuring wealth distribution, as it overlooks many gradations. Nevertheless, it offers a snapshot of devastating social and economic inequality. Most notably, among the 80 percent at the base of the pyramid, a vast difference in the standard of living exists between those nearer the top and those near or on the bottom. And a substantial number of people, nearly 20 percent of the population, actually live *below* the bottom of the pyramid with negative financial wealth (that is, more debt than assets).

Historically, the United States has always had a steep economic pyramid with a large concentration of wealth in the two richest classes. But in the last thirty years, the distance between the ruling and managerial classes and the rest of the population has increased dramatically. Class mobility has decreased, and the economic well-being of the poorest 80 percent has substantially deteriorated. Those on the bottom of the pyramid have fared the worst. During this period, most of those in the top 20 percent have thrived, because they have substantial assets providing them with social and economic security as well as access to power, resources, education, leisure, and health care. Those at the very top have consolidated their power and privilege.

The Ruling Class/Power Elite

We refer to the top 1 percent as "the ruling class," because members of this class hold positions of power as corporate executives, politicians, policy makers, and funders for political campaigns, policy research, public-policy debates, and media campaigns. They "rule," because they are positioned to make decisions that govern the public world. This is not to say that they collectively act as kings or dictators; most of or all ruling-class members would deny that they "rule" at all. Often enough, their actions contradict and conflict with each other rather than representing a monolithic governing front. Nevertheless, it is the economic structure — the culture of power — in American (and, increasingly, global) life that places them in the role of decision makers and reproduces that role from generation to generation, even when it is not individually pursued.

The ruling class maintains the power and money to influence, and often to determine, the decisions that affect our lives, including where jobs will be located and what kinds of jobs they will be; where environmental toxins are dumped; how much money is allocated to build schools or prisons; and which health-care, reproductive-rights, civil-rights, and educational issues will be discussed and who defines the terms of these discussions. In other words, when we look at positions of power in the United States, we will almost always see members or representatives of the ruling class. We cannot call our country a democracy when 1 percent of the population controls nearly half the available resources, and the top 20 percent controls 93 percent of the wealth and the access to power that wealth produces. This vast concentration of wealth produces conditions of impoverishment, violence, and marginalization.

The Professional/Managerial Class

The next 19 percent of the economic pyramid, the professional/managerial class, are people who work for the ruling class. Members of this class may not gain the same level of power and financial rewards as people at the very top, but their work provides the research, managerial skills, expertise, technological development, and other resources that the ruling class needs to maintain and justify its monopolization of political and economic power. This class also carries out the direct management of the largest public, private, and nonprofit enterprises in the country.

The Bottom of the Pyramid

The majority of the population, the bottom 80 percent, produces the economic wealth benefiting those at the top. Laboring in factories, fields, classrooms, homes, sweatshops, prisons, hospitals, restaurants, and small businesses, the individuals composing this enormous class keep our society functioning and productive. Meanwhile, entire communities remain entrapped in endless cycles of competition, violence, and insecurity that those at the top are largely protected from.

Certainly the gradations within the bottom 80 percent (middle class, working class, and the dependent and working poor) produce additional security and benefits for some of its members, specifically those in the middle class, and keep many of us blaming and attacking those worse off than us rather than looking to the economic system and the concentration of wealth at the top of the pyramid as the sources of our problems. The role of many of our institutions is to keep our attention away from those in power and to manage and to control our efforts to survive in the bottom of the pyramid. These functions are necessary, because people on the bottom rungs of the pyramid have always organized to gain more power and access to resources. Most of the progressive social change we have witnessed in recent US history resulted from the work of disenfranchised groups of people fighting for education, living-wage jobs, accessible health care and child care, civil rights, reproductive rights, safety, affordable housing, gay and immigrant rights, and a safe, clean environment.[13]

The Buffer Zone

Over time, people in the ruling class have developed legal, educational, and professional systems to create a network of occupations, careers, and professions to deal directly with the rest of the population while protecting their own wealth and power. This buffer zone includes all occupations that carry out the agenda of the ruling class without requiring ruling-class presence or visibility; it acts as a buffer between those at the top of the pyramid and those at the bottom. The buffer zone is not an economic position indicating income or wealth; it is the roles that some people perform through their work that help the system run smoothly and without change. Some of the people employed in the buffer zone fall into the 19 percent section of the pyramid; however, most have jobs that put them somewhere near the top of the bottom 80 percent. These jobs give them a little more economic security and just enough power to make decisions about other people's lives — those who have even less than they do.

Functions of the Buffer Zone

The buffer zone has three primary functions:

1. *Caretaking:* The ruling class holds such a concentration of wealth that there is not enough to go around for the rest of the population, especially those who are poorest. Millions are without basic necessities, and every year hundreds of thousands of people die from the effects of poverty, racism, sexism, homophobia, ableism, and ageism. If these people died in the streets, mass uprisings would occur constantly.

   Because most people receive minimal levels of care, and those who die do so individually in hospitals, at home, in rest homes, or in prisons, it is less likely that people will be able easily to recognize the total impact on all of us of the concentration of wealth. Thus, women are pressed into unpaid service providing care for our loved ones, which results in elevated rates of poverty among women. Further, many *social-service* jobs — nurses, attendants, social workers, teachers, youth workers, child-care workers, counselors, all jobs that are primarily held by women and that provide minimal services to those in need — allow people to take care of those at the bottom of the pyramid. Taking care of those in need is valuable and honorable work, and most people do it with generosity and good intentions. But in our society, this work is also unsupported and low-paying, and serves to mask the inadequate distribution of jobs, food, and housing, hiding the full impact of the concentration of wealth.

2. *Keeping hope alive:* Moms, dads, and other caregivers always want their young people to have a better quality and longer life than they may have. For people to think they or their children have a chance to escape poverty, unemployment, low wages, high rents, and the violent conditions in their lives, they need to see a few people make it. They need to believe that if they have it together, work hard, and persevere, they can succeed. Sadly, success, in this way, often becomes synonymous with escaping from family, class, and ethnic/racial backgrounds. Indeed, one of our tasks as educators is to choose the "best and the brightest" from disempowered groups and push them up the ladder. We are supposed to encourage them to stay in school, to study hard, and to become leaders. From our trusted position, we reinforce the notion that education is the key.

   The reality is that the very few who do make it out of poverty leave their communities and join the middle class, leaving their communities unchanged.

These few success stories foster the illusion of hope and keep our work focused on helping people escape, one by one. They also distract us from understanding why economic opportunity is unequal in the first place and taking steps to change it.

These stories of individual achievement serve another purpose — they provide a way to blame those who don't make it. It appears that success goes to the hard-working, competitive, self-confident, and smart. Those who don't succeed are told and come to believe it is their own fault, and if they worked a little harder or were smarter, they could have made it like these individuals. The many professionals ready to step in with training in self-esteem, assertiveness, and study skills merely reinforce self-blame, a principal weapon of internalized oppression. The fact that the economic system is set up to allow only a few people through the gates to success is kept carefully hidden.

3. *Enforcing the rules:* Some of us are trained to enforce the rules of the economic system by punishing and monitoring or simply controlling those on the lower levels of the pyramid. Deans and principals, probation officers, police, security guards, welfare investigators, immigration officials, the National Guard and state militias, and even therapists and mental-health workers are all empowered to intervene punitively in the lives of people who are disruptive.

Men predominate here. Many boys are trained for occupations that help control people and maintain the system for the ruling class. The power elite has used government troops and state militias to control workers, police and prison guards to control communities of color, immigration officials and border guards to control immigrants, soldiers to control other countries, security guards to control petty theft and access to personal and business property, and the FBI and the CIA to control dissidents here and in other countries. Millions of men are employed in jobs that are explicitly enforcement roles. These jobs tend to be better paid than the caring work that women do, giving men the message that the work they do is more important than "women's" work.

Managing the Buffer Zone

At the top of the buffer zone are members of the managerial class. They set the standards and norms for their professions, determine policy and curricula at the main training and educational institutions, and run the professional associations. They often have connections with funders and other members of the power elite. They determine and certify who is allowed to move up in their professions, what are acceptable practices, and the standards to contain and to control those at the bottom of the pyramid.

It is the job of the members of the managerial class to promote those workers and programs in the buffer zone that accept the system and to screen out, to render ineffective, or to get rid of those who challenge it. They usually have no choice, because their funders — government agencies, foundations, and individual donors — are prepared to hold them accountable for maintaining the status quo.

What about Us?

Many of us have become social workers, teachers, probation officers, child-protection workers, medical professionals, therapists, counselors, and other providers of educational services to youth, because these jobs allow us to care and to advocate for those who have less power and opportunity than we do. Most of us have a little more education and job privilege, if not money, than many of the young people and their families with whom we interact. Most important, we have the ability to make decisions and to interpret the institutional rules that affect the lives of those we "serve." The ruling class determines the context of our work. We are a buffer zone, operating between society's institutions and the people under the institutions. We must ask ourselves: What purpose does our work serve? Whom does it really benefit?

QUESTIONS TO ASK YOURSELF: WHERE DO I FIT?

▶ What are the historical roots of the work that you do? If you are a teacher, how much do you know about the movement that created public education? If you are a violence-prevention activist, how familiar are you with the work done by women to address men's violence? What do you know of movements for economic justice, a root cause of interpersonal and youth violence?

▶ What were your motivations or intentions when you began doing this work? Did you think of yourself as the answer to those people's problems? Did it seem like a good thing for your resume? Did you believe your well-being depended on working for a just society?

▶ Who are you in solidarity with in the pyramid?

▶ Which group does your work benefit most: people at the top of the pyramid, people in the buffer zone, or people at the bottom?

▶ In what ways have you come to enforce the status quo or to train young people for their role in it? Where can you get support to reflect on your answers?

For those of us in the buffer zone, the challenge is figuring out how to do our jobs subversively. How can we take the meager funds we receive for direct services and use our resources to educate people about the issues, to empower them to make changes in their own lives, and to help them organize with others to demand change in the system?

One way to do this is to recognize the professionalization of our work as part of the problem. Assume that youth, domestic-violence survivors, and people deprived of homes, pushed out of schools, and working outside the formal job structure can do the work that we do if given the information, skills, and opportunity. Another part of being subversive is giving people information from the inside of agencies and institutions about what is really going on. Who makes decisions? Where does most of the money go? Who really benefits from these programs? Instead of advocating for people's interests, we can help them learn how to advocate for themselves. We can focus on leadership skills just as much as survival skills, social change just as much as social service. Numerous ways to work subversively from within the buffer zone reveal themselves when we think less about how to help some individuals get ahead and more about how to help the community get together.

Getting Together for Social Justice

Young people and adults all need effective strategies for surviving and thriving in a system with such disparities of wealth, power, and opportunity. Many options exist, but they can be described within a limited number of strategies, each with quite different consequences for ourselves and our communities.

Young People's Strategies

Young people are very aware of the limited opportunities for most people, given the current economic system with its extreme concentration of wealth. They are concerned about their own survival in such a system. How are they going to support themselves? How can they pursue educational opportunities or support a family? Not all strategies lead to the same results. Some may help them survive in the short term but be destructive to them or to those around them in the long term. Now we look at survival strategies that young people use and see where they lead.

Getting ahead: All children start out doing what their parents and teachers tell them. They want to work hard, to stay in school, and to succeed. They want to get ahead. However, they soon learn that getting ahead in the present structure means stepping on other people in order to move up. It can mean isolation, alienation, adopting mean-spirited values, and competing with, rather than cooperating with, others.

In addition, the road to success for many is filled with obstacles that become increasingly clear as they grow up. Poverty, racism, sexism, homophobia, lack of parental support, lack of role models, inadequate schools, lack of accommodation for mental or physical disabilities, teasing and bullying, physical and sexual assault, and limited opportunity resulting from the concentration of wealth all keep youth from being able to get ahead. So they turn to other strategies:

Getting by: Many young people give up trying to get ahead and just try to get by. They adopt an attitude of, "Just tell me what to do, and I'll do the minimum." They are waiting for the end of class, the weekend, summer vacation, or high-school graduation.

Getting over: Some youth are committed to getting ahead but don't have the resources or opportunity to do so by legitimate means, so they turn to illegitimate ones. They lie, cheat, or turn to illegal activities, trying to get over the system without getting caught.

Getting around: Some don't try to confront the obstacles in their way but try to get around them by playing the system or the people within it with whatever skills, connections, or resources they can muster.

Getting out: Some become so discouraged by the inequality of the current system that they just want to get out. They drop out of families, out of school, and out of community life, or they turn to alcohol and other drugs, computer games, and other escapist activity. And some commit suicide, the ultimate way out.

Getting back: Some are angry at those they perceive to be in the way of their getting ahead. Males especially will pick up guns or other kinds of weapons to get back at those in their lives, perhaps the people who teased them or those whom they have been trained to scapegoat for their problems: girlfriends; people of color; lesbians, gays, bisexuals, and transgender people; or recent immigrants.

Getting caught: For many young people, the only way to get some adult attention, caring, and resources is to get caught. Often the attention they receive is punitive, but it is attention, and for young people in despair, it can feel like support.

Getting together: Getting together with others to work for change is how people have always made gains, and this advancement happens through organized struggles, such as those we have cited elsewhere. On a smaller scale, people have been getting together in workplaces, in schools, in neighborhoods, and in many other arenas to gain access to power and resources, and to eliminate exploitation, discrimination, and environmental destruction. We share a long history of people getting together.

Adults' Strategies

As adult allies, each of us also chooses strategies for our survival. Are we getting together with others for social justice? Social justice education is about young people learning to choose strategies that allow them not only to get ahead but also to get together with other youth and adults to work for change. Therefore, we must look at our buffer-zone roles and strategically transform them into roles that support young people getting together.

Each of us who does not want to play out our preassigned role must constantly remind ourself that we are all in this together. Any temporary middle-class privilege, power, or status we have is very fragile. A major medical crisis, disability, or cash-flow problem quickly reminds us of our own economic vulnerability. We are also vulnerable and dependent, because we too need jobs, references, and benefits. If we get out of line, plenty of punitive apparatuses are in place to put us back into line. We can be reprimanded, disciplined, put on probation, or just plain fired, which returns us to the frightening role of "client." We each must heed someone with authority over us who may encourage us to pass on abuse to those with less power.

Incorporating education about the system of economic power into our work helps young people identify unproductive strategies, confront internalized self-blame and self-destructiveness, and interrupt violence. In doing so, we provide support and alternatives and help them understand the costs (emotional, physical, and economic) of these counterproductive patterns. We also enable students to see themselves as allies rather than as competitors and enemies. Finally, it is important that we examine our own needs for power and security to ensure that they're not acted out against the people who have less power than we do. Teaching for social justice means that we must learn to recognize the underlying cause of our fears and frustrations and not let our own feelings of anger, frustration, or powerlessness lead us to hurt others.

It is worth reacknowledging that we have socially sanctioned power over young people's lives, including those from families in the lower echelons of the pyramid. Some of us, through our work, can take children from families, provide or deny benefits, allow or prohibit access to various programs and community resources, and recommend people for jobs, housing, or academic placement. How can we use the power we have in the best interests of those whose lives we affect, *as they define their own interests*?

QUESTIONS TO ASK YOURSELF

▶ Is the primary goal of the work you do to help young people get ahead or to help them get together?

▶ How do you connect people to others in similar situations?

▶ How do you develop leadership skills in the people you serve?

▶ How do you use your access to open doors so young people can represent themselves in the levels of decision making that affect their lives?

▶ Do you provide them with information not only about their own needs but also about how the larger social/political/economic system works to their disadvantage?

▶ Do you create situations in which they can experience their own power, their connection to others, *and* their ability to work together for change?

▶ Do you help people understand and feel connected to the ongoing history of people's struggles to challenge injustice?

▶ Do the students in your classroom see themselves as part of a community of learners, activists, and change agents? Are you helping people see that they are not alone, that their problems are not unique, and that their struggles are interrelated? Are you helping them come together for increased consciousness, resource sharing, and mobilization?

We live in conservative political times and in a contracting economy in which racial, gender-based, religious, and homophobic violence is widespread and accepted. You may feel discouraged about the possibility of doing effective social justice education in this context. You may be fearful of losing your job if you take risks. This is a real concern. But this is also a time of increasing and extensive organizing for social justice. It is an opportunity for many of us to realign ourselves clearly with those organizing efforts and to reclaim the original vision of an end to the violence and exploitation that brought us into this work. This is a vision of social justice and true equity.

RACISM

Racism is another system of oppression — an institutionalized structure that confers power and privilege on one group and makes another group vulnerable to exploitation and violence. As "The Power Chart" on page 33 (Section 2) shows us, each such system has similarities but also has a unique historical development and current features that are important to understand. The systems are all intertwined and mutually reinforcing, and they affect young people. Anti-Jewish oppression and Islamophobia are discussed in this section, because they are systems of oppression closely interconnected with racism, and because historically all three grew out of Christian dominance. Racism specifically grew out of concepts of religious difference, and people who are not Christian are often treated as racial others; for example, as Jews were treated during the Jewish Holocaust. Although our treatments of these forms of religious oppression are brief, they should alert you to another area of social justice education to explore with young people.

The Oppression of Racism

Racism is the systematic, institutionalized mistreatment of one group by another when the groups are differentiated by perceived physical or cultural differences. These differences are said to be found in or attributed to skin color, smell, brain size, genes, blood, DNA, or other bodily aspects. Although "racism" as a term is most often used to describe the belief that one "race" is superior to others, we use it here to describe the structure of oppression itself. In the United States, white people are the group whose members originally founded and now continue to benefit from a hierarchical system of racial differentiation. We live in a society that, in general, grants to white people more prestige, benefits, opportunities, and social, political, and economic power than people of color. The groups targeted for exploitation and violence are people of Arabic, Middle Eastern, Asian, Pacific Islander, African, African American, Afro-Caribbean, Latin American, and Native American descent and people of mixed or multiple racial or ethnic heritages. Even though many white people do not consciously or actively seek such power, simply by being "white" they enjoy material benefits unavailable to people of color.

Prejudice and stereotyping are not in and of themselves racism. Given the misinformation, stereotypes, and lies in our textbooks, media, and everyday culture, we all have prejudices and false beliefs about other groups of people. We each have a responsibility to unlearn the misinformation we have accumulated. But if a person has prejudice and possesses the power to commit a socially sanctioned and structurally reinforced act of discrimination, harassment, exploitation, marginalization, disrespect, or violence against a group of people labeled as racially inferior, then that person is perpetrating an act — a "microaggression" — of interpersonal racism. From this perspective, in the United States, *interpersonal* racism consists of abusive and discriminatory actions that white people commit toward people of color and people of mixed racial heritage.

Looking to the larger, institutional level, interpersonal racism is caused by and in turn reinforces institutional racism. *Institutional* racism is racial dominance, power, and privilege built into the institutions of a society regardless of the intentions of individuals involved.

For example, I can be a white teacher and treat all my students, white and students of color, equally, helping each master the class material and move on to the next grade level. However, if the school tracks students of color into lower-achieving classes, disciplines students of color more harshly than white students, doesn't hire faculty of color, or uses curricula that don't include the contributions of people of color, then, regardless of my personal practices, I am supporting an institution that enforces racism. Low-income white students might also be treated unfairly in my school. This situation would not disprove the presence of racism; it would simply mean discrimination against low-income students (classism) also is at play.

Many white people claim "reverse racism" if they have experienced mistreatment or prejudice from people of color. But because racism is institutional, the power is always on the side of those who, at least with regard to race, run and benefit from the dominant institutions — white people. Anyone from any group can have personal attitudes of prejudice toward others. Racism is not about prejudice but about power. People of color may have positions of power within white-dominated institutions. They can certainly abuse their power and discriminate against white subordinates. In other words, they can engage in acts of interpersonal racial discrimination. But in US society, only white people have the power to enforce systematic, institutionalized racism.

Human beings are members of the same species. Few biological differences exist between any racial groups, and none hold any significance. The Human Genome Project has demonstrated that all people share 99.9 percent of the same genes. But in the United States, we are born into a society in which white people have established racial power imbalances. It is a cycle: Institutions enforce established inequalities, which in turn teach us that the power imbalance is natural and appropriate. The exploitation of one group by another is justified by statements about the inferiority of that group. These supposedly inferior group members are said to be less than human in various ways — less smart, less hardworking, less patriotic, less honest, less intelligent — judgments also handed out to the first waves of immigrants from Ireland and Mediterranean and Eastern-European countries until, in succeeding generations, they became "white." This racialized system of power functions at great cost to all involved, and people of color disproportionately bear the burden.

The history of each group designated as a racial group is different, the history of racism it has experienced is different, and the strategies of resistance each has employed varies. In particular, the issues of land, sovereignty, sacred sites, and environmental destruction that Native American peoples experience are unique to the various Native American nations and not parallel to or subject to the same remedies as issues that other groups of people of color face. The oppressions of East, South and Southeast Asian, and Pacific Islander groups have centered on histories of occupation in countries of origin and immigration, exclusion, and imprisonment in the United States. Latin American and Chicano peoples have undergone colonization, occupation, subsistence labor, and hate-related violence. Arab, Middle Eastern, North African, and central and south Asian people identified as Muslim face outright violence. And the oppression of African, Afro-Caribbean, and African American people is inextricably tied to the legacies of the Middle Passage, slavery, and Jim Crow segregation.

But racism itself has direct common results for everyone who is categorized as a person of color:

- shorter life spans for people of color
- higher infant mortality and poorer health care for people of color
- less access to jobs, lower wages, and more dangerous working conditions for people of color
- economic and cultural exploitation of the labor and culture of people of color
- less access to education for people of color
- more vulnerability to violence for people of color
- lack of recognition for the tremendous contributions that people of color can make and have made to society
- fear, mistrust, anger, and violence between whites and people of color
- narrowing and distortion of history and current reality among white people
- disillusionment, despair, fear, and hopelessness among whites and people of color
- violence enacted by both white people and people of color who function as the public face of institutions carrying out polices of exploitation and exclusion
- denial and suppression of cultural differences among white people
- total eradication of certain native peoples and cultures

One of the exercises we conduct with racially diverse groups, designed to increase understanding of the effects of racist oppression more clearly is the following pair of stand-ups.

PEOPLE-OF-COLOR EXERCISE

The exercise begins with everyone sitting down. People of color are asked to rise whenever a statement applies to them. A person may pass, but they are asked to notice their feelings if they do so. As with other stand-up exercises, facilitators should pay attention to the racial balance and level of safety in the participating group. Although some of these statements may apply to white people, the purpose of this exercise is to focus on the experiences of people of color, and you may need to explain this to white students to avoid confusion. This exercise is also effective for people-of-color support/discussion groups. People who are physically unable to stand are encouraged to raise their hands, if they are able, for each statement that applies to them.

Instructions for Conducting the Exercise

Direct the group members as follows:

Please stand up silently, if you are able, or raise your hand if...

1. your ancestors were forced to come to this country, were forced to relocate from where they were living in this country—either temporarily or permanently—or were restricted from living in certain areas because of their race or ethnicity

2. you ever heard or overheard people saying that you or your people should leave, go home, or go back where you came from

3. in your family, as a child, you were the intermediary between your parent/s and store clerks or public officials (social workers, school officials, and so forth) because of language or other differences

4. you were ever called names or otherwise ridiculed by someone you didn't know because you were African American, Latino, Asian American, Native American, Arab American, or of mixed heritage

5. you were ever ridiculed by a teacher, employer, or supervisor because of your racial heritage

6. you have ever been told by a white person that you are "different" from other people of your racial or ethnic group

7. you were ever told that you didn't act black/Latino/Asian/Arab/Indian enough

8. you were ever told you were too sensitive about racial matters or were acting too black/Latino/Asian/Arab/Indian

9. you have ever been told by a white person that you are too sensitive, too emotional, or too angry when talking about racism

10. you have ever received less than full respect, attention, or response from a

doctor, police officer, court official, city official, or other professional because of your race or ethnicity

11. you ever saw your racial/ethnic group portrayed on television or in the movies in a derogatory way

12. you ever tried to change your physical appearance (such as your hair or skin color), mannerisms, speech, or behavior to avoid being judged or ridiculed because of your race or ethnicity

13. you have ever been told to learn to speak "correct" or "better" English

14. you were ever discouraged or prevented from pursuing academic or work goals or tracked into a lower vocational level because of your racial or ethnic identity

15. you were ever mistrusted or accused of stealing, cheating, or lying because you were African American, Latino, Asian American, Native American, Arab American, and so forth

16. you ever picked up that someone was afraid of you because of your ethnic or racial background

17. you were ever stopped by police on the street because of your racial or ethnic identity

18. you were ever refused employment because of your race or ethnic background

19. you were ever paid less, treated less fairly, or given harder work than a white person in a similar position

20. your religious or cultural holidays were not recognized on your job or at your school (for example, meetings and work time were scheduled during those periods)

21. you ever were refused housing, were discouraged from applying for housing, or had to leave housing because of racial discrimination

22. you ever felt conspicuous, uncomfortable, or alone in a group because you were the only representative of your racial group

23. you ever felt uncomfortable or angry about a remark or joke made about your race or ethnicity but didn't feel safe enough to confront it

24. you ever felt the threat of violence because of your race

25. you or close friends or family members were ever victims of violence because of your race

An alternative format is to start out with a couple of these questions and then ask people of color to take turns asking "Please stand up if you ever..." questions of each other, which they create from their own experiences.

To close the exercise, the group processes their feelings about the experience.

Internalized Oppression

When people of color are treated as inferior and exposed to lies and stereotypes taught over generations, they internalize them. When they act that experience out on themselves and other people of color, we call it *internalized oppression*. The patterns of internalized oppression may look different for each racial group (for example, Asian Americans may sometimes believe they are the "model minority" and should be good in math, Latinos/Latinas may learn that Spanish accents mean lower intelligence, and African Americans may be taught to value light skin or, conversely, to worry about whether they are "black enough"). The end results are the same: to pit people of color against themselves and to pit different racial groups against each other.

Internalized oppression may also take the form of separating people within a group from each other. If you come to believe the lies that are told about your group, or if it is dangerous to associate with members of your group because of discrimination and violence, then you may respond by not wanting to hang out with or be identified with members of your group.

People develop many different survival strategies to deal with oppression. Some of those strategies can seem dysfunctional according to the standards developed by members of the dominant group who don't experience the oppression. Sometimes those survival strategies work for short-term safety but have long-term costs. White people should be cautious about judging the strategies of people of color as internalized oppression when these strategies may be creative and effective ways to survive in an oppressive society.

Anti-Jewish Oppression

In our antiracism workshops over the years, we have had to address two oppressions closely linked to race but separate — the oppression of Jews and the oppression of Muslims. The oppression of Jews has been complicated in the United States, because although the stereotyping of Jews and hate-motivated violence against Jews continue day to day, many Jews are "white" and consequently possess white privilege. Anti-Jewish oppression itself is minimized or denied in US culture.

Jewish people are a diverse religious and cultural group. *Anti-Jewish oppression* (often labeled anti-Semitism) is the systematic mistreatment of Jews by Gentiles (non-Jews). Jews are not a racial grouping, as Latin, Arabic, white, black, and Asian people may be Jewish. In fact, the majority of the people in the world who are Jewish are people of color. However, anti-Jewish oppression follows a structure of oppression and internalized oppression similar to racism.

Although Jews have been persecuted around the world throughout history and endured the Holocaust in recent history, their oppression is less visible than it was previously. Jews are said to not have it so bad now: They have a lot of money, they are very powerful, and so forth. In other words, the old stereotypes about Jewish people continue to exist, but their vulnerability to discrimination and violence is denied. In the meantime, Jews experience discrimination in a Christian-dominated society, whether in direct acts of persecution, such as personal attacks, the bombing of synagogues, and the desecration of cemeteries, or indirectly, from jokes, stereotypes, and in the more general invalidation of Jewish culture.

In the United States, Jewish people are, as in other countries, pitted against people of color and blamed for social problems. Jews who are light-skinned (of European descent) have relative privilege over Jewish and non-Jewish people of color. This in turn separates people of color and European-descended Jews and sets them up as antagonists.

Anti-Muslim Oppression (Islamophobia)

The oppression of Muslims, in turn, is complicated, because many Muslim Americans (and others perceived to be Muslim) have been categorized until recently as "white" in the federal census or as foreign, exotic, and therefore outside the usual parameters of racist discrimination. This oppression has increased dramatically since September 11, 2001. Instead of "Islamophobia," we use the phrase "anti-Muslim oppression" to keep focus on the oppression and the institutions behind oppression rather than on the putative "phobia" some non-Muslims may have.

Just as individual Jews in the twenty-first century are held accountable by some for killing Jesus, Muslims are individually held accountable for negative actions by Muslims anywhere in the world. These oppressions are only accentuated by the long-standing confrontation between Jews and Muslims in the Middle East.

It is misleading to avoid talking about anti-Muslim or anti-Jewish oppression in discussions of racism, because these are forms racism takes in current US society. Like other forms of racism, anti-Muslim and anti-Jewish oppression take our attention away from the white-male-Christian-dominated ruling class and place it upon scapegoats — in this case Muslims and Jews as well as people of color, poor people, and other groups targeted for oppression.

Muslims are a diverse religious and cultural group. More than 1.6 billion Muslims live worldwide. Anti-Muslim oppression is the systematic mistreatment of Muslims and such people as Sikhs, Iranian and Palestinian Christians, and others who are perceived to be Muslim by non-Muslims. Muslims are not a racial grouping; Latin, Arabic, white, black, and Asian people can be and are Muslim. In fact, the majority of the people in the world who are Muslim are people of color. In the United States, anti-Muslim oppression follows the same structure of oppression and internalized oppression as racism but with added complexities because of the addition of religious difference within a Christian-dominated society.

Alliance: On Being White and Being a White Ally

Understandably, white youth may resist the definition of racism outlined above and may even resist being categorized as "white." They may feel blamed for conditions of racial inequality they did not create. They will have been told repeatedly, especially in the "post-Obama" era, that racism is not a problem anymore. As European immigrants assimiliated into the United States, youth — especially from Irish, southern and eastern European, and European Jewish cultures — became white, losing touch with their cultural origins. White culture itself is popularly branded as bland, whitebread, and boring — after all, other cultural identities are said to have better food, better music, and better dancing. And some want to separate themselves from the violent extremism of white-pride hate groups. Any of these factors may make white students want to refuse to be white.

These specific factors count as the harmful socialization of white young people — segregating them from youth of color and hindering them from seeing the way the world really is. Transformative education must work against this socialization, inviting white youth to be proud allies of youth of color. What does being a white ally mean?

White people must clearly understand the devastation that racism produces for people of color, individually and collectively. To cite just one example for one group: In 2004 the *American Journal of Public Health* reported that in the 1990s nearly nine hundred thousand African Americans died from causes that could have been prevented had health-care services been race-neutral. In other words, in the United States, nearly one hundred thousand African Americans die annually because of the impact of racism.[14]

White people must also understand the social and institutional nature of racism in order to move beyond self-guilt or the blaming of other white people. This understanding enables us to see that although changing personal views and behaviors is useful, acting to change social practice is where real community building will happen.

Furthermore, white people who act as allies must understand that racism is also a white issue — racism is and has been devastating for white people. Their early experiences of learning about racism often were hurtful (for example, hearing hateful comments or being told not to play with other children who are different). These messages often come from people, such as parents, whom they trust or love but who are passing on the hurtful messages they heard themselves. Racism also operates to deny the different ethnic heritages of white people, persuading whites they have no cultural heritage but instead come from a bland monoculture. And it assigns different statuses to different white ethnic groups, based upon structures of domination inherited from European culture: Eastern European, Mediterranean, and Irish people are often established "one level down" within white society; as they immigrated to the United States, each group was subjected to exploitive labor, jokes, stereotyping, and discrimination — the charge that they were not "white enough." Racism falsifies white people's views of the world. It robs them of moral integrity through living lives based on exploitation. It saddles them with resentfulness, lack of awareness, fear, guilt, or hate when the subject of racism is brought up. And it is necessary to understand that all these effects are happening to white children now.

The following exercise for white people helps demonstrate just how racist training takes place and what the costs are for white people.

WHITE EXERCISE: SOCIALIZATION

White participants are asked to stand up if a statement applies to them, to notice who else is standing, and to notice their feelings. Those who cannot stand are asked to raise their hands if they are able to indicate response to the statements. Everyone has the right to pass, but participants are asked to pay attention to how they feel if they do. People of color, if any are present, are invited simply to observe the exercise.

Instructions for Conducting the Exercise

Please stand up silently if…

1. you don't know exactly what your European/American heritage is, what your great-grandparents' names are, or what regions or cities your ancestors came from

2. you have ever been told or believe you are just "white" or just "American"

3. you grew up in a household where you heard

    a. derogatory racial terms or racial jokes

    b. that racism was bad, so you were never to comment out loud on racial differences (for example, people told you, "It doesn't matter if you're purple or green, we're all equal, so don't notice a person's color")

    c. that racism was bad, that some or all white people were racist, and that you would always have to fight against it

4. you grew up, lived or live in a neighborhood, or went to a school or a camp that, as far as you knew, was exclusively white

5. you grew up with people of color who were servants, maids, gardeners, or baby-sitters in your house

6. you were ever told not to play with children of a nonwhite ethnicity when you were a child

7. (For this category, after you stand, stay standing if the next item also applies to you.) you ever saw pictures or images in magazines, film, or television, or heard in music or on the radio of:

   - Mexicans depicted as drunk, lazy, or illiterate
   - Asians depicted as exotic, cruel, or mysterious
   - Asian Indians depicted as excitable or "silly"
   - Arabs depicted as swarthy, "crazed," or terrorist
   - black people depicted as violent or criminal
   - Pacific Islanders depicted as fun-loving or lazy
   - American Indians depicted as drunk, savage, or "noble"
   - movie and TV roles depicting nonwhite cultures played by white actors

8. you did not meet people of color in person, or socially, before you were well into your teens

9. you ever find yourself trying to pretend "not to notice" the ethnicity or race or skin color of people of color

10. you ever felt like "white" culture was bland culture—empty, boring—or that another racial group had more rhythm, more athletic ability, was better with their hands, was better at math and technology, was better at trade or handling money, or had more musical or artistic creativity than you

11. you ever felt that people of another racial group were more spiritual than white people

12. you have ever been sexually attracted to a person from another racial group, because it seemed exotic, exciting, or a challenge

13. you ever learned to be afraid of or to not trust people of a nonwhite racial group

14. you ever felt yourself being nervous or fearful or stiffening up when encountering people of color in a neutral public situation (such as in an elevator or on the street)

15. you ever worked in a place where all the people of color had more menial jobs, were paid less, or were otherwise harassed or discriminated against

16. you ever ate in a public place where all the customers were white people and the people of color who were present were service workers

17. you have ever been in an organization, workgroup, meeting, or event that people of color protested as racist or you knew or suspected to be racist

18. you ever felt racial tension in a situation and were afraid to say anything about it

19. you ever had degrading jokes, comments, or put-downs about people of color made in your presence and felt powerless to protest

20. you ever witnessed people of color being mistreated in any way by white people

21. you ever saw people of color being put down or attacked verbally or physically and did not intervene

22. you ever felt guilty or powerless to do anything about racism

23. you ever felt embarrassed by, separate from, superior to, or more tolerant than other white friends or family members

24. you have ever been in a close friendship or relationship with another white person where that relationship was damaged or lost because of a disagreement about racism

25. you have ever been in a close friendship or relationship with a person of color where that relationship was affected, endangered by, or lost because of racism between you or from others

This exercise ends with the group breaking into dyads to discuss how they felt during the exercise. A whole group discussion then follows.

After the exercise, someone may ask, "Are you saying all white people are racist?" Labeling people as racist is hurtful and not useful. It is clear that every white person, at least to some extent, gains concrete benefits (sometimes labeled "white privilege") from being white in this country. Most white people have been socialized from an early age to perpetuate racism. Many white people have also resisted and challenged racism. Individual white people are not responsible for the system of racism, which preceded them by centuries. But they are responsible for the choices they make to collude with, to perpetuate, or to challenge racism in their daily lives.

For Adults Working with Young People on Racism

We must be clear: No one is born a racist, and no one is born inferior. This training starts early and is intense, but it takes years to train children to believe some people are racially different, inferior, and justifiably mistreated. It takes years to train people of color that they are less able than white people. Young white people resist these lies as best as they can. But many end up believing and passing on the lies. Young people of color also resist the lies and violence as best they can. But the oppression takes its toll, and many end up internalizing it to some degree. Our work as adult allies is to hold up a different mirror, to openly counter the training, and to support strategies that connect youth to each other and challenge the seeming inevitability of the structure of racial divide.

The situation is not hopeless. Every day we fight back and see others fighting back against the realities of racism. To strengthen ourselves in this struggle, we can take specific steps.

It is crucial for adults who work with children who are white, Muslim, Jewish, and of color, often in the same classroom or group, to be completely clear about what racism is, what anti-Muslim and anti-Jewish oppression are, and how they operate to divide us from one another. In fact, it is doubly important, because adult society elsewhere may be actively feeding these children lies and confusions about these issues. This task means several things for adult workers:

1. We must be able to identify how racism operates and affects us from day to day, looking at our own ethnic heritages, our early memories of learning about other groups, and areas where we might get stuck when issues are flying in the classroom.

2. We must be prepared to initiate frank and open dialogue about racism in the classroom. Open discussion contradicts young people's experience in a society where adults often pretend racism doesn't exist or have great ambivalence about discussing it. We have also noticed over the years that racism will not be addressed in class unless adults bring it up; young people's experience of adults' volatility and denial makes them reluctant to risk discussion. But once the issue comes up, the discussion takes off.

3. We must ensure that cultural diversity is represented in our numbers — that whites and people of color, Muslims, and Jews are all working together and modeling cooperative relationships for young people. Of course, this is not easy, because we are usually working within white, Christian-dominated institutions.

4. We must analyze and understand how racism works in the youth-serving institution we are a part of. We must put on a racial lens and analyze how the curriculum, classroom management, school discipline and tracking, hiring and firing decisions, and all other aspects of the institution have racial aspects built into them. You are not alone in your discontent with training young white people to be the next generation of gatekeepers of privilege and young people of color to accept their subordination. It gets easier to talk with people in authority once you have identified others who will stand with you.

5. To work effectively with young people on racism, we need to understand the effect of racial oppression in their lives and to enable them to heal from its violence as well. Each oppression is a system; the oppressions altogether are an interlocking system. One will not be lessened while others, with their own sets of abuse and hopelessness, are left in place. This means making racial issues a part of all classroom work, naming them, interweaving them in role-plays and exercises, and never "forgetting" to address them.

6. We can acknowledge the strong and powerful things we and others are doing to end racism.

7. We need not blame ourselves for racism or for times when we failed to do more. Blame isn't useful for adults, and it is absolutely useless for young people. Nothing is quite as useless to people of color as guilty white people.

8. We can make mistakes, fix them, take responsibility for our actions, analyze and learn from them, and go forward.

9. We can assume that no one wants to participate in this racist system. Everyone is doing the best they can with the lies and ignorance they were given — even white supremacist groups and white corporate CEOs!

10. We can assume that living with structured inequality is harder than taking action to change it.

11. We can recognize that we all come from cultural and ethnic traditions. By taking pride in our own, we are less likely to fear and to attack others (see "For Nontarget Groups" on page 39).

12. We can examine how we learned about racial and religious difference and discrimination through early experiences and impressions and give healing attention to what was hurtful.

Potentially endless exercises and techniques allow us to do personal work on combating racism. This manual contains several, such as "The Power Shuffle," "The Power Chart," "The Speak-Out Process," and "The Class Race" (on pages 29, 33, 54, and 69). Because we experience and learn the system in groups, from and with those around us, it is particularly powerful to unlearn it in the company of others. Working in multiracial groups to end racism is perhaps the most effective way of all to counteract our training.

Safety in Classroom Discussions

Issues of racism have great emotional pain attached to them. Creating relative emotional safety among people we work with has to be of prime importance in designing our work. In part, this requires an understanding of the differing definitions of safety young people of different racial and economic cultures might have. What might "feel safe" for white youth with relative privilege (for example, to not feel blamed or guilty) is not actually safety but comfort. Making white students feel comfortable might in turn pressure youth of color to be silent about or to downplay their experiences of racial inequality or to assure white youth in the room that they're not the problem, therefore losing the safety they need to be able to talk about their experiences. We cannot guarantee nor is it possible to create absolutely safe spaces, and the task is not to make everyone simply comfortable. Yet we should aspire to foster enough mutual respect and safety that young people can learn how to have the discussions they need to have about difficult subjects, such as racism.

Relative safety for people of color, multiracial people, Muslims, and Jews must be established so we minimize the risk that:

▶ they become targets of further abuse

▶ they become isolated from the group

▶ they are set up to be spokespeople for their races or ethnic identities

The goal of the work is to strengthen the individuals and their connection to one another. It is not useful to attack individuals for holding the ideas and assumptions they have learned as members of society. We structure the experience to increase the possibility that white people (and Christians, where anti-Jewish or anti-Muslim oppression are in play) will:

▶ get in touch with and heal from the lies of the early painful "learning" process they have had and not be faulted for what they have been told

▶ be able to bring up doubts, confusion, anger, and other painful emotions

▶ listen attentively and supportively to people of color, Jews, and Muslims speaking out

▶ be able to support and to challenge each other to continue working on this issue

Finally, increased safety comes only from mutually respectful relationships within a just society. This work is designed to facilitate the making of a culture inside your classroom that promotes the change we all want for our society. For all young people, safety is enhanced when adults are clear and the information presented is direct, basic, and consistent. If we can create relative safety for the process, each young person will become better informed, stronger, and closer to others. The group itself will increase its interest, experience, and strength in challenging racism within the group and within the larger society.

WHITE EXERCISE: BENEFITS (PRIVILEGE)

For white youth who may wish to take steps on becoming allies, the following exercise enables them to examine unearned advantages—privileges—that white people accrue in the United States. The exercise is conducted as a stand-up exercise; see the instructions for conducting stand-up exercises and follow-up activities, like the "People of Color Exercise" and "White Exercise: Socialization" exercises on pages 89 and 94.[15]

Stand up (or otherwise signify) silently if…

Origins

1. your ancestors were legal immigrants to this country during a period when immigrants from Asia, South and Central America and Mexico, or Africa were restricted

2. your ancestors came to this country voluntarily and have never had to relocate unwillingly once they were here

3. you live on land that formerly belonged to Native Americans

4. your family received homesteading or land claims from the federal government

5. you or your family or relatives receive or received federal farm subsidies, farm price supports, agricultural extension assistance, or other federal benefits

6. your ancestors employed people of color as slaves or indentured laborers

7. you grew up with people of color who were servants, maids, gardeners, or baby-sitters in your house

Housing

1. you lived or live in a city where housing discrimination prevents people of color from getting housing loans or allows them to receive them but on less favorable terms than white people receive.

2. you lived or live in a neighborhood from which people of color were prevented from residing because of visible or hidden discrimination

3. your first language is English, and you never heard or had to learn any languages other than English or other "European" languages (such as German, French, or European Spanish) while you were growing up

4. you grew up, lived or live in a neighborhood, or went to a school or a camp that as far as you knew was exclusively white

5. your race is not a factor in where you choose to live

Education

1. you or your parents went to racially segregated schools

2. you live in a school district or metropolitan area where more money is spent on the schools that white children attend than on those that children of color attend

3. you live in or went to a school district where children of color were more likely to be disciplined than white children or more likely to be tracked into nonacademic programs

4. you live in or went to a school district in which the textbooks and other classroom materials reflected your race as the norm and depicted people of your race as the heroes and builders of the United States while mentioning little about the contributions of people of color to this society

5. you were encouraged to go to college by teachers, parents, or other advisers

6. you attended a publicly funded university or heavily endowed private university or college, or received student loans or other financial support

7. your race is not a factor in where you send your children to school

Military

1. you or someone in your family served in the military when it was still racially segregated or achieved a rank shared by few people of color or served in a combat situation where large numbers of people of color held dangerous combat positions

2. you or someone in your family had options for avoiding military service that may have not been as available to people of color

Work

1. your ancestors were immigrants who took jobs in railroads, streetcars, construction, shipbuilding, wagon or coach driving, house painting, tailoring, longshore work, bricklaying, waiting tables, working in the mills, or any other occupation where people of color were driven out or excluded

2. you ever worked in a place where all the people of color who were employees had more menial jobs than yours and those of other white employees

3. you received job training in a program in which few or no people of color participated

4. you received a job, job interview, job training, or internship through the personal connections of family or friends

5. you worked or work in a job where people of color made less for doing comparable work

6. you have worked in a job where people of color were hired last or fired first

7. you work in a job, career, or profession or in an agency or organization in which few people of color are employed

8. you receive small business loans or credit, government contracts, or government assistance for your business

Civic Life

1. your parents were able to vote in any election they wanted to without worrying about poll taxes, literacy requirements, or other forms of discrimination

2. you can always vote for candidates who are members of your race

3. you live in a neighborhood that has better police protection and municipal services, and is safer than where people of color live

4. the hospital and medical services close to you or that you use are better than those available to most people of color in the region in which you live

5. you have never had to worry about whether public facilities, such as swimming pools, restrooms, restaurants, or nightspots, would be closed to you because of your skin color

6. you see white people in a wide variety of roles on television or in the movies

7. you never have to think about your racial identity when driving at or over the speed limit on a public roadway

Daily Life/In Public

1. you ever experienced being treated more favorably or with more attention or courtesy in a public situation (for example, by a store clerk or police) than a non-white or non-English-speaking person

2. you ever ate in a public place where all the clientele were white, and people of color who were present were service workers

3. you don't need to think about race or racism every day, or you can choose when and where you want to deal with and respond to racism

Process this exercise in dyads and then rejoin for a group discussion. Conclude by asking the group, "Taking into account the tremendous costs of racism to people of color and both the costs and benefits of it to white people, why should white people step up as allies in this struggle?

The work to end racism goes hand in hand with the work to end economic oppression, just as it joins efforts to stop anti-Muslim oppression, anti-Jewish oppression, and violence against people who are transgender, gay, lesbian, bisexual, elderly, working class, or poor. It is part of our lifework to help young people create a world that is safe, empowering, and based upon personal and collective liberation, equality, and respect.

Sexism and Heterosexism

When we wrote the first edition of this book, no transgender liberation movement existed, even though transgender resistance and activism have existed for centuries. Most people thought male and female identities were opposites — two distinct and separate identities. Some people believed gender was more like a continuum from extremely male to extremely female but with a clear line down the middle and with most people falling close to either end of the continuum. Most of society went to great lengths to perpetuate the view that gender was an inclusive binary system that was both natural and normal.

A simple understanding of sexual orientation follows from this idea about gender identity. Sexual orientation was defined by where the people you were attracted to were located — on the same side of the line as you, on the other side, or on both sides (bisexuals). It took the courage, organizing, analysis, and pioneering work of the people involved in the transgender liberation movement to shatter those assumptions.

Sexism, the oppression of girls and women; *heterosexism*, the oppression of lesbians, gays, and pan- or bisexuals; and *transphobia*, one name for the oppression of queer and transgender people, are all built upon the basic assumption that there are two sexual identities, one female and one male, and that every person falls into one of those two categories. Sexism operates by giving each of the two gender identities a unique and mutually exclusive set of qualities or attributes as well as privileging men with power over women. Heterosexism and transphobia police the boundaries of those gender roles and impose a heterosexual orientation and gender identity on everyone, whether female, male, or transgender.

The simple truth is that not everyone falls into one side of a simple gender-binary system. Tens of thousands identify as gender queer, transsexual, transgender, or any number of other self-identifications that are not simply female or male (these terms are explained below and in the Glossary). Some people's sexual identities are androgynous, while others don't identify as either male or female. Some children have their sexual identities misidentified at birth. Some have their bodies surgically altered, and others change their identity without changing physically. Sexual identity is complex, incredibly rich, and varied, and it is not subject to an either/or classifying process. Nor is it possible to determine a person's sexual identity from their appearance; people can perform gender in all kinds of ways that others easily misread. Finally, gender identity/ies (how I identify my gender/s) is completely separate from sexual orientation (what gender/s I find myself attracted to).

How does this work in day-to-day life? *Gender presentation* means the way I decide to express my gender identity in public: I can be said to *perform* it. My presentation can change a great deal from day to day, even from minute to minute. It involves such aspects as how I dress, how I walk, how I fix my hair, how I talk, what I say, my mannerisms and body language—all the ways that I show up to people around me. In a society structured along a male/female continuum, most people are trying to present as normal for the genders that they identify—or are identified—with. It is often safer, easier to communicate, and more acceptable to do so in work, at school, in the neighborhood, and in other settings. Many of us cannot even imagine not living on this continuum or not presenting ourselves and interpreting the identities of others in accordance with it. And we might get very uncomfortable when people challenge our interpretations of their identity by passing as a "man" if they are "female" or as a "woman" if they are "male."

Visualizing the Continuum

Imagine the female/male continuum as a line across the middle of a room, with one end representing extreme masculinity and the other extreme femininity. Sometimes we conduct an exercise with a group by asking participants to take a position on the line according to how they primarily present themselves by gender daily—how they think or intend other people see them on the gender continuum. Most people quickly find a place on the continuum relative to others in the group and toward the end that represents how they present themselves to the world.

We then ask participants to find a place on the continuum that represents their inner feelings about their gender identities: not how people see them, but how they identify themselves. Again, most people find a place, usually not too far from where they were before, but often noticeably closer to the center of the continuum.

At this point we ask participants how they feel about the labels "man" and "woman." What does it mean to be identified or to self-identify as one or the other? How does it feel?

Finally, we say that gender is not really a line or continuum at all—it contains all the space within the room. It is not one dimensional but, at a minimum, two dimensional. We ask people to move to anywhere in the room that they feel comfortable. Many people are confused or disoriented or simply cannot imagine gender not being a binary continuum. They often are unable to move. Others are relieved to move off the continuum, because they have never felt that being on a gender-binary continuum represented their reality. Others have trouble from the very beginning of this exercise, because they have never lived along the continuum and have always recognized its inadequacy.

This exercise represents an admittedly crude picture of gender identity but serves as a useful way of understanding the assumptions and limits of the gender-binary system in which we live. Imagine the force it takes to make everyone, normally spread out through a room, sort themselves out on the continuum and crowd together in its inadequate space. You can then begin to articulate the lengths to which our society goes to make sure that anyone who steps off that line and challenges that binary classification will be punished, marginalized, violated, and quickly rendered invisible so that others do not join in resisting the "line." You can imagine the pain, anger, confusion, shame, embarrassment, resentment, vulnerability, and loneliness that any young person might experience as they are forcibly socialized into a male or female gender role and placed on the line. Think about the impact on a two-year-old boy with long hair who is asked, "What are you?"; a twelve-year-old girl dressed as a tomboy being told that she will never get a date dressed like that; or a sixteen-year-old young man told that he talks, walks, or throws like a girl.

You may have students in your class or program who have never lived on the line. They have always known that they were neither simply female nor male. You may have students who are beginning to question the gender binary, to feel uncomfortable with the categories, and to try out other ways to live in the world. You may have students who have been raised as boys or girls and have found those designations to be incorrect. They identify themselves as a boy who has been raised as a girl or a girl who has been raised as a boy. They may be actively changing their gender presentation or even in the process of transitioning to the gender identity they feel most aligned with. Many of your students will identify with being male or female but will be uncomfortable or upset, wanting to reject the binary male/ female gender socialization that restricts their behavior, their relationships, their safety, and their life options. Others will question their sexual orientation and the gender-binary heteronormative system that presents multiple obstacles to their figuring out who they are, to whom they are attracted, and how they might establish healthy and respectful relationships. And every student will be aware and may well have experienced the violence that is used, including by young people, to enforce this system.

None of this will surface unless you create enough safety for it to be talked about. Even then, you can expect that the way that students will circle around deeper issues of gender identity will be through discussions of sexism, homophobia, and heterosexism, because these are the ways in which the system is enforced.

FACING SEXUAL AMBIGUITY EXERCISE

Although many young people claim to treat everyone as individuals and to not notice differences, most are uncomfortable with gender or sexual ambiguity. It is important for them to be able to examine this response.

Ask young people, "When you see someone walking toward you and you don't know if they are a man or a woman, how do you feel?"

Most of them will say that it is hard to know what to think about this person and that if they meet someone and are not immediately sure of their gender, it is difficult to know how to talk to them, whether to address them as a man or a woman.

Ask them what difference it makes. What choices are they consciously making about how they treat people? What is behind the choices?[16]

All people, including young people, have the right to self-identify and to perform and to "be" their gender in whatever ways feel right and appropriate to them. Adult allies have the responsibility to ensure that they can do so in safety and with respect. This environment obviously does not exist in the overwhelming majority of schools and other youth spaces. Creating some emotional space so young people can at least talk about these issues is part of our task as such allies. In what follows, we look first at how to work with youth to address sexism and violence against girls and women, turning then to consider heterosexism and transphobia.

Talking about Sexism and Sexist Violence: Working Assumptions[17]

Acts of violence against girls, women, and female-identified people, acts such as rape, battering, trafficking, and sexual harassment, are rooted in *sexism* — the systematic, daily, routine, institutionalized degradation of, exploitation of, and violence against girls, women, and female-identified people by boys, men, and male-dominated institutions. It is systematic because it extends throughout society, taking physical, emotional, spiritual, political, social, and economic forms, and because it affects every one of us — adults, elders, and young people. It is intensified and compounded by the other systematic imbalances of power among people differentiated by class, age, race, sexual orientation, and physical and mental ability discussed throughout this section. And, like other systems of oppression, it helps maintain the power and wealth of ruling elites who divide us by gender and use males to exploit, to harass, and to abuse females. All men and some women benefit from having one portion of the population — women — made primarily responsible for the unpaid work of child raising, housekeeping, caring for elders, and caring for people with disabilities as well as the underpaid work they do on farms, in sweatshops, in factories, and in other people's houses. Men, in general, also benefit from the paid or unpaid sexual, emotional, psychological, and physical care and services that women are expected and often forced to provide them. However, the bulk of the benefits from this system accrues to those who are at the top of the economic pyramid.

Part of the task of working actively to break down institutionalized sexism is to unlearn sexist attitudes and beliefs. A much larger part, of course, is what follows — organizing and acting to stop the violence and to promote gender justice. But in the classroom as a learning community, the first priority may be "unlearning." Sexism and sexist violence are already profoundly present in the lives of young people, and many students have already experienced or witnessed various forms of male violence, including family violence, dating violence, sexual harassment, intimidation, domination, disrespect, and the cutting off and silencing of the voices of girls and women. Some students will have already actively confronted institutional sexism and male violence in such forms as war, gangs, police brutality, the criminal legal system, pornography, and prostitution.

Below are our working assumptions on how to unlearn sexism and to combat the sexual violence that is its expression. Use them as guidelines for your work.

Assumption 1

Like all forms of oppression, sexism — the systematic abuse of girls and women — is based on tremendously high levels of exploitation and violence. This process hurts all of us and devastates our communities. Exploitation and violence isolate and divide us from each other. They dull our sense of what is possible, condition us to accept injustice, lead us to rationalize unacceptable human suffering, and keep us from our strength in human community. We learn, simply, to give up on one another.

Assumption 2

Sexism is not biological or natural. No human being is born a male chauvinist, a darling housewife, or a rapist; anatomy is not destiny, and boys need not be boys. Physical differences between human beings are not the cause of sexism but are used to excuse it. In particular, male/female roles are socially constructed; the prescriptions of gender are present in the culture before our births and become part of how we learn who we are and how to identify. They are taught to us as children and enforced by teasing, harassment, threats, and abuse. The very first question asked about us is, "Is it a boy or a girl?" Completely different treatments await us based upon the answer. Anatomical difference is used to justify already established male/female stereotypes — misinformation — that in turn justifies already existing mistreatment, abuse, and economic exploitation. For example, all of us have the capacity to care for and to nurture others, but men are specifically taught that these are "feminine," motherly characteristics. They learn on the playground and in the living room to devalue these traits in women, other men, and themselves — indeed, to bond with other men by ridiculing "feminine" behavior (all those jokes). Caring and nurturing are human traits. However, the stereotypes are still used to justify keeping men in higher paid work while women work double shifts doing low-wage work during the day and unpaid housework and elder or child care in the evening.

Assumption 3

A further deadly function of gender roles is the enforcement of heterosexism and related violence against transgender people, discussed later. Boys first learn discrimination against gays, lesbians, and bisexuals when they are taught that their major job in life is to "have" a woman and to be tough and aggressive with other men. Girls are pressured to catch and to care for men as their job.

The insistence that two and only two genders exist is itself an assumption, buried in our day-to-day practices, operating finally as a background justification for sexism itself and its role in maintaining the economic pyramid. We make an opposing assumption: that gender is flexible. How one identifies by gender can be an ongoing process that changes over the course of one's life and across a spectrum of possible identities. The violent responses to the expressions of this flexibility are a reflection of how deeply sexism itself is policed and enforced.

Assumption 4

Lies, misinformation, and conditioning are harmful to all young people. Having attitudes and beliefs that are sexist is like having a clamp on one's mind — it distorts one's perceptions of reality. No one believes lies voluntarily. Young people retain sexist attitudes and beliefs because that is the only information they have, because it is the best thinking they have been able to do at the time, because no one has been able to relieve them of this misinformation, and because the surrounding culture continually reinforces such attitudes through the media, advertising, public policy, and the use of violence against those who challenge sexism.

Assumption 5

Young people will change their minds about deeply held convictions when (a) a new position is presented in a way that makes sense to them, (b) they trust the person who is presenting this new position, and (c) they are not being blamed for having believed misinformation.

Assumption 6

People hurt others because they have themselves been hurt, and because they have been trained to turn their pain, anger, and frustration toward those with less social and political power. In this society we have all experienced systematic mistreatment as young people, often through physical violence, the invalidation of our intelligence ("girls are stupid"), the disregard of our feelings ("act like a man"), and the discounting of our abilities ("you're only a kid").

Because of these experiences, we tend to internalize this mistreatment by accepting it as the way things are and to externalize it by mistreating others. Externalized mistreatment may be directly sexist (for example, in sexual harassment on the street) or it may be indirect (as when a man, feeling guilty or blamed, trashes other men for their behavior or accuses women of "reverse sexism").

Assumption 7

The situation is not hopeless. People always come together to work for social justice, and the world as it stands is not built in stone. Everywhere, women actively fight violence and inequality in campaigns for economic, environmental, racial, and gender justice. They are not "helpless" but rather are strong and powerful leaders. And everywhere, men do not voluntarily approve of or engage in disrespect, discrimination, or abuse and work to stop their own and other men's violence. Men can take responsibility for men's violence; they are logical allies for women, because most men pay huge costs for the small benefits that accrue to them from sexism. Women can and do support and love one another and expect men to rise to the level of being allies. Men do achieve long-lasting intimate relationships with other men based on love and not on the oppression of women. Sexism can be examined, analyzed, and unlearned, and structures of power based on gendered and other forms of oppression can be dismantled.

Assumption 8

There are many different ways to be male, female, and transgender; many different kinds of personal and collective relationships develop between people.

Assumption 9

We cannot make permanent change acting from guilt or hopelessness. We each come from personal heritages and traditions that have a history of resistance to sexism, and every person has their own individual history of resistance. When we recall and celebrate that resistance, we contradict the lies of separation, powerlessness, and inevitability. When people act from a sense of informed pride and joy in acts and traditions of resistance, they will be more effective in all struggles for justice.

Assumption 10

Men who challenge sexism contradict the assumptions that men are inevitably abusive to women, that men will never change, and that men cannot work for gender justice. If you are male, you can expect that when you make mistakes, say the wrong thing, or act on your own sexism inadvertently, women will be angry at you. You will, through your actions, however well-intended, have reinforced the distressing, hopeless feeling that men will always be the same, and you will have hurt women directly with sexist behavior. To be a true ally to women is to hear the anger and to understand its source in feelings of hopelessness and experiences of mistreatment, to listen, to take criticism, to make changes, and in general to make it clear that you are delighted to do so. This work is not just another way to earn women's attention, approval, gratitude, or trust.

Other men may be angered when you stop colluding and instead work to challenge sexism in your school, workplace, and organization. They may feel betrayed when you support women's leadership and interrupt sexist practices. They may feel deserted or unfairly blamed when male dominance and inequality are identified as problems. To effectively contradict men's defensiveness (and potential cynicism), it is crucial to remember that the problem is not men themselves but male collusion in a system of gender-based exploitation. Rather than faulting or attacking men for their misinformation, keep focused on behaviors and institutional practices that benefit men and disadvantage women. It is especially important for men to speak out to other men about sexism and male violence against women. Men hear other men's voices differently. However, this privilege should be used carefully and wisely. By caring for and accepting other men even while confronting their beliefs and attitudes, you demonstrate the potential for strong and loving alliances against injustice among men.

Assumption 11

Lies about gender reinforce and reflect social inequality. For example, the stereotype that women are naturally better than men at taking care of children justifies not paying them very much, or at all, for child care. Lies do not cause inequality but rather are caused by it. They serve to justify or to cover up the domination of many women and men by a few men, because they give all men limited rights to dominate.

The full unlearning of sexism involves the active undoing of gender-based injustice. Unlearning or changing an attitude is not enough; understanding sexism is not enough. This unlearning is something we act upon as a community. The point of understanding the world is to change it.

GENDER-SOCIALIZATION EXERCISES

We sometimes use the following stand-up exercises in high-school and college class-rooms and adult workshops to explore how boys are hurtfully conditioned and girls are directly victimized in the process of being taught to "act like a man" or "act like a woman." The exercises are introduced with the following points:

The questions are different for the raised-male and raised-female exercises. Men and women do share some of the same experiences, but this exercise focuses on the overall different kinds of experiences (sometimes painful) that raised-female and raised-male youth experience as they grow up, and how they affect each group. The raised-male exercise is explicitly about violence that is done to or among those socially identified as boys and young men as part of the "act-like-a-man" training. It was developed to enable young men to be able to talk about the training as a prelude to learning about sexism against women. The raised-female exercise is explicitly about the violence of sexism itself against those socially identified as girls and young women.

Of course, the very idea of a gendered stand-up exercise raises difficulties for transgendered or queer youth and adults, putting before them, again, the requirement that they choose one gender or another, not to mention acknowledging it publicly if it has been concealed. You will have to evaluate the safety for queer and transgender youth in your group. Making sure it is safe for them to participate (or to abstain) will be part of the work for you and for the entire group.

Explain to the group that the exercise will be done in two parts: one for those who were raised male and one for those raised female. Those who identify as neither male nor female can observe the entire exercise, or they can decide for themselves which part—or both parts—they want to participate in.

If both exercises are being conducted, we begin with the "raised-male" exercise.

Instructions for Conducting the Exercise

1. Preselect categories, based on the profile of your group and the need for relative safety, using at most twenty categories.

2. Explain the following:
   - The exercise is to be done in silence.
   - Everyone must decide for themselves whether the category fits them—you will not explain the category but will simply repeat it if asked.
   - Everyone has the right to pass, participating at the level at which they feel most comfortable, but you will ask them, whether standing or sitting, at least to notice personal feelings that come up.
   - At the close of the exercise(s), students will form dyads to take turns talking about how it felt to do the exercise.

3. If any participants have limited physical mobility, conduct the exercise by saying, "Please stand up or otherwise signify if…"

4. Call each category calmly and clearly, leaving time for people to stand; for each person standing, repeat the words, addressing all the people in the room:
   - "Notice who's standing, and who's not."
   - "Notice how you feel." (Pause.)
   - "Please be seated." (for people who are standing)

5. If any participants have visual limitations (that is, they can't see other people standing or sitting), simply state, "Notice how you feel… [pause]; please be seated."

6. Let people know when you have only a few categories left.

7. Close by having participants sit in silence for a few moments. Then break into pairs for participants to take turns talking about what feelings came up.

Male Socialization

All the people in the room who were raised male are instructed to stand for each of the following statements that applies to them:

Please stand up (or otherwise signify) if you…

1. have ever worried you were not tough enough

2. have ever exercised to make yourself tougher

3. were told not to cry or were hit to make you stop crying

4. wanted to be held or hugged or shown affection by an adult but were denied

5. were called a wimp, queer, bitch, pussy, gay, or fag

6. were told to act like a man

7. have ever been hit by an older man

8. have been forced to fight or were in a fight because you felt you had to prove you were a man

9. grew up with a father who was absent most of the time

10. grew up with a father who was abusive

11. grew up with a father who was present but emotionally distant or absent

12. saw an adult man you looked up to or respected put down, yell at, threaten, hit, or beat a woman

13. were physically injured in competitive sports or on a job

14. were in a sport, in the military, or in any other program where you were taught to hide your feelings and to hurt other people

15. have been physically injured and hid the pain or kept it to yourself

16. stopped yourself from showing affection, hugging, or touching another man because of how it might look

17. or a man you know has been stopped by police on the street

18. or a man you know has been arrested or done time in the juvenile justice system or jail

19. or a man you know are (or plan to be) in the military

20. or a man you know got part of the information you have now about sex with women from viewing soft- or hardcore pornographic images of women in magazines, in videos, or on the Internet

21. or a man you know ever felt addicted to or out of control about looking at pornography

22. engaged in sports or other activities in which, when you think about it now, you took unnecessary physical risks

23. or a man you know got so mad that, while driving, you or he drove fast or lost control of the car

24. or a man you know drank or took drugs to cover feelings or to hide pain

25. don't get enough sleep or have a hard time getting uninterrupted sleep

26. have a health problem right now that you are ignoring, not dealing with, or putting off dealing with

27. or a man you know has a physical scar from a knife, baseball bat, gun, or other weapon

28. or a man you know felt like blowing yourself or himself away

29. know a male who was beaten regularly or terrorized as a child or young person

30. know a male who was touched sexually without his consent as a child or young person

31. or a man you know hurt another person physically

32. or a man you know hurt another person sexually or were sexual with another person when they didn't want to be sexual, whether they said so or not

Female Socialization

All the people in the room who were raised as female are instructed to stand for each of the following statements that applies to them:

Please stand up (or otherwise signify) if you…

1. have ever worn makeup, shaved your legs or underarms, or worn nylons

2. have ever worn uncomfortable, restrictive clothing, such as heels or clothes that felt too tight or too revealing

3. have ever been afraid you were not pretty or feminine enough

4. have ever changed your diet or exercised to change your body size, body shape, or weight

5. have ever been told you were too fat or to lose weight

6. have ever made yourself, or thought about making yourself, throw up to lose weight or to avoid gaining weight

7. started a diet this year

8. have ever been told that you are too angry or to "be nice" or to smile

9. have ever been not encouraged to pursue or actively discouraged from taking academic courses such as math, chemistry, or physics

10. have ever felt less important than a boy or a man

11. have ever been ignored or talked over by a boy or man or unable to speak because the boys or the men were doing all the talking

12. have ever pretended to be less intelligent than you are to protect a boy's or man's ego

13. have ever felt limited in what careers were open to you

14. have ever been paid less than a boy or a man for doing equal work

15. have ever been expected, without discussion, to take care and responsibility for children or younger siblings in your vicinity (for example, in your family or congregation)

16. have ever been expected to cook, to clean, or to serve because you are a woman

17. have ever been forced to give affection (hug/smile) when you didn't want to

18. have ever been sexually pressured by a man in your workplace or at your school

19. have ever been sexually harassed or sent sexually explicit comments or threats online

20. have ever been yelled at, had your body shape or size commented upon, whistled at, touched, or harassed by a boy or a man in a public place

21. have ever been called a bitch, cunt, slut, freak, ho, or whore

22. routinely or daily make plans for or limit your activity because of fear for your physical safety

23. have ever stopped yourself from hugging, kissing, or holding hands with another woman in public for fear of how it might look

24. have ever been expected to take full responsibility for birth control

25. know a woman who was pregnant when she didn't want to be

26. know a woman who considered cutting, hurting, or killing herself

27. have ever been afraid of a man's anger

28. have ever said "yes" to a man because you were afraid to say "no"

29. have ever been pressured to have sex with a man when you didn't really want to

30. have ever received repeated unwanted or bullying phone or text messages, sexting, instant messages, e-mails, or social-media messages (Facebook or MySpace) directed specifically to you from another person

31. have ever been followed, tracked, watched, communicated with when you didn't want to be, or stalked over time by a man

32. have ever used alcohol or other drugs, undereaten, overeaten, cut yourself, or done something dangerous or unsafe to cover your feelings or hide your pain

33. have ever been hit by a man

34. know personally a woman who was sexually abused or assaulted by a man

35. know personally a woman who was molested

36. wished you were a boy instead of a girl

The exercise(s) closes with students being paired up in dyads to discuss how it felt, followed by group discussion.

Sexism and Male Privilege

The point of these exercises is to explore the costs to males and females of sexism and to establish the reasons why all people have much to gain from its eradication.[18] However, sexism works to the advantage of males; if they perform well as men they are offered substantial benefits, such as better pay, more respect, credibility, safety, and access to women's caretaking (or, as the media highlights it, power, money, sex, cars, and stereos) that women of their class and race do not have equal opportunity to acquire. Of course, for many men, these are false promises that they will never achieve. Nevertheless, a discussion of male privilege is an important component of work on challenging sexism. The following exercise has proved useful in all male groups or in mixed-gender groups with a significant percentage of males.

MALE EXERCISE: BENEFITS (PRIVILEGE)

Read the instructions for previous exercises before starting.
Stand up (if able, or raise your hand) silently if...

1. your father or grandfathers had more opportunities to advance themselves economically than your mother or grandmothers

2. your father had more educational opportunities than your mother

3. you or the other boys in your extended family had more encouragement or financial support for pursuing academic, work, or career goals than the girls

4. in the schools you went to, the textbooks and other classroom materials depicted more men in roles of heroes, political leaders, and creative artists than women, or little mention was made of women's contributions to our society

5. in the schools you went to, the textbooks or other classroom materials reflected male viewpoints or male characters as the norm

6. you attend or attended a school where boys were more encouraged to take math and science than girls

7. you attend or attended a school where boys were called on more often in class

8. you attend or attended a school where boys were given more attention and funding for sports than girls

9. you received job training in a program where few or no women participated

10. you obtained school admission, a job, a job interview, job training, or an internship through a personal connection with other men

11. you work or worked in a job where women made less for comparable work or did more menial work

12. you work in a job, career, profession, agency, or organization where few women hold leadership positions, or your work has less status *because* women are in leadership positions

13. you take medications or undergo medical procedures that you can assume or have been assured were tested and proven safe on other men

14. on TV you more often see men as heroes, athletes, leaders, experts, or authorities than women

15. you have seen or heard men in positions of authority belittle women's contributions, writing or musical abilities, intelligence, or physical strength

16. you have received child care, cooking, cleaning, nursing, or clerical services from women earning less than you do

17. in your family, women do more of the cleaning, cooking, child care, or laundry than you or other men in your family do

18. in your community, it is as a rule harder for women to obtain housing loans, small business loans, agricultural loans, or car loans than it is for men, or they receive them but on less favorable terms

19. at car dealerships or auto-mechanic garages, you have ever noticed male cus-

tomers being given more information than or charged less or otherwise treated differently than women customers

20. you have access to sexually revealing images of women in magazines, in bookstores, in video or pornography outlets, or on the Internet

21. you know, regardless of whether or not you act on it, where you can obtain sex from women for money in the city or region in which you live

22. you generally feel safe when hiking in the woods, in the mountains, on the beach, or in other rural settings

23. you do not, in the normal course of your daily life, experience situations in which you fear being a victim of sexual harassment, sexual assault, or domestic violence

After the exercise, facilitate discussion in dyads and then with the whole group.

Although all males gain some benefits from sexism, most males gain little and pay substantial costs. Why is it in the interests of all people to challenge sexism?[19]

Young White Men: Scared, Entitled, and Cynical—A Deadly Combination[20]

When we talk about social injustice, we are often talking about the violence that maintains systems of oppression. When we talk about violence, we are often talking about young men, especially young white men — yes, young *white* men.

White men are convicted of perpetrating nearly 72 percent of the devastating violence we experience in our communities, and young white men between the ages of fifteen and thirty commit nearly 40 percent of that violence, contradicting the usual, stereotypical association of young men of color with violence.[21] What kind of violence? All kinds: domestic violence, rape, incest, male-on-male fights, serial killings, racist hate crimes, gay bashing, arson, campus riots, bombings, and barroom brawls.

The violence of young white men maintains a society in which some older white men have most of the power and benefits.[22] Some young white men will become part of that privileged group, but most won't.

Young white men see older white men at the top of nearly every corporation, court, government office, military command, university post, and other site of authority visible in our society. Like everyone else, they are flooded with an unrelenting stream of history books, TV, movies, video games, and ads for guns and cologne displaying white men on top, in control, in power, and in charge, while others are portrayed as inferior and undeserving of the same power. Parents reinforce this vision when telling boys that they are special, they are leaders, and they can be anything they want, and that it is up to them to achieve and to be successful. Boys so treated can easily come to feel entitled to special attention; time devoted to their interests, resources put into their activities, and money invested in their future. The messages of entitlement lead them to expect care and sex from women and service, deference, gratitude, sacrifice, and self-effacement from everyone else. They can become confused and then angry when their sense of entitlement is not responded to, when others demand access to what they do not want to share, and when their ability to get to the top is threatened.

Young white men learn that white men should be on top, but they also know that this is a dog-eat-dog, competitive culture that only rewards a few. Men who get ahead get the prize regardless of what they do to succeed; what counts is winning. Of course this is not all they learn. They also learn about positive roles men can play, acting with courage, integrity, and generosity on behalf of their communities. But they can see — in work, politics, athletics, and academics — the compromises in integrity and the sacrifices in dignity and self-respect that adult men around them have had to make to get ahead. They learn in countless ways that lying, dishonesty, manipulation, racism, violence against and exploitation of women, and criminal activity are more or less justified means for coming out ahead. They see the success of greed and violence, and they learn to put aside the natural optimism and integrity all young people possess to better play the game. They learn cynicism.

Young white men know that others are not necessarily going to play fair. So beyond entitlement and cynicism, they learn to watch their backs; they learn to fear. At some point they realize that only a few will come out on top, and they might not be among them. And they will hear that everyone who is not a white male is trying to get what white men are entitled to. Many end up being scared. Their fear can come to dominate their thinking. Their fear, combined with cynicism and a sense of entitlement, can lead to desperation and violence. Why violence?

One of the aspects of US history that our school textbooks and media outlets portray accurately is white men's routine recourse to violence to achieve their goals. It is not surprising that young white men would see violence as a primary way to solve problems.

Entitlement, cynicism, and fear, coupled with a cultural history of white-male violence, lead some young white men to sexually assault, to beat up, or to kill their girlfriends, because they are not receiving the sex, deference, and services they are told they deserve. The same factors lead them to commit gay bashing and racist hate crimes, because they are taught that homosexuals and people of color are the cause of their problems. And these factors also lead to relentless male-on-male competition, fights, and other forms of violence, because every other white male is perceived to be in the way of their own success and a potential saboteur of their efforts to succeed. Even the use of violence — the perception that one has the right to control others and to force them to do what one wants — comes from a sense of white-male entitlement.

Young white men need another choice, a choice that says they can be part of our joint efforts, as adults who work with young people to prevent violence, to change a social system that does not work for most of us, a choice that shows them they can live with integrity. We need young white men to be active participants in our struggles for social justice. They bring vital energy, insight, creativity, passion, and caring to our efforts. But to enlist their participation we must see through their fear, their cynicism, and their sense of entitlement. We must look past their appearances, their attitudes, and their behavior to the caring and responsible young people that they are. We must draw them in rather than pushing them out.

How do we counter fear, entitlement, and cynicism? We have to start with their fear: If we challenge their entitlement first, we only reinforce their fear. They need safe places — groups, classrooms, and one-on-one discussions, by turns light and serious — where, with adult and peer facilitation, they can talk about their feelings, hopes, and fears. In particular, they need time and attention to learn how to express the fear, to hear the fears that others share, and to see how the fear has been constructed through segregation, stereotypes, scapegoating, and the creation of economic scarcity.

Once their fears have been expressed, acknowledged, shared, and understood, we can begin to address their sense of entitlement. We can help them understand the distortions of history, science, politics, and culture; the false values; and the actual exploitation upon which that sense of entitlement is built. That can become a process through which we build a new sense of human entitlement to the fulfillment of basic human needs for food, shelter, respect, decent work, education, culture, and leisure for all people, including white men.

Finally, we can counter cynicism by retelling the real histories of the many different people from many different times and places who have fought and continue to fight for equality, full participation, and social justice. We can point to their achievements and note how far we have to go. We can recount the stories of white men who have been active participants and allies in those struggles. And we can bring the story up to date by providing information about the vast number of community struggles currently being waged and the various ways people are organizing for change. In doing this, we are really extending an invitation to young white men. We are inviting them to join us in our efforts to transform a system of such limited and unacceptable options.

There is no better way to overcome the fear, the cynicism, and the sense of entitlement among young white men than to invite them to stand on the front lines with us in our efforts to achieve social justice. This cause is a long and glorious one, and everyone has a role in it. We cannot hope to stop the violence that young white men perpetrate without giving them better choices than they presently have. The choice to get together, to become participants, and to play that role is the one choice that will benefit all of us and will restore the sense of connection, purpose, and moral integrity that young white men need and that we so desperately need from them.

Out Proud: Unlearning Heterosexism and Transphobia

Probably the most routinely explosive subject that comes up in a group or classroom is gay/lesbian/bisexual/transgender (LGBT) identity. Typically it comes up when we talk about the "Act-Like-a-Man" Box and the "Act-Like-a-Lady" Flower and the names boys and girls are called when they attempt to act outside these parameters (see *Making the Peace,* Session 9, and *Making Allies, Making Friends,* Session 2.10). When students call out some of the names — "gay," "fag," "dyke," or "queer" — that keep people in the gender boxes, the discomfort is palpable: giggling, side conversations, finger pointing. Other things happen, too:

- Some students may immediately disclose to the group that they aren't gay or lesbian. Sometimes this is done verbally ("Well, I'm not gay, but…," "No homo!"), and sometimes it is done physically (the participant may shift their posture or voice levels to appear more "manly" or "womanly").

- Some students question the facilitators about their sexual identities.

- Some students adopt a detached attitude, as if lesbians, gays, and bisexuals were an odd species and required sanction from others even to exist ("I don't care what they do behind closed doors, but…").

- Some students presume that everyone (at least every youth) in the room is heterosexual or has no questions about their own sexual identity.

- Some students show complete incomprehension — blank stares — at the mention of "transgender."

- Not infrequently, some students express violent disgust.

As facilitators, we can easily become hooked in by the same anxiety. We may subtly or openly identify at once as heterosexual (regardless of our sexual orientations) with the same sort of cues, such as "casually" referring to one's heterosexual partner, or rush to bury, to drop, or to change the subject. Somehow the discussion, once the subject of "gay" comes up, never quite returns to where it was. What is this anxiety about?

A classic word for it is *homophobia*, a dislike, disdain, or even hatred of homosexuals rooted in fear, or even panic, about closeness among members of the same sex. In the last several decades, this idea has extended to the new concept of "transphobia."[23] This panic is learned, not biological or instinctive. It is also the source of the astounding level of violence surrounding this issue among youth. The violence against lesbians, gays, and bisexuals that is often called "homophobia" we call "heterosexism" to highlight it as an oppression. The violence against transgendered, intersex, or gender-neutral people, often called transphobia, doesn't yet have an accepted or common phrase that identifies it as oppression; here, we use the term "transgender oppression" to refer to this violence.

Some Facts

1. No generalization can be made about how (or whether) one is or becomes lesbian, gay, bisexual, heterosexual, or gender queer. Each occurs normally, with no identifiable cause, and is experienced differently by different people. Indeed, every sexual orientation occurs naturally not only among people but within many different animal species, such as sheep, lions, seals, bedbugs, bonobo chimps, and quite a few kinds of fish and birds. Some of us "know" from birth what gender we are and don't experience "choice" at all, some of us choose, and some of us simply find ourselves where we are.

2. All cultural groups (people of different ethnicities, ages, and so forth) at all times in history have had gay, lesbian, bisexual, gender-queer, and heterosexual members. At a minimum, one in ten people is gay or lesbian, and more are bisexual. Human sexuality studies conducted by Alfred Kinsey (which are dated and may underrepresent the facts) reported that overall at least 37 percent of us have had same-sex sexual encounters — up to 50 percent of adult men, 28 percent of women, 60 percent of boys, and 33 percent of girls.

3. Many ways of being gay or lesbian exist, as do many ways of being heterosexual and many ways of being male, female, or transgender. This means that gay men as a group are no more "feminine" than other men, and lesbians are no more "masculine" than other women. Masculinity and femininity are not measures of sexual orientation. They refer to how people act out, display, or "perform" their gender identities and how closely these roles conform to societal norms of female and male behavior in different historical/cultural periods. Not all people are either straight or gay. Many are bisexual or pansexual; some of us elect to change the gender identities assigned to us at birth by changing our

names, changing our clothing and comportment, or undergoing hormone replacement and surgery; and many fall elsewhere on the continuum of sexual orientation — or off it entirely, as we point out in the introduction to this section. Some of us change orientation over the course of our lives, and others don't. That is to say, human sexuality encompasses a wide variety of orientations and attractions. Exclusive heterosexuality and homosexuality are two convenient social definitions but fall far short of describing the range of human sexual interaction.

Heterosexism and Transgender Oppression

Heterosexism is the systematic, day-to-day, institutional mistreatment of lesbian, gay, bisexual, pansexual, and gender-queer people by a heterosexually dominated culture; *transgender oppression* is the systematic, day-to-day, institutionalized mistreatment of transgender people. We are expanding the meanings of these terms from the usual ones — the beliefs that heterosexual practices and lifestyles are superior — to include the types of violence associated with other "isms," including stigma, economic exploitation, harassment, isolation, lack of civil rights, physical and emotional abuse, and murder. Homophobia is one of the major expressions of heterosexism, and transphobia is one of the major expressions of transgender oppression and a way each of us — whether heterosexual or LGBT — internalizes the oppression.

Heterosexism and transgender oppression are among the few oppressions sheltered in the legal system (that is, to be homosexual or transgender is illegal in many places). When we published the first edition of this book in 1990, twenty-eight states criminalized same-sex partnerships with antisodomy laws. Although the US Supreme Court *Lawrence* decision in 2003 decriminalized such partnerships, except in about a half dozen states in the country, same-sex domestic partners still cannot be legally married in most states, expect to secure custody rights or visitation with children from divorced partners, or obtain tax breaks. In 1990 gays, lesbians, bisexuals, and transgender people could be prohibited or dishonorably discharged from military service and the Boy Scouts; despite ongoing national campaigns to end such strictures, in practice these exclusions continue in the present.[24] Only at the end of 2010 was the "Don't Ask, Don't Tell" prohibition against "out" lesbians and gays in the military abolished, and it will take years to change the culture that supported the ban. LGBT people can also be discriminated against in housing and in employment opportunities. For example, a lesbian/gay identity could cost a public-school teacher, hospital worker, or child-care worker their job. This amounts to nothing less than a denial of basic civil rights and unequal protection under the law.

Every American institution, from the family to the medical establishment to the high-school prom to Top-Forty radio, presumes that we are all normally heterosexual and that each person is attracted to the opposite (binary) gender. Even TV programming now featuring gay characters can make their gayness itself the plotline, unlike the plotlines for heterosexual characters. This presumption of "normal" sexuality is nowhere enforced so powerfully as in the family. If you face oppression in the larger society as a person of color, a disabled person, or a worker, you may find people in your family who support you, but in coming out to your family, you may experience immediate and severe abuse.

The presumption of heterosexuality makes gayness invisible and conceals homosexuality behind anxiety-ridden stereotypes. Fixed-gender identity makes *any* departure from this norm aberrant. Transgender people are made, conversely, to become most visible as not-quite-human freaks or comic or demonic figures. Some of these stereotypes are that gays proselytize, that same-sex child molesters are gay, that AIDS is a gay disease, that gayness comes from excessive mothering, that gayness is a simple matter of choice (or the opposite: that all sexual orientation is innate, having to do with brain chemistry), that lesbians just haven't met "the right man," or that transgender people are confused, sick, or evil.

A more ominous form of the oppression, beyond invisibility, is stigma, found in the medical treatment of homosexuality as an aberrant or unnatural mental condition and in the religious demonizing of gayness as a moral evil to be exorcised. Stigma is motivated by larger moral anxieties and myths about sexuality that dominate US life. Strongly influenced by the dominant Christian culture, sex is still a morally frowned-upon activity and a forbidden topic in most classrooms and living rooms, so it becomes an obsession for most of us. The alternatives youth are given to cope with the obsession — to repress sexual feelings or to act them out — are set along exclusively heterosexual lines. Even the idea of questioning one's sexual identity out loud is prohibited to teens, because it is too dangerous to consider.

And finally, we consider violence. The label of "queer," "dyke," "gay," "lesbian," or "fag" is one of the most physically dangerous to carry in a high-school setting. A boy can start a fight to the death just by calling another boy "fag." And as gays become more outspoken and visible, the rate and intensity of gay bashings climbs. For example, the battles over legalization of gay marriage brought violence against LGBT people in 2009 back into prominence as the leading form of hate-crime violence in the United States. Overall, gays and lesbians are seven times more likely to be assaulted than are heterosexuals. The historical precedents extend from European witch burnings to the extermination of lesbians and gays in the Nazi Holocaust. It was only in late 2009 that a bill labeling acts of violence against people based on sexual orientation or gender as hate crimes was signed into federal law.

Ultimately this violence touches all of us; each of us can be targeted by heterosexism and transgender oppression. It is rooted in the socialization that every child receives. Think of the physical actions alone that each of us has learned to perform when in public, on a daily basis, to avoid being labeled as gay or lesbian. Think about how we negotiate physical contact with members of the same gender — how we carry ourselves, how we dress, how we walk, how we sit in a chair, how we drink our tea, what we joke about. Then think about how some of these negotiations have become so automatic that we don't even think about them.

Internalized Oppression

LGBT people internalize some of the effects of heterosexism and homophobia. The ways in which gayness and transgender identity have been penalized as crimes, treated as diseases, or preached against as sins have made self-doubt, guilt, shame, outright denial of one's identity, or attacks upon other queer-identified people a common feature of queer life. One must decide a dozen times a day whether to be out, and each setting provides different challenges. The absolute intolerance of homosexuality in most youth settings makes for the ultimate internalization: Adolescent lesbians and gays account for one-third of teens committing suicide. None of these actions, of course, is part of being lesbian, gay, bisexual, or transgender; rather, all are caused by attempts to survive in a hostile environment and amid the stress and pain of having to negotiate a stigmatized identity.

Vibrant LGBT cultures have always existed, challenging dominant paradigms of social behavior; taking leading roles in battles for civil rights and women's liberation; thriving in political, social, creative, and religious communities; sustaining alternative families and healthy parenting; and, most recently, emerging as the gay and transgender liberation and feminist movements. All of these circumstances must be recognized, remembered, celebrated, and called upon when we think about internalized oppression.

Alliance: Working with Young People on Heterosexism and Transgender Oppression

As adults committed to young people's liberation, we must decide, regardless of personal or religious beliefs or feelings or our own sexual orientation, that discrimination and violence against gays, lesbians, bisexuals, and transgender people must be stopped. It is a matter of safety and justice for all of us. Making this decision means stating publicly that this violence is wrong. Challenging heterosexism and transgender oppression creates safety not only for young people of these identities and others who are questioning their sexuality but also for heterosexual youth being pressured to be intolerant or violent to "prove" they are indeed heterosexual.

We may all broadly agree that discrimination by race, gender, physical ability, and the like should be eliminated. But because most of us possess insufficient information about what heterosexism is or transgender identity even means, it is incumbent upon each of us to examine our own convictions and the assumptions that prevent us from accepting differing sexual identities and orientations.

A good starting point is any early experiences we remember of learning that closeness between men or between women has strict boundaries — and the boundaries of these genders themselves are strict. We should look particularly at early religious teachings we may have received. How did these experiences affect us or limit our activity? Whatever our sexual orientation is, how do these experiences affect our work with youth now?

The next step is to strategize how to address these issues in our work with youth. Based on our experience, it is best to develop classes, workshops, and groups devoted explicitly to unlearning heterosexism, facilitated by lesbian/gay/bi/transgender and heterosexual presenters. This presentation can be done in tandem with the programs on sexism, racism, and adultism outlined in this book. In workshops on heterosexism for young people and adults, we often use the exercises below.

COMING-OUT ROLE-PLAY

One facilitator plays an older teen or young adult who is lesbian or gay or who is deciding to begin the process of changing their gender identity, unknown to their parents. Two others (or one other plus a teen volunteer) play the parents. The father and youth are in the driveway, working on a car (or in the living room, watching television). The father pressures the young person about who they are dating, and the latter finally decides to come out. The father reacts explosively. The mother enters, finds out what is going on, and chimes in with her shock and disapproval.

This is an interactive role-play. After the first few minutes, participants are encouraged to come up, tap any one of the characters on the shoulder, and take their place. Make sure that each of the parts gets replacement actors and that the LGBT character doesn't devolve into a stereotype. After a few minutes, the role-play is stopped and the group processes how it felt.

Alternative scenarios you may want to try include a straight student supporting a student under attack or standing up as an ally for their rights by interrupting interpersonal or institutional homophobia, a worker coming out to two unsupportive friends on the job, or a young person coming out to two disapproving friends from school. The point is for participants to try out the roles and for lots of feelings to be aired. Facilitators should ensure that (as in reality for many gay/lesbian/transgender youth) at least one "parent" at some point threatens extreme violence and orders the youth out of the house. This scenario can lead to a general discussion about what heterosexism and transgender oppression actually are, the connections with sexism, and the conditioning young people receive to be heterosexual and fixed in their identities.

One reason discussion of these issues can be difficult is that young people may have deeply felt religious convictions that gender identity or sexual orientation that is not male/female and heterosexual is sinful, immoral, or unnatural. You will have to facilitate the discussion so that while people's personal beliefs are respected, the social-justice goals of safety, inclusion, and civil rights are upheld for everyone.

In doing this work, we have developed certain approaches in our youth classes and groups addressing gender and racial violence:

1. Assume, act, and speak as if lesbian, gay, bisexual, transgender, and questioning youth are present. Notice any tendency to presume that everyone is heterosexual.

2. Continue to raise the issue of heterosexism and transgender oppression wherever you mention the other "isms." Much of heterosexism is about silencing and hiding, so it is always appropriate to discuss it and to be prepared for feelings that come up — not only young people's and other adults', but your own.

3. *Always* question or interrupt derogatory or joking uses of the words "queer," "fag," "dyke," and so forth. It is important to remember that young people who use these words are not simply being abusive nor are they simply being funny. The names and accompanying behavior are about the fear that has been instilled in them. Leaving this unchallenged lowers everyone's level of safety.

4. Assume that if you are heterosexual, you also lack information on this issue. Research LGBT history and consult the abundant new writings by LGBT people in various cultures and races about their experiences. Provide as much of this information to young people as possible, and don't fault them for not having it previously.

5. If you are heterosexual, in a situation where you are spontaneously asked what your sexual identity is, avoid as much as possible identifying your own sexual orientation. Identifying as heterosexual may silence and separate LGBT or questioning youth who are present. It is fine to return the question, asking them why they want to know or how it feels not to know. Use this as a chance

for young people to express and to question their fear or concern and to talk about the dangers of "coming out." (Practice this response a lot, ahead of time.)

6. If you are lesbian, gay, bisexual, or transgender, you may decide, on strategically picked occasions, that it is appropriate to be out. Being out to young people from the beginning carries its own power. Most young people have never been allowed to meet an "out" adult, and it can be a crucial experience in pride, understanding, and self-assertion for them. However, this openness is a choice based on your gauge of your own safety.

7. Evaluate your program not only for anti-LGBT violence but also for the missing connections between heterosexism, transgender oppression, and sexism. We cannot effectively address male violence unless we speak to the homo- and transphobia that keep it in place. Other areas to look at include the pictures on the walls of your classroom; how queer and transgender people are reflected in the curriculum (have they been rendered invisible?); what vocabulary is used in the halls; how gay, lesbian, bi, or transgender parents are treated at teacher conferences and at other school events; and how safe it is for teachers and staff to be out at the school.

8. In the previous analysis, no oppression is lessened if any is left in place. Try what you can, make mistakes, and try again. Every attempt will make more room where lesbian, bisexual, pansexual, gay, transgender, and gender-queer youth and adults can be out and proud.

ACCESS NOW! DISABLING ABLEISM

All human beings have basic sets of capacities and abilities that enable us to live, to function in, and to move through the world; this is what we have in common. What distinguishes us from each other are our very differing capacities and abilities to cope — differences in body, mind, and feelings, among many others. We may experience some of our own differences as limitations and others as special abilities.

It is part of every human life to be able to do some things and to be unable to do some others. And most of our "abilities" are constantly changing over our lifespans. These amount to basic features of human beings: Whatever our mental, physical, and emotional capacities and limits, each of us is a whole human being just as we are.

ABILITY VISUALIZATION

1. Pick a favorite animal other than human beings—mammal, fish, bird, or reptile. Visualize it, forming an image in your mind.

2. Visualize your animal as it is in the world: how it lives, functions, and moves day to day.

3. Now think of something that your animal does—an ability it has—that human beings, including you, don't have; for example, if you are picturing a bird that can fly, flying is one thing it does that you can't do without help. If you are picturing a fish with gills, it can live and breathe underwater, whereas you would need assistance. Make a clear picture for yourself of this ability that you lack. Now think of the following questions silently:

   ▸ Would you have noticed, without this visualization, that you "lacked" an ability?

   ▸ How is your life impacted by being without this ability?

   ▸ How do you get along without this ability?

   ▸ How do you compensate for lacking this ability (for example, if the ability is flying, what do you do instead of flying or being able to fly)?

   ▸ Do you feel that you are "less than" a regular organism because you "lack" this ability?

As humans, we and those around us possess many different kinds of capacities. It is normal for us to be able to do some kinds of things and not to be able to do others. Mostly, we do not experience the things we can't do as a lack or something that diminishes us. In fact, we may not even notice these "limits." For such limits we figure out, living our everyday lives, how to do what we need and want to do and how to compensate for or to handle the limits.

Think about the people in your family and community. Maybe you have a grandparent who is having trouble with memory. Maybe someone in your school survived a car accident or gunshot wound. Maybe you have struggled with depression or anxiety. Maybe you wear glasses, and the state requires that you wear them when you drive. You may know young women and men who have returned from war who are experiencing mental or emotional disturbances or have amputations. A group of students in your school, which may sometimes include you, undoubtedly has been identified as "learning disabled." We are at all times in the presence of people who are different from each other in what they can do.

Part of the process of being acculturated involves learning what in this society is considered "normal" and what is labeled as a limitation or "abnormal." Some of our labeled "disabilities" simply are incapacities, but others are seen as disabilities, because the larger culture does not accommodate them. For example, stairs are seen as a "normal" way to ascend or descend from a height. We don't consider it a disability not to be able to jump to and from the next floor, so stairs seem an appropriate accommodation. However, if I use crutches, canes, or a wheelchair, steps will not accommodate me. Ramps can help, but the wider society considers them to be special accommodations to disability.

These ranges of limitations are quite broad and include the following:

- physical, mental, and emotional disabilities
- short-term, or temporary, and long-term conditions
- disabilities related to illness or injury
- visible and invisible, "hidden" disabilities
- learning disabilities
- less involved ("milder") conditions, such as allergies, skin conditions, and so forth, and more involved ("more severe") issues, such as mobility impairment, blindness, deafness, and so forth
- conditions that may at least seem to be (or are labeled as) voluntarily contracted by people, such as obesity, or addictions, such as alcoholism

Even making such a list is tricky. Many disabilities are classified with stereotypical words or medical terms that devalue what they name. Medical terms may not be familiar to people with disabilities or adequately name their own experiences of their disabilities. Just to call something a "limitation" makes the assumption that something is there, natural and fixed, that counts as a limitation.

The labeling process—how society pictures disability—can easily slide into oppression. Like sexism, racism, and other "isms," it sets a group of people apart as "different" and "abnormal." Merely using the terms "limitation" or "incapacity" hints at tagging people with disabilities as "less than."

One form this labeling takes is the equating of disability with illness. Although this correlation may apply to some kinds of disabilities, obviously illness and disability are different; I am not ill if I use glasses, have a stutter, use a cane or a wheelchair, or need extra time to take a test. But the lingering effect of this confusion is to associate people living with disabilities with disease or unhealthiness, thus separating them into a group outside the norm. This is reinforced by the terms we use: "*dis*-abled," "handicapped" and "impaired."

Furthermore, within this framework, a person who is perceived to have a disability is often an object of pity or scorn. An abled person's obligation, in turn, is to help "the blind" or "the lame"—enhancing the virtue of the helper while relegating the helped to the status of hapless dependent.

Other versions of labeling equate disability with ugliness and even outright evil. Western images of beauty, although they have changed over time, always portray a particular era's notions of physically unflawed, perfect bodies. Such physical features as warts, moles, or skin rashes have operated as symbols for danger, evil, contagion, and infectiousness.

None of these forms of labeling may be conscious in students or staff. But after centuries of common use, they can still deeply affect people's perceptions of someone with a disability and the willingness to make accommodation for and to support them.

As humans, we are all vulnerable to changes in our physical, mental, and emotional statuses. Most of the people who are living with disability became disabled after birth. Challenging ableism also means understanding how we learn to blame disabled people for the problems our society causes them. In some cases, the disability itself is caused by policies that promote war, environmental degradation, and other behaviors that reduce human capacities, in service of the wealthy. What is the cost to us when we learn to shun or to stigmatize people who are disabled?

Picturing Disability

How does society picture "normal" and "abnormal" in physical, emotional, and mental human capacity and behavior? How does it picture "disability," and how do young people become aware of these distinctions? Paradoxically, perhaps the first picture young people experience is the *lack* of a picture: the segregation of children classified with mental, emotional, or physical differences/disabilities or "developmental delays" from mainstream populations of children in day care, preschool, and grade school. The justification for treating people identified as having particular kinds of "limits" begins to happen in the stereotypes young people learn about what is supposed to be "normal" for human beings and what is "abnormal." The following short set of exercises highlights this scenario in the classroom.

THREE FIGURES

A commonsense description of human activities comes up with three general parts of what it means to be human—what it is like for a human to have a body, to think, and to have emotions. In each of these areas, what kinds of things count as normal/abnormal?

Draw three human stick figures, labeled "body," "mind," and "emotions." Draw boxes that enclose each of the figures. If each box stands for the "shaping" that happens to humans—the way social institutions train all of us in what is normal and what isn't normal—what shaping happens around disability?

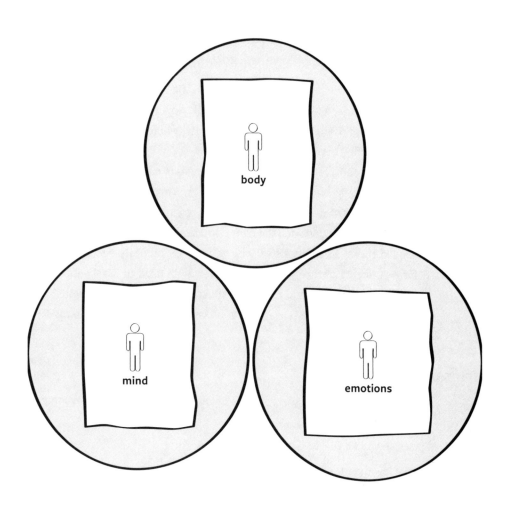

For the following, write responses for each of the boxed figures:

1. Write these words *into* the appropriate box.
   - What are words we use to describe a person with a "normal" physical body?
   - What are words we use to describe a person with a "normal" mind or mental state?
   - What are words we use to describe a person with "normal" feelings?

2. Write these words *around* the exterior of the appropriate box. Draw a circle around the whole.
   - What are words we use to describe an "abnormal" physical body?
   - What are words we use to describe an "abnormal" mind or mental state?
   - What are words we use to describe the "abnormal" feelings of a person?

3. Write these words *around the exterior* of the appropriate circle.
   - What are the names we sometimes call or use as stereotypes for people identified as having "abnormal" bodies?

- People identified as having "abnormal minds"?
- People identified as having "abnormal" feelings?

Look over what you've written. How do the words on the outside of the boxes work to "box" or shape the figures, telling people how they should act and behave, how they should appear? These boxes are used to justify *ableism*—discrimination against people with identified disabilities.

Finally, consider the commonplace images in cartoons, video games, magazine covers and ads, TV, and films of people with "normal" bodies. What groups of people by race, age, and class are typically represented as models of beauty, ability, intelligence, and virtue? Then consider the commonplace imaging of people with "abnormal" bodies. Do these expectations vary by gender? By race? By economic background? How have concepts of race, class, and gender been used to label entire groups of people as having abnormal, and therefore substandard, bodies and minds? What groups of people, categorized by race, age, and class, are typically seen in media images, compared to the above?

WITNESSING DISABILITY

Identify silently an early experience of witnessing or being shown someone with a visible disability:

▸ How did it feel to witness this person?

▸ How did other people act around this person?

▸ Think of any ways the person with a disability was treated as "different" and how that made you feel.

▸ If another person was with you, how did this person react? How might they have told you to act?

▸ If you were told to act in a certain way, how did that make you feel? How might it have made you feel about having a disability?

▸ When you think about it now, what information about the person with the disability or their experience would you have liked to have had? If no one gave you information then, why do you think that was?

▸ If you had been able to ask any question you wanted to of the person with a disability, what would you have wanted to ask?

▸ Describe any way that you think this experience might have gotten in your way of having a normal human relationship with the person with a disability.

▸ What do your early experiences show about how you were able to picture disability and people with disabilities?

Ableism

Ableism means the discrimination against or abuse of people identified or labeled as living with mental, emotional, or physical differences and the elevation of "normally" abled people into positions of privilege, with power over people with these differences.

The target group includes people with visible physical differences — those who use assistance with mobility, hearing, sight, speech, and so forth; people with mental differences in speech, type of intelligence, behavior, emotional affect, "learning" ability, and so forth; and people whose differences are hidden — people who can hide or mask physical or mental differences. The stereotypes, names, and physical exclusions most likely to be known to young people now are just the surface of a much deeper and more violent history of the treatment of people with differences ranging from isolation, quarantine, confinement, warehousing, and imprisonment to physical and sexual abuse, medical experimentation, enforced drugging, and finally the killing of infants and adults alike. Some features of ableism include the following:

▸ *Anyone can be a target:* Unlike some of the other "isms," anyone can be a target of this "ism" and will be at some time in their life. Anyone can have or contract a visible or hidden disability, illness, or injury, and anyone's "normality" can be called into question.

▸ *Being seen as disabled:* Virtually all people with visible disabilities have undergone the experience of being stared at, perceived and treated as different or "abnormal," or identified simply by or reduced to the disability they have (for example, a "cripple," "AIDS victim," "a blind person," and so forth). Others are even more directly targeted with the onus of the disability, especially with mental differences (for example, "special ed," "retard," "wacko," "lunatic").

▸ *Pity/abhorrence:* Bearing the label of "disabled" almost invariably means the labeled person at one time or another will experience being treated as an object of pity or being avoided altogether: two forms of invisibility.

▸ *Disability and illness:* Ability and disability are not the same as health and illness. People living with most kinds of physical or mental differences can at any time be ill or well — what distinguishes their experiences are socially defined categories of "normal" and "abnormal."

▸ *Ableism and other "isms":* Ableism has often been used historically to justify other "isms." For example, women have been labeled as "too emotional," "irrational," or "hysterical," while various groups of people of color have been labeled as less intelligent, even "primitive" or "savage," particularly when they were resisting exploitation and violence. The labels imply that these groups are "less than" men or white people because they possess these (abnormal) features.

Sometimes target groups, doing their best to resist, having internalized the oppression, have responded to this mistreatment not by challenging the ableism in these labels but by proving that the labels don't fit them, thereby leaving the labels in place — for example, women rightly fought to prove that women are not "irrational" or "hysterical" but equally as rational or stable as men; people of color have rightly fought against being labeled as mentally deficient and to be accepted as being as intelligent as white people. But this can inadvertently leave uncontested the assumption that anyone so labeled deserves to be treated as "less than."

▸ *Real disability:* What we call disabilities are often, of course, genuine limits on "normal" human functioning. A person with such a disability may need assistance — a person with paraplegia may need a wheelchair, and a person with a learning disability may need tutoring. Because ableism attaches a stigma to disability, people who need such assistance may deny their disability or refuse to ask for assistance.

▸ *Medicalization:* Most identified "disabilities" have, only in the last century, come to be defined by developing medical institutions as "disabilities" to be "treated." People identified with disabilities have become "cases" or "patients" (or "test cases"), depending upon medical institutions not only for care but even for the very concepts of the disability or illness they "have." Advances in medical care have meant prolonged and improved lives for many people, but they have also brought about segregation, dependence, medical experimentation, lack of understandable information, overprescription of drugs or outright drugging, wrongful diagnosis and treatment, and premature death of people with disabilities.

▸ *Exclusion:* From "tracking" in schools to the creation of wards, "sheltered" workshops, nursing homes, "treatment" houses, and asylums, people with various disabilities have been bodily removed from mainstream social life. Some exclusions are justified as providing for better treatment of and care for various conditions. But much of the exclusion has been inappropriate — a denial of human rights — and has led to gross abuses and exploitation. Regardless of intention, exclusion amounts to incarceration, a life "less than," separate, and unequal.

▸ *Mental-health oppression:* Abuse of people identified with mental-health "issues" rates in a category of its own. School systems can abuse designations made through testing, grading, and determination of acceptable student behavior, especially when diagnosing youth with attention-deficit disorders. Signs of this abuse are reflected in the phrases that young people (and even teachers) sometimes use to put down someone who isn't intelligent, such as "retard" and "stupid." The above-mentioned examples of women deemed as irrational and people of color as mentally deficient show how mental-health oppression continues into adulthood.

▶ *Violence:* Ableism can involve outright violence — restraints on movement; medication against one's will; neglect and abuse by "caregivers"; involuntary incarceration or segregation; physical, emotional, or sexual violence; neglect; "pulling the plug" on people perceived to be near death or "not worth reviving"; genetic engineering to select for and to produce "healthy," "normal" children with socially valued traits, which is a form of eugenics; and selection and criminalization of certain populations of people based on "scientific" theories of violence related to genetics, brain structure, or other variations.

▶ *Institutionalized mistreatment:* Finally, ableism occurs when institutions exclude people with disabilities. These range from schools, public education overall, and workplace hiring and setup, to public stores and buildings, public transportation, movie theaters, public recreation areas, amusement parks, and city sidewalk curbs.

Resistance

Resistance is not about resisting being disabled or coping with it "heroically" but rather resisting the oppression of ableism — the stigma, exclusion, and abuse that might attach to having a disability. On that score, people labeled as "disabled" have always resisted the mistreatment that accompanies the label, although this resistance may have been hidden. Disabled resistance is often "invisibilized" (because disabled people are largely kept invisible in mainstream culture), and ableism works by assuming that disabled people are helpless and need to be "helped," whether they ask for help or not. Well-intentioned allies may take over by "helping" without asking whether their help is needed, once again taking power from the targeted group.

Beyond acts of personal resistance, disabled activists have participated in long-standing organization against ableism. Just within the last thirty years this organizing has taken the form of the following:

▶ *Patients' rights:* Organizing among disabled recipients of medical care for informed consent for medical treatment, against forced incarceration or medication for people with mental disabilities, and around other similar issues.

- *Organized communities:* Establishing advocacy groups organized by and on behalf of particular constituencies — for example, the blind community, the deaf community, and others.

- *Independent-living movement:* Organizing to enable disabled adults to live independently of institutions, establishing and maintaining households and employment.

- *Disability-rights movement:* Activists organized to change existing laws and to create new legislation ensuring public access and accommodations for all disabled people and schools and workplaces that integrate abled and disabled people ("mainstreaming" people with disabilities). A major achievement of the movement was the passing of the Americans with Disabilities Act, securing rights from access to public buildings to protection from discrimination in the workplace for people living with disabilities.

- *Cultural access:* People with disabilities organize their participation in sports (Special Olympics), the arts (Access Theater for actors with and without wheelchairs, National Theater for the Deaf, and so forth), and other arenas.

- *Access/Accommodation:* One of the most important things disability activists have fought for is *access*, the right for people with disabilities to be enabled to participate in all areas of civic life that abled people can access. Activists have continually shown that pity, denial, minimization of the problem, or complaints that changes "cost too much" are themselves part of the oppression of ableism. Highly visible public demonstrations, wheelchair blockades of inaccessible buses and buildings, and "curb-cut" campaigns are among the actions that produced the first Americans with Disabilities Act, which requires that all public buildings be accessible.

To close, the following are role-play and follow-up exercises on resistance we have used in workshops.

"You Poor Thing"

Have three students who have previously volunteered and been prepared for this role-play take their places in front of the class. Bring one chair to the front of the room. One student sits in the chair, while the others face them. All three are same-age students. The chair is a wheelchair, the person in the chair—the first patron—is paraplegic, and the scene is in the first-floor lobby of a movie theater. One of the other students plays a second patron who is not paraplegic, and one plays the (student-age) assistant theater manager. Remember that if real-life students in wheelchairs volunteer to participate, they have the option of playing any of the three roles.

Scenario

In the following scene, the second patron plays the part of someone who wants to help, but their chief feeling about the chaired person is *pity*: "It's so sad that you have this handicap." The chaired patron has bought a ticket to see a film on the second floor, but the only access is by stairs (the elevator is broken, as it often is at this theater). This has happened before, and this time they refuse to leave until something is done about the elevator. The manager plays an overworked, embarrassed employee who is trying to talk the chaired person into leaving. They might offer to have the chaired person taken out of the wheelchair and carried up to the theater by other employees (the other patron might offer to help do this), they might argue that it costs too much to fix the elevator, or they might end up angry at the chaired person for complaining too much and making things too inconvenient. The chaired person refuses to be lifted out of the chair and holds to the principle that the theater is responsible for making movies "accessible" to everyone.

Invite students to play out the role-play with the above directions for two to three minutes. Encourage the students enacting the second patron and the theater manager to play their character parts fully, saying all the "wrong" things.

Freeze the role-play. Have the actors take turns talking about how it felt to be in their roles, beginning with the chaired person. Then have other students report what they observed. Ask the following, based on this role-play:

▶ How was the chaired person mistreated?

▶ How did the chaired person resist mistreatment?

▶ Does the person in the chair need assistance in this situation?

▶ What kinds of assistance were not helpful? Why?

▶ What could a chaired person do to change this situation? What could an ally do?

No One Left Out

Explain that students will now turn to a group project on making a place, the room in which the class gathers, accessible not only to abled people but to people with different disabilities—"no one left out, no one left behind."

Break students into small four-member workgroups. Assign each group accessibility planning for one of the following groups of people with disabilities (if you have more than twenty-four students, you may make six-member groups; if fewer, you may use fewer categories).

1. visually impaired
2. hearing impaired

3. in a wheelchair

4. learning disabled

5. "special ed" or "developmentally disabled"

6. breathing allergies/asthmatic

When groups are assembled within their assigned categories, put them through the following process.

My Day So Far[25]

Have students form dyads within their groups. Each student will have two minutes to talk in their pair. The topic is going through "my day so far" as someone with this particular disability:

▶ What happens when I wake up?

▶ What happens with breakfast and getting ready for school?

▶ How I get to school?

▶ How I enter school and go to class as the person I am, with this disability?

If the student has the disability in question, they will speak about their own experience; if not, they are to imagine what happens. Explain that when students don't have enough information about the disability in question, they should just do their best to think about what it would be like, without using stereotypes, and notice how it feels not to have the appropriate information.

Time the dyads, telling students when to switch. Complete the dyads, and have students, while still in their groups, process for a few moments what it was like to talk about the topic, including any difficulty or discomfort. In particular, they might address:

a. what *extra* things they had to do that were different from what they normally do and may take for granted

b. what attitudes they might have experienced from others, whether at home or on the way to school

c. what barriers they experienced

d. what they would want an ally to know, do, or not do

Access Brainstorm

Now the task of each group is a brainstorm exercise about a day at school for students who have the disability assigned to the group:

1. *Barriers:* Brainstorm all the barriers a student with this disability will face in the school-building architecture, environment, room setup, teaching process and

classroom procedure, school "tracking" of students into segregated groups, or attitudes from other students or teachers. Write as many barriers as they can think of on butcher paper (five minutes).

2. *Changes:* Brainstorm what should be different in room setup and space, class presentation, teaching process, etc. (five minutes) to enable the student with this disability to participate fully as an equal and as a "heart" with everyone else. A central part of the task is to incorporate the standpoint of people with the disability: How would a person with this disability design the room to be accessible? Be as specific as possible. Someone in each group should take notes of changes for ready reference.

3. *Allies:* Brainstorm how able-bodied students can help and not help students with this disability in making the room fully accessible (five minutes).

The Accessible Classroom

Using their notes about changes, have groups take five minutes, all at the same time, to make any changes in the room setup they have devised. Then close the entire process by having students as a full group evaluate what they have done and what else they would recommend. Then have a few respond to a final question:

▶ How would improved access that benefits students with disabilities *also* benefit able-bodied students?

The Accessible School

What would it take to bring these changes to an entire school? As a final project, diagram a map of the school facility and have students study the map to brainstorm short- and long-term changes or improvements in the building design, building services, and school events that could improve access. As a class project, students could study the process by which recommendations for change could be brought to the school administration and the school district, design a petition (and even research costs for different recommendations), and begin a lobbying process to achieve access.

CHRISTIAN HEGEMONY

Approaching the topic of Christian culture in US schools in the twenty-first century means entering a battleground of school boards, parents, administrators, and teachers — all of whom are adults — about what young people are to learn. Conflicts range (and rage) over evolution versus creationism and intelligent design, prayer in school, observed and ignored religious holidays, school attire, sex education, and the separation of church and state.

The ferocity of these conflicts is exacerbated by the perception that wider global conflicts are generated by "clashes of civilizations," most notably Christian and Muslim, with the subtext that US life possesses (Christian) values that are "under attack." The widespread belief that mainstream US culture and its educational institutions have become secular or even antireligious further shapes these debates. To even suggest that Christian institutions, beliefs, and practices dominate US culture can bring sharp denials.

How does this look in the classroom? Young people can be anywhere on the spectrum of religious involvement, in any religion, from fundamentalist conviction to occasional observance to indifference to active atheism. The kinds of Christian practice some students observe vary widely based on the differing roles of churches in communities of different racial, ethnic, and socioeconomic backgrounds. Some evangelical denominations actively market to youth and train them to proselytize. For groups targeted for oppression by race, class, or other differences, Christian (and other) religious communities may function as bulwarks, or at least familiar community settings, against daily experiences of mistreatment. Finally, some forms of Christian practice, such as fundamentalist or evangelical forms, may be frowned upon or made fun of by student and adult culture at a given school, making individual Christian students feel persecuted.

Of course, Christianity is the dominant religion practiced in the United States—recent polls show that about 75 percent of the population believes in a Christian deity.[26] The structural role of Christianity in the formation of the United States, from justifications for bloody conquest of the continent to laws governing citizen behavior, is a well-known part of the US narrative. Christian doctrines of hard work, individual responsibility, industry, and development, sometimes popularly called the "Protestant ethic," have played a role in the creation and maintenance of a global capitalist economic system. Overtly Christian movements have been active, sometimes violently so, in formats from right-wing talk radio to governmental lobbying; speaking against reproductive rights and lesbian, gay, bisexual, and transgender rights; and other issues that affect non-Christian minorities.

Christian institutions have also played a deep, founding, and shaping role in US school systems. The spiritual practices of students and their families and communities are not the issue here but rather how all students become oriented in a society in which Christianity plays a dominating role as Christian hegemony. *Hegemony* in this sense refers to whatever is part of the systematic, day-to-day, institutionalized, taken-for-granted routine in a given culture: the "default position." Because we identify "oppression" as the systematic, daily, routine dominance and mistreatment of a target group by a nontarget group, we in effect identify such "isms" as racism and sexism as hegemonies. An easily understood, obvious example of Christian hegemony in the United States is the observance of Christmas, observed throughout the business and civic world as a holiday that saturates all aspects of US culture for believers, nonbelievers, and "secular" Christians alike for more than a month every year.

It may not be as openly acknowledged that education in US and European societies is, to a great extent, modeled on a conception of education as moral training, development, and maturation of what is designated as the human soul—the training of individuals in how to behave, how to strive, and whom or what to obey—found in Christian-based pedagogies begun in medieval Europe. The use of Christian parables and moral instructions in the early New England primers for learning the ABCs are easily cited examples. Even today, many of our taken-for-granted assumptions about how teachers are to educate young people and what young people should be taught reflect Christian concepts of good and bad, light and dark, chosen and condemned, and educational progress as the analogue of salvation. These assumptions are implicit in the pedagogical approaches taken in most US school systems, quite apart from more explicit expressions of Christian hegemony to be found in such practices as Christian prayers in classrooms, school assemblies and sports events, and dress codes in some schools that forbid the Islamic head-scarf while ignoring the crucifix.

What other taken-for-granted practices in US life are based on Christian values? We use the following exercise to promote students' awareness of the influence of these values, regardless of the particular religious practices, if any, they have been raised to observe. As with previous exercises in this book, this is a stand-up exercise using categories you may preselect from the list. If any participants have limited mobility, they may participate by raising hands if they are able.

LIVING IN A CHRISTIAN-DOMINANT CULTURE

Please stand silently if…

1. you have been baptized or otherwise ceremonially introduced, as a child or adult, into "being a Christian"

2. you have ever attended church of a Christian denomination regularly

3. you have ever attended Sunday school as a child or attended church periodically (for example, during Christian holidays)

4. you have ever attended a Christian-based recreational organization as a young person, such as the YMCA or YWCA, or church-based summer camp or

participated in a program of a nonreligious youth organization that was based in Christian beliefs, such as the Girl Scouts and Boy Scouts

5. you have ever been told or instructed that things that you do with your body, sex with others, or sex by yourself was sinful or unclean

6. you have ever been told that sexual acts other than intercourse between a man and a woman or sexual orientations other than heterosexual are sinful or unclean

7. you have ever heard heaven and good described as light or white and hell and evil described as dark or black

8. you have ever been told something you did was sinful or evil or that you were sinful or evil

9. you have ever been approached by family members, friends, or strangers trying to convince you to become Christian or a Christian of a particular kind

10. you have ever been rejected in any way by family or community members, because you were not Christian or were not Christian enough

11. you have ever experienced the church in your community as a major center of social life that influences those around you and that would be difficult to avoid if you wanted to

12. you have ever taken Christian holidays, such as Christmas or Easter, off, whether you observe them as Christian holidays or not, or have taken Sunday off or think of it, in any way, as a day of rest

13. you have ever been given a school vacation or paid holiday related to Christmas or Easter when school vacations or paid holidays for non-Christian religious celebrations, such as Ramadan or the Jewish High Holidays, were not observed

14. public institutions you use, such as offices, buildings, banks, parking meters, the post office, libraries, and stores, are open on Fridays and Saturdays but closed on Sundays

15. the calendar year you observe is calculated from the year designated as the birth of Christ

16. you have ever seen a public institution in your community, such as a school, hospital, or city hall, decorated with Christian symbols (such as Christmas trees, wreaths, portraits or sculptures of Jesus, nativity scenes, "10 Commandment" displays, or crosses)

17. you can easily find and access Christian music, TV shows, movies, and places of worship in your community

18. you can easily access Christmas- or Easter-related music, stories, greeting cards, films, and TV shows at the appropriate times of the year

19. anyone in your family have ever received public services—medical care, family planning, food, clothing, shelter, or substance-abuse treatment—from a Christian-based organization or one marked by Christian beliefs and practices (for example, Alcoholics Anonymous or other twelve-step programs, "pro-life" family planning, hospital care, and so forth)

20. you daily use currency that includes Christian words or symbols, such as the phrase "in God we trust"

21. you have ever been told that a war or invasion, historical or current, was justified, because those who were attacked were heathens, infidels, unbelievers, pagans, terrorists, sinners, or fundamentalists of a non-Christian religion

22. your parents or ancestors were ever subject to invasion, forced conversion, or the use of missionaries as part of a colonization process either in the United States or in another part of the world

23. in your community or metropolitan area, hate crimes have been committed against Jews, Muslims, gays, transgender people, women, or others based on or justified by the perpetrator's Christian beliefs

24. you have ever attended public nonreligious functions, such as civic or governmental meetings, that were convened with Christian blessings, references, or prayers

25. you have ever been asked or commanded to sing or to recite, in public, material that contains Christian references, such as the Pledge of Allegiance or "America, the Beautiful"

This exercise, like the other stand-ups, ends with students breaking into dyads to discuss how they felt during the exercise. A group discussion follows.

A good starting point for such a discussion, and for conducting the above exercise, is to assure students that their and their families' individual religious commitments are not at issue. Christianity itself is not at issue. Professing Christians have been part of almost every social justice movement in the United States and elsewhere in the hemisphere, from the abolition of slavery to antipoverty work to civil disobedience against war to liberation theology across the Americas. As noted above, some churches have served as sources of family and community protection against and healing from oppression. To make being a Christian as such seem wrong or misguided only plays into popular stereotypes about Christian believers, alienating observant youth and giving credence to their potential self-righteous feelings of being persecuted while enabling everyone else to ignore the presence of hegemony in their lives.

What is at issue, rather, is the seventeen-hundred-year history of Christian institutional dominance in European and US internal governance and external, exploitive colonizing "missions," as well as the oppressive effects of this history that persist in our society. The history is difficult to tell, partly because it is hidden by Christian hegemony itself, and partly because the history is ridden with horrible events committed in the name of or under the auspices of Christianity, including "witch" burnings; inquisitions; pogroms; justifications of slavery; Christian boarding-school kidnappings of Native American youth; clergy sexual abuse; the killing of lesbian, gay, bisexual, and transgender people; the bombing of mosques and temples; the murder of reproductive health physicians; and many other acts. Like the histories of the real effects of racism, sexism, heterosexism, and adultism, the depths and reaches of these brutalities extend far outside the classroom and what students can absorb and understand in the classroom space.

The persisting effects of that history, in turn, can be hard to define, because they are so deeply layered in the institutions that shape our lives now. To take other examples besides educational practices: In our mainstream Western medical/health-care systems, the concepts of dirt and cleanliness, hygiene, germs, infection, illness, disease, quarantine, healing, cure, twelve-step programming, and sexual and reproductive health reflect Christian ideas and values. Our legal systems are built upon Christian concepts of sin and innocence, aberration, error, confession, guilt, judgment, punishment, penitence, obedience, rehabilitation, and redemption. Our workdays and civic lives are ordered by the Christian-based structure of the work week, the cultural meanings of T.G.I.F., Saturday night and Sunday morning, and the year-round schedule of holidays: Halloween, Christmas and "Christmas bonuses," Good Friday, and Easter. From within such frameworks, it is hard to see what alternative ways to deal with such social systems as health and law would look like.

What we can do is build awareness of Christian hegemony among our students. To begin with, students should be enabled to recognize the contemporary effects of Christian hegemony on those who are not from Christian households. Elements of those effects can be seen in the stand-up, in the invisibility of non-Christian religious holidays, and general culture-wide unawareness about and often demonization of some religious practices (for example, Islamic) and the romanticization of others (for example, Native American).

On the surface, invisibility may mean that if you are from a household with a spiritual affiliation other than Christian, your holidays and practices, such as dietary concerns, will not be recognized, honored, or allowed for at school or in the workplace. Your normative cultural beliefs about such topics as physical contact, dress, and gender and family relationships may be ignored or ridiculed. Your peers can ostracize you. If you are Native American, your sacred sites, including cemeteries, can be desecrated or archaeologically plundered, your rituals legally prohibited, your ritual objects sold as tourist objects, and your entire culture appropriated or turned into degrading symbols and mascots. If you are Jewish, your religious background can be lumped together with, and thereby absorbed into, Christianity under the label "Judeo-Christian." If you or your family is openly atheist, you can be targeted for condemnation, proselytization, or both. If your family or you are Muslim, you can be called a terrorist, be treated as dangerous, and have your loyalty to this country questioned.

But more deeply, invisibility can mean a profound assumption about the normality of Christianity and the abnormality of everything else: that your or your family's faith or practice — or refusal to follow any faith or practice — can become caricatured or stereotyped, which can mushroom into discrimination and violence. These distortions can show up, for example, in persecution of Muslims, Native Americans, Jews, or other religious minorities, from epithets and name calling at school to violent attacks on religious centers and subjection to airport searches, profiling, and surveillance in a national setting — in other words, a full-scale climate of fear and hatred of people perceived to be not Christian. Many of your non-Christian students will have family members (or they themselves may be) experiencing such persecution, and most will know stories of such persecution occurring within the last several decades in their communities.

What are the effects of hegemony on students from households that are actively or tacitly Christian? At the top of the list are the presumptions of Christian-based value systems passed on to Christian children. Like those of other world religions, Christian practices have as one function the reproduction of such systems generation by generation. Children learn early on the do's and don'ts of human behavior — what's right and wrong, what's good and bad, as structured by Christian beliefs — well before developing capacities to understand, to judge, to challenge, or to freely subscribe to the deeper imports of these lessons. Even such a binary framework reflects a Christian worldview.

Our survival as human beings depends upon our healthy relationships with each other, and Christian practice is one form of such learning. But one major institutional form Christian practice has taken historically is a demarcation between those who are Christian and those who are not. This demarcation implies a separation between those who know what is good and bad and those who don't; those who are "clean" and those who are "dirty"; and, by further implication, those who are good or capable of being good and those who are ignorant of good or actively evil. This inculcation can generate fear and hatred of others and the fostering of the stereotypes that appear throughout the Christian era from "ignorant savages" and "Godless sinners" to Jewish financiers and Islamic terrorists. A final aspect of hegemony Christians may internalize is the confusing feeling that one is good *and* bad, divided within oneself—subject to feelings of self-righteousness and innocence juxtaposed with self-doubt, self-hate, and guilt. Commonly, this split happens around the body, which is considered unruly and in need of discipline or punishment, while one's thoughts and intentions are considered virtuous and "good." A Christian's feelings of innocence can make it possible to stay unaware of the benefits that accrue to them as an active or secularized Christian in the United States; treat any criticism of themselves as persecution; and justify remaining on guard against, uninformed about, afraid of, and hostile to those defined as other than Christian. Pervading all this, guilt can make one feel helpless about addressing any of the above.

What can be done to offset effects of Christian hegemony that might be affecting students? The following are some bottom lines:

1. Social justice work with young people is always about fostering community. This effort always means building alliances across lines of race, gender, ability, and other differences to bring everyone into the room. In such a community, people of all religions and those eschewing religion are recognized and welcomed. At least one intent of the First Amendment of the US Constitution was to separate matters of church from matters of state, freeing all churches from the state persecutions that many immigrants from Europe experienced. It is in the spirit of that intention that full recognition from the community and the separation from government-based and hegemony-based mistreatment be extended to institutions *beside* churches, including other religions, indigenous practices, and the rights of those outside religious practices—an inclusive community.

   In the classroom this means, minimally, that students are not to be joked about, faulted, or ignored for religious practice or nonpractice outside Christianity but rather acknowledged and respected. To the extent that religion is a topic of discussion, you (and your students) can research and call upon liberation practices within Christianity, within other religious traditions, within practices of agnosticism and atheism, and within democracy itself to build this inclusive community.

2. Much of the educational process, especially as encoded in the hidden curriculum, is about teaching students how to behave "properly": *decorum*. The

decorum invariably reflects mainstream conceptions of "appropriate" behavior or comportment; invariably, this task places school authorities, including you, in the position of enforcing this decorum. And students are judged according to this decorum — indeed, they may stake out positions in relation to it, from model student to rebel/outsider. The judgment amounts to an evaluation of student character. So to the extent that the decorum is modeled on Christian conceptions of right and wrong, students' characters are being evaluated according to their conformity to Christian standards. And if a Christian worldview is hegemonic, deeply imbedded in our social structures, it can be very difficult to understand what is right and wrong, appropriate and inappropriate, outside the automatic reference to such standards.

This difficulty can play out in how people judge other groups of people: to divide female students, for example, into good girls and sluts; or to label non-Christian students as different, exotic, or weird. By mid-adolescence, young people have certainly internalized such standards, using them to brand and to separate from each other.

To call such standards into question is not to forgo having standards. It is important to continually invite students to think about moral action. It is crucial to be clear with students (and with other teachers and school authorities) that personal integrity and moral action are not dependent upon quality of religious affiliation or practice, nor adherence to one particular moral code. It is always appropriate to bring into discussion how students treat each other and how adults treat them. It is always appropriate to act as allies against mistreatment. Examples of these forms of "decorum" can be found in social justice movements within and outside all religions and spiritual practices.

3. A more difficult matter to address in the educational process has to do with what actually counts as "knowledge" or "truth" in our curricula, particularly in the sciences. The practices of Western science are grounded in academic systems set up in the Christian abbeys and schools of medieval Europe and, as a result, focus on determining what is true. The notion is that a universal truth exists, and those in authority, whether priests or scientists, have found and possess it. Little room for complexity, nuance, and multiple perspectives exists within this framework. Most of our standards of evaluation, most prominently the vast multilayer system of testing of students to determine how much of this truth they know, rely on the assumption that knowledge is discrete, noncontradictory, and knowable. In this view, students must learn the right answers and put their different perspectives, understandings, and creativity aside to succeed in the educational system.

Generally, the story of how the "truth" has been decided at different times — who decides and in whose interest those decisions have been made (by historians, physical and social scientists, and political leaders) — is not taught. This omission thwarts students' participation as active learners in the educational process, undermining their ability to understand movements for social justice. One way to undermine the impact of Christian hegemony within the classroom is to teach students how to analyze competing truth claims, how to assess the interests of the groups that decide what counts as truth, and how to increase or "complexify" their abilities to hold different perspectives.

4. With the participation of your students, inventory your school rules, protocols, ceremonies, newsletters, bulletin boards, sports games, theater productions, and, of course, holidays to determine how Christian hegemony might show up day to day at school. Enlist students' help in identifying the issues and promoting forums in which to bring other traditions of belief — and nonbelief — into school life. In doing this, you are performing one of the basic functions of all spiritual practices — to acknowledge our dependence upon and need for each other and for meaningful connection to the natural and social world.

ANTI-IMMIGRANT OPPRESSION

Each year, more than eight hundred thousand people are in the process of migration worldwide, displaced by the forces of globalization, finance capital, environmental disaster, war, and outright trafficking. They are either leaving countries of origin permanently or following long-established depart-and-return routes to earn funds for their families. The United States is one of the world's principal destinations, a country with disproportionate wealth, a high demand for low-paid labor, and a global image as a land of prosperity. Population figures from 2008 show 12.6 million first-generation (born in another country) documented "lawful residents" and an additional 10.8 million undocumented immigrant residents.[27] These figures do not include the millions more second-, third-, and fourth-generation Americans who still identify or are identified with a different country. Whether in the states with highest immigrant populations (California, Texas, New York, and Florida) or beyond and whether (as most current immigrants are) from Mexico, Central America, the Philippines, India, China, the Caribbean, or Canada, nearly a quarter of all young people now in elementary and high school in the United States are immigrants or the children of immigrants.[28]

Each day, the presence of people who have left their home countries to come here impacts all of our lives. From the people who work in fields and factories growing and processing our food to the people who work in factories manufacturing clothing to people working in hospitals, nursing homes, and other care facilities, the US economy depends on immigrant labor. Slave and immigrant labor constructed much of the infrastructure of the United States. Bringing the issue of immigration to your classroom means filling in students' understanding of how interdependent we all are and what it means to have the contributions made by Latinos, Asians, Pacific Islanders, Africans, and Native Americans ignored, appropriated, or erased. This segment is an opportunity to build relationships across the difference of national origins on the basis of an honest accounting of the roles all our people have played in the development of this country.

Reasons people immigrate vary. Some are joining family members who came in earlier waves, sometimes fleeing war, violence, or economic deprivation. But young people end up together from all the groups — those whose families have been here for many generations find themselves in your classroom with those who have come recently. They all bring with them questions of belonging: Where do I come from? Where do I belong? Who do I belong with? These questions by themselves are, of course, recurring features of school life, part of what it means for young people to become young adults. Belonging is obviously a theme in the formation of cliques, clubs, gangs, and the barriers built between groups of people in school discussed elsewhere in this book. For most young people, navigating where to fit in may be excruciating, but the process rests on a bedrock, taken-for-granted certainty — whoever I am, I belong here: If I'm from here, if not from this town or region, then at least from this country, the United States.

The school has as one of its missions building upon that taken-for-granted base: to turn each young person, through the daily school routine, the hidden curriculum, the background practices of American culture, and the trajectory toward adult livelihood, into a US citizen. What about immigrants and the children of immigrants, students for whom the bedrock is not a given but may (or may not) be something still to be achieved? What messages are they receiving, openly or implicitly? There may be messages such as, "You don't belong here," "Why don't you go back to where you came from?" and "Where are you from? No, really, where are you from?"

The United States has styled itself from the beginning as a "melting-pot" nation built by immigrants, whether free, indentured, or enslaved. Acknowledged less often is its early history as an occupying, colonizing enterprise; this version of history also renders invisible the presence of Native Americans. Detailed even less often is its history of identifying, managing, selecting, and excluding immigrants. US government policy has ensured that, although successive waves of European immigrants — Irish, Mediterranean, Central and Eastern European, and Jews — have over many generations more or less successfully assimilated as "Americans," generations of African, Asian, Latin American, Pacific Island and Caribbean immigrants have repeatedly been barred from entry, much less full assimilation. White ruling elites have worked hard to make sure that assimilation has only been possible for people possessing light-skin privilege, people who could become "white" — an effect of racism.

The latest expressions of that history can be found in the current chilling political climate immigrants face in the United States. Tighter residency requirements, borders militarized by government and "citizen" militia border guards, frequent unannounced raids on homes and workplaces by Immigration and Customs Enforcement (ICE) officials, multistate initiatives to detect and to criminalize immigrants, undisclosed massive detention and deportation practices, post-9/11 fears about "illegal aliens" fostered by media and the Patriot Act alike, and, more broadly, the elimination of affirmative-action and bilingual education programs across the country are among its most visible forms. How have your students been impacted by the current anti-immigrant climate? How are your colleagues and administrators dealing with increasing pressure to enforce anti-immigrant policies?

The Oppression of Immigrants

Anti-immigrant movements in the United States are part, finally, of *anti-immigrant oppression* — the daily, systematic, routine, institutionalized discrimination and violence against people perceived to be or identified as immigrants, especially those from non-European countries. This system offers small-scale benefits to people identified as "native born," or citizens, and large-scale benefits to a governing class that can keep wages low, workers divided, and the general population distracted from the real sources of political and economic problems. It is most obviously manifest in the names and stereotypes in daily parlance: "illegals," "aliens," "day laborers," "temporary workers," "wetbacks," "FOBs." Mixed in as well are class-based characterizations of these immigrants as poor, illiterate, opportunistic, violent, unlawful, and robbers of welfare, medical care, and "American" jobs. Recent immigrants have also been labeled terrorists. In short, they are often defined as a problem, or even, for some, *the* problem.

Intentionally stirred up by economic and political leaders, *xenophobia*, the fear of foreign others, is a staple of US life in times of economic stress. The wars and economic politics overdeveloped countries deploy to accumulate wealth in the global North by extracting it from the global South set into motion the pressures for people to immigrate to the United States. The overdeveloped United States benefits from cheap, exploitable immigrant labor in its industries and agribusiness. The result of such deliberate economic policies is the policing of borders; the ICE raids and the minutia of conflicting, constantly changing requirements for entry or temporary and permanent residence; and licensure and identification of all kinds—passports, visas, green cards, and the rest—that have become a fixture of first- and second-generation immigrant life.

What is rarely noticed is that immigrant labor in the United States, whether directly exploited or not, stimulates the economy and profoundly benefits the culture; studies show that reducing immigration reduces economic production and even job opportunities for nonimmigrant workers. However, what makes the headlines are conflicts, especially ethnic conflicts, primarily between whites and immigrant communities. As in other oppressions, the governing class uses immigrants as scapegoats, naming them as the problem rather than the inequalities of power and wealth that are the source of worker exploitation. Organized immigrant resistance, large pro-immigrant public demonstrations, and increasing involvement of some immigrant communities in local and national politics ensure that these issues will remain in the forefront of public life. On immigration matters, school is a microcosm for the larger society; immigrant students made invisible or treated as problems reflect the widespread stereotyping of immigrants as burdens. As a result, whether discussed or not, the stereotypes will be features of school life for immigrant students and those whose families have been in this country for generations. Although immigrant students may well be aware of these economic and political dynamics, nonimmigrant students are unlikely to know them.

Who Are Immigrant Students?

The federally defined, legal category "immigrant" technically applies to permanent immigrant residents, temporary "guest" workers or students, undocumented immigrants, people seeking political asylum, and refugees. However, even naturalized citizens might socially or quasi-legally be treated—and experience daily life—as immigrants. Your classroom may include young people from any of these classifications. They, their parents, or their grandparents come from cultures with different values, customs, family structures, gender relationships, codes of conduct, economies, first languages, educational systems, standards of health and medical care, and spiritual practices. They will be profoundly influenced by their generation in the United States, whether first generation (born elsewhere), "generation 1.5" (born elsewhere but arriving before age five), second generation (born here of parents from elsewhere), or third or fourth. There may be a pronounced difference between their family's educational and economic status in their country of origin and their likely significantly lower-income status in the United States. They may be transnationals, moving back and forth between countries. They may be the children of war. They each have a story that they may or may not have been able (or allowed) to tell. They may not even want their stories or statuses as immigrants to be told; they may fear the danger to their families if they tell. Without their stories, the end result is the unlikelihood of their full participation and the continuation of their invisibility.

Immigrant Student Issues

Here we use the term "immigrant youth" to apply to young people in all the above categories, regardless of citizenship status. In addition to the complexities they must navigate, immigrant students have in common some of the following barriers to full participation in US life:

- *Conditions of emigration:* Recent immigrants may be economic refugees, but they also may be and often are political refugees, having left situations of devastating armed conflict, some of these resulting from direct or indirect US involvement. Some will have fled countries ravaged by tsunamis, earthquakes, other disasters, or simply severe impoverishment. Some will have been adopted as children by US parents. And some will have arrived through the labor or sex trafficking of family members or outright child trafficking. Their situations may be traumatic and may include the abrupt loss of extended family and familiar culture.

- *Differences in generation in the United States:* Young immigrants' experiences vary in the extreme based on how long they have resided in the United States. To take one example, first-generation youth face all the barriers their parents face, but the "1.5 generation" of youth arriving by the age of five is much more likely to have mastered English and begun to understand—and embrace—US culture by adolescence. In turn, they may often function as the interpreters and moderators for their parents or other family in interactions with the US medical, legal, and educational systems, thereby driving a new wedge between themselves and their families.

- *Citizenship status:* A profound factor in young immigrants' lives is their and/or their families' citizenship status, in particular their documentation or lack of it. A pervasive and always changing lexicon of citizenship classification haunts immigrant families: Terms such as "illegal/legal," "documented/undocumented," "recently arrived/permanent resident," and many other terms are part of it. Youth in the United States from undocumented families face serious legal obstacles to work, higher education, driver's licenses, and the ability to travel freely. The simplest interaction with a store clerk, employer, school official, clinic doctor, highway patrolman, or airline ticket agent could result in deportation of their family or themselves. Even if the youth themselves were born in the United States, threats of deportation haunt them and their families. Finally, even youth from documented families will face questions, disbelief, and threats about their "legality."

▸ *First language:* The periodic US "English-only" movements — to require all education, voting, and legal materials and services to be conducted only in English — highlight the oppression for immigrant youth whose first languages (and thereby cultures) of their homes, families, and nearest and safest communities are not English-based. In school, this situation will mean longer hours required to study, limited comprehension of course materials, lower performance on standardized (and possibly culturally biased) exams, and a ghettoizing process that isolates youth from their peers.

▸ *Class:* For some immigrant families, migration from the original country means the loss of educational and professional status because of the refusal of US institutions to honor their degrees and licenses. For these families, a considerable drop in economic status, and thereby prestige and recognition, is likely to occur. Youth from families who fled impoverished or devastated homelands may be the first in the family with the possibility of graduating from high school and entering college. Students from impoverished families with limited earning ability may be required to work in family businesses or in independent jobs or even to drop out of school to contribute income to the family. Other immigrant youth may have to stay home regularly to take care of younger family members so that all the adults can work. The families of some immigrant youth may have to move a great deal because of economic insecurity, making it difficult for students to establish relationships or stability in a neighborhood or school.

▸ *Gender:* How is gender defined in different cultures? How do youth (and youth and elders) act toward each other, culture by culture, across genders? What is correct dress in public? When is it appropriate for a person of one gender to touch, to shake hands with, to embrace, or just to be alone with a person of another gender? When might these actions be frowned upon or forbidden or be perceived as improper or insulting? Entry into customary ways of being and presenting oneself in US gendered culture can be jarring for immigrant families, who encounter both the continuing dangers of sexism and sexual violence and the contradictory messages about gender, a highly (hetero)sexualized American youth culture, and feminist struggles for equal education, pay, and rights for women.

▶ *Acculturation:* To be born and raised in the United States is to know the unspoken givens of American life: how close to stand to someone you're talking to and how loudly or softly to speak; how to appropriately greet, address, and say good-bye to other youth and adults; how to shop in a mall; how to dance; what music to download; how to date, to dress, to walk, to play; and how to talk (or talk back to) teachers and other persons in authority (or elders in general) as well as what topics around race, gender, class, and the rest are likely to be unacceptable for open discussion. So youth without this taken-for-granted background will invariably be regarded and treated as outsiders by their acculturated peers and adults.

▶ *Assimilation…and race:* In the melting-pot story of immigration, assimilation over several generations into an "American" way of life was a given and desired destination for newcomers, part of the American story dating from the writings of Benjamin Franklin and Thomas Jefferson, which proposed a homogeneous culture and racial stock amounting to white supremacy. The acculturation process virtually assures that young people from immigrant communities will be pressured to assimilate, driving a further wedge between these youth and their families and cultures of origin. They feel additional pressure to fit in at school as well as to be part of the broader, much-vaunted US youth culture. For the first generations, this is a pressure to fit in; for the later generations, it can mean a felt loss of connection with the languages and cultures of their families' countries of origin, amounting to a loss of family as such. For all, rifts may develop among immigrant students from the same cultures about who really fits in and who doesn't.

However, unlike the multigenerational experience of European immigrants, the pressure for assimilation for immigrant youth of color is countered by the realities of racial discrimination in the United States that they face, which likewise date from the proposal for a homogeneous nation. Recent histories have documented the fabrication of that homogeneity, as early as 1691, in the concept of "whiteness" in the early United States. This racial reality resulted in generations of Irish, Mediterranean, Eastern European, and Jewish immigrants, among others, taking generations to be assimilated as "white people." A clear divide prohibits that assimilation for darker-skinned immigrants of Latin American, Asian, Pacific Island,

West Asian, and African descent. And the internalized oppression of racism brings about further well-documented cross-racial and intraracial tensions between native-born and immigrant youth of color, crystallized in the barriers between those designated as recently arrived and those who are the children of immigrants, one-up in (limited) economic and political power.

The ultimate barrier, of course, is anti-immigrant oppression itself. Altogether, the barriers amount to a simple, graphic divide between immigrant and nonimmigrant youth. On one side, students of immigrant backgrounds may be aware enough of the divide that they want most of all to ignore or to step away from it in order to fit in; on the other, nonimmigrant students carry attitudes ranging from simple unawareness of the issues to a touristlike interest in other cultures to outright xenophobia. How can this divide be addressed?

Taking Stock and Improvising

Youth from immigrant backgrounds need time in their lives, inside and outside school, to adjust, to be heard and seen, and even to heal, without their stories becoming exoticized for native-born students. Native-born youth themselves need perspective on the background and history of their people and on the political and economic relationships between the United States and the countries represented in their school and community. Given the potential risks of open discussion about immigrant backgrounds and statuses in your work with young people, in the beginning, be prepared to do a lot of improvising, building personal relationships among youth across the divide without explicitly addressing immigration. In the area of immigrant status, as with race, gender, and other divides, activities and informal gatherings that match up students across their differences and promote their social interactions through shared tasks, games, projects, and other activities are always recommended. In these situations, stories, bit by bit, may begin to be told. For these and other strategies, the guidelines we previously outlined for adult allies can be helpful.

Beyond this, you may wish to inventory the culture of power with regard to immigration issues as it may show up in your classroom, your school or youth center, and the wider community, enlisting your students in the study. What are the features in your class or group room — wall posters; types of world map depictions, if any; decorations; texts in use; intercom announcements; social media and Internet sites; flag symbols; and even desk arrangements — that may mark this space as specifically "American," white, and English-speaking? Are languages other than English visible in any of these sites, in particular related to those spoken by your students? What messages about other cultures or countries come through? How does the "American" perspective shape them? What non-US-centered cultures are represented in the history, social studies, math, and English curricula? How are they portrayed? How do these show up in the institution and the wider community?

In turn, how do your own and your institutional policies and practices shape your relationship with immigrant students? In your classroom, how might English-language and American or Anglo-centric cultural values show up in such areas as initial student placement, testing, grading, promotion, and who is called upon most often and easily in class?

Finally, you may wish to gauge the local and regional communities your students inhabit. Do cultural organizations, community-based associations, parent groups, advocacy groups, or faith communities serve and speak for immigrant families in the area? How does your institution relate to them, and how could these relationships be deepened? How could these sources provide you with information about the social, legal, and political climate for young people and their families, including any discriminations and dangers they face? What steps could you and your institution take, including developing and changing your physical environment and policies, to build public alliances with these groups?

Nonimmigrant students are living and growing into adulthood within a diverse and international society. They must have an understanding of immigrant communities and of the systematic oppression these people face so that they are prepared for respectful interaction and alliance with immigrants. And all students need to have an understanding of the powerful role that immigrants have played in the history of the United States, despite ongoing efforts by the powerful to rewrite that history.

Immigrant youth have the right to full and equitable education as well as fair and just treatment, including safety and due process in all negotiations for citizenship. They have the capacities, like all youth, for leadership, civic engagement, and voice. All your students have the capacity to challenge unfair immigration practices and advocate, not for assimilation but for justice, an end to exploitation and a genuine opening and welcoming to differences and full inclusion. Each next step you take supports that opening.

ENVIRONMENTAL JUSTICE

Obviously, social justice is concerned with human's social, economic, and political relationships. But what about human relationships with our environments? This section addresses environmental justice: a concept that suggests there is a system of oppression — humans over the rest of the natural world — and provides an opportunity to use the social justice framework presented in Section 2 to analyze issues that touch everyone's lives and are of immediate concern to many young people. How do we apply concepts of social justice to our relationship with the natural and manufactured worlds in which we live? How do we navigate our cohabitation of the planet with plants and other living families and species, land, water, and air masses — the life and spirit of which the environment is composed?

Environmental justice can be loosely defined as the fair and equitable sharing of and care for the earth and its life-forms as well as remediation for the costs of human-caused damage to natural and human en-

vironments, especially as this touches on the new discoveries about global warming in the last two decades. Those costs, in the forms of rapid depletion of natural resources and related environmental degradation, clearly show up in the vast differences between those who consume most and those who consume least as well as the toxic environments in which targeted populations live and from which nontargeted populations are insulated. Insofar as human and other-than-human habitation and survival are at issue, environmental justice may actually be of the most importance for young people who are in the process of coming to grips with social justice, because it moves beyond our human-centeredness to include all life. Here, too, who "we" are and how "we" are going to live together are of ultimate concern.

Human supremacy, sometimes described as "speciesism," human-centeredness, or anthropocentrism, names the deep cultural beliefs that humans are superior to and should be in charge of all life on earth. Citing such factors as our ability to develop language, our use of tools, or our superior minds, some Western philosophies proclaim our separation from animals and plants. Christian belief systems, for example, underscore this, citing the Old Testament teachings that God put humans in charge and gave them dominion over all life.

Multinational corporate capitalism has also emphasized human dominance over and use of the earth and its resources, justifying almost any form of exploitation and destruction of the natural environment. People are encouraged to consume tremendous quantities of disposable, unrecyclable products to support the economy and to distract us from deeper personal needs for security, intimate social connections, meaningful work, health, leisure, creative expression, community service, and a sustainable economy not based on the exploitation of land or people.

The belief in human entitlement, the disconnection of our lives from the animal and plant life around us, and the lack of a sense of the sacredness of all life are deeply rooted in our society. But social justice education requires us to go deep — to reflect on the roots of the problems we face and to help young people become critical thinkers about these issues. Really, nothing less will do. We cannot address the environmental crises we face with half-measures or less-than-radical solutions.

Indigenous peoples around the world who understand themselves to be interdependent and in mutual relationship with the earth and all life around them have recognized this fact for a long time and reflect this understanding in their daily practices. Recognition of the need for a deep rethinking of our values is also reflected, for example, in the new constitution of Ecuador, adopted in September 2008,[29] that gives nature the "right to exist, persist, maintain, and regenerate its vital cycles, structure, functions, and its processes in evolution" while mandating that the government take "precaution and restriction measures in all the activities that can lead to the extinction of species, the destruction of the ecosystems, or the permanent alteration of the natural cycles."

Within our culture in recent years, the concept of dominion has evolved somewhat toward a concept of human stewardship for the earth. This change is a positive sign. If our political and economic policies were pursuing environmental stewardship, we could halt a great deal of our most environmentally destructive corporate, governmental, and individual practices. But the concept of stewardship still assumes that humans should be in charge, that we understand best how to care for the earth, and that animals, plants, and the earth itself have no natural rights. Rather than becoming more responsible stewards, humans need to learn to live in balance and harmony with the natural world.

The injustice of the devaluation and exploitation of human life that racism, sexism, and economic inequality represent is part of a belief system that devalues and exploits all life and denies the living spirit in all things. An exploration of environmental justice and the ecological crisis the world faces is one way to tie together young people's current concerns to issues of social justice. More importantly, it can provide an opening for an exploration of the deepest values of our society and the way that these values provide a foundation for all types of exploitation and violence. Such a focus can also provide an opportunity for young people to explore their values and their vision of the healthy, life-enhancing, and sustainable communities they would like to work toward during their lifetimes.

Many young people, of course, come to school and enter other youth programs with a deep concern about the future of the earth and life on it. They may have been watching with dismay as world leaders at international conferences, such as Copenhagen 2009 and Cancun 2010, fail to agree on or to pass significant accords addressing environmental problems while catastrophic environmental disasters, such as the 2010 Gulf oil spill, continue to occur.

Young people may have already been bombarded in their classes with suggestions for what they can do personally to save the planet—consume less, drive less, recycle more, buy local, buy fair trade—admonitions that in themselves are incommensurate with the magnitude of the environmental problems we face. Seen this way, the admonitions make it seem that changing how and what we consume—buy—count as the solutions for these problems. Accordingly, corporations can "greenwash" their actions and products by making outrageous claims about the environmentally healthy impact of buying more and more green items. In the end, while highlighting personal choice and responsibility, these admonitions mask the deeper social forces that produce these problems and the unequal burdens they place on target and nontarget populations, not to mention their effects on other species.

Those of us with privilege in "overdeveloped" countries do need to simplify our lives and make more environmentally conscious decisions. However, consumer choice is not a substitute for organizational and institutional change. A great deal of the most destructive environmental impact is produced by wars, such as those in which the United States is engaged, or by oil, gas, and mineral extraction, logging, agribusiness, and fishing by multinational corporations that bring back profits for the "overdeveloped" world. The impact of colonialism and neocolonialism have created extreme inequalities of wealth; "overdeveloped" countries contribute a disproportionate share of global-warming effects and "de-developed" (exploited) countries take the heaviest part of the burden with the least amount of resources to compensate for the impact. A leading instance of the disproportion is extreme weather—likely caused by global warming—such as Hurricane Katrina in the United States or the tsunamis, droughts, and floods in South and East Asia, the South Pacific, Africa, and the Caribbean. These impact women, poor people, and men and women of color much, much more than wealthier and whiter populations. We cannot begin to talk about environmental justice without at the same time talking about gender, racial, and economic justice and the relationship of humans to the rest of the planet.

All this is to say that, because many young people care about environmental issues, have already been exposed to some information about them, and have many local opportunities to plug into and participate in environmental actions, environmental justice is an excellent issue to use to give them an understanding of the interconnections between social justice issues as well as a chance to participate actively in making a difference in their own community. It can also lead to an examination of the deeper values that justify the exploitation and violence of all life.

The following are some of the environmental topics that can be used for research and discussion within a social justice framework. Any of these topics can be explored not only in terms of their environmental impact but also in terms of sexism, racism, economic inequality, and other issues of oppression:

▸ water availability, quality, usage, and environment impact

▸ food production

▸ waste management and toxic-waste disposal

▸ energy

▸ plastic

▸ oil

▸ pollution

▸ transportation

▸ genetic modification of plant and animal species

▸ mining

▸ timber

▸ toxic environments

▸ sacred sites

▸ urban sprawl

Questions to Ask Regarding Environmental Justice

1. Picking any of the above topics as a starting point, what are the environmental issues with respect to this topic?

   • locally   • regionally   • globally

2. Where can you look and who would you look to for accurate and real-life information about this topic?

   • locally   • regionally   • globally

3. Who on "The Power Chart" (see page 33) is more likely to receive the benefits in this area, and which groups are more likely to bear most of the cost?

   • locally   • regionally   • globally

4. Research and map your school and local environment on this topic, making an environmental inventory of the following:

    a. How does this topic actually show up in your environment? List any examples of how it is produced or what it looks like.

    b. Which human beings are likely to benefit, and which are least likely to benefit?

    c. How are other species and environmental conditions affected in this area?

    d. What are the human institutions or people who are most responsible for the way this topic shows up in your local environment?

    e. If your entire class or larger local community were to take on a plan to alter the local conditions to produce a healthier environment regarding this topic, what/who would be your
       i. goal
       ii. people who should be involved in achieving the goal
       iii. first three steps to take to achieve this goal
       iv. plan to make this effort sustainable

Beyond this, in a history, social-studies, or economics class, you can study examples of how different political and economic decisions reflect different relationships to the natural world and have had different impacts upon it. In math, provide examples and problem sets that come from environmental situations: energy distribution and consumption, water flow, the economics of oil spills, and more. In health and social-living classes, address the impact of environmental dumping, toxic waste, and other forms of pollution on public-health.

The issue of environmental justice is particularly useful, because it can lead to deeper discussions about beliefs, values, and individual and social practices in our society that tie together all issues of social justice. But issues other than environmental justice can also easily be used to broaden the social justice framework and to enable young people to make connections with their own lives and actions. War, sweatshops, economic inequality, violence in the community, hunger, homelessness — each of these topics draws together individual-, interpersonal-, communal-, national-, and international-level concerns; issues of race, gender, class, and other identities; and history, politics, economics, literature, art, and culture. Although explorations of these topics lie beyond the scope of this book, they are the content of the discussions leading to deeper understanding and practical application of the concepts presented throughout *Helping Teens Stop Violence*, foregrounding most importantly the role of people organizing to bring about lasting change toward a world for all.

Being in the Classroom

Beyond what we teach is how we teach it. This section speaks to the "how." "Teaching as an Activity" discusses overall strategies for facilitating a classroom or group process; "The Agreements" are guidelines we ask young people (and ourselves) to agree to and to practice together to build safety and participation in the group. Finally, "The First Two Minutes" describes a process young people can follow to measure the "climate" in their school, to practice intervening in situations where they or their peers are facing emotional or physical mistreatment, and to take the next steps on the road to becoming full allies against violence. We close with a guide to the Making the Peace curricula — the detailed middle- and high-school programs, full-school campaign, children's workbook, and separate specific curricula for young women and men — in which the social-justice concepts of this book are applied.

TEACHING AS AN ACTIVITY

Walking into a classroom means entering an institution: a designed building, of course — and a room with desks, chairs, a board, artificial light, a front and a back of the room, and a teacher's place, in a building of many similar rooms. But it is also a legal institution, a place where youth are supposed to be during certain hours of the day, certain days of the week, certain months of the year; a social institution, where youth are permitted to be with each other as a group and to have relationships with adults not based upon family or local community connections; and a political institution, where adults are charged with supervising and training young people to become productive and law-abiding adults and to take their expected places in society based on their class standing, race, gender, ethnicity, immigration status, physical and mental abilities, and disabilities. In such a setting, how do young people learn? And what do they learn?

The Banking Concept of Education

Brazilian educator Paulo Freire has described one traditional model of education: The student or, more graphically, the student's head or brain, is a safe-deposit box, a "bank," into which the teacher makes deposits of bits of knowledge — the periodic table, the battle of Waterloo, how to enter a computer command, the life cycle of the paramecium. The teacher must be an expert in a field, a lone expositor of accumulated information. The communication — the deposit — moves in one direction. What is communicated is "outside" the student, in a separate world, impersonal, made up of hard and fast "facts."

In this model, education is an investment in the student and in the future of society, a passing on of knowledge/wealth. To learn is to accumulate as much wealth as you can and to be able at any time to display it. After so many deposits, so much wealth, you can get a monthly balance statement: the report card. The seats have built-in desktops, placing and bounding the student, while making a surface to write down, line by line, the facts to ingest and then to regurgitate on a test.

The classroom might look like what is shown in Figure 4.1.

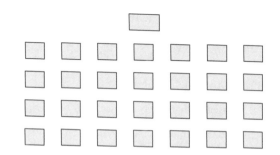

Figure 4.1. A typical classroom desk layout, with one larger desk in the front

Obviously, many classrooms are arranged differently; obviously, many other kinds of teaching occur. But our educational system, our method of performance evaluation (grading), and the arrangement of school grades and "tracking" of students into college-bound and non-college-bound segments turn people into containers to be filled, the world into bite-size objects to fill those containers, and education into the process of making deposits.

The Hidden Curriculum

What do young people actually learn, beyond the unrelated data or "deposits"? Education reformers have for years used the term "hidden curriculum" to describe what youth learn just by virtue of being present in a school and sitting in the room schematized above. Among the teachings of the hidden curriculum are the following:

- Obey those in authority.
- Be on time.
- Work on a schedule.
- Dress appropriately.
- Behave appropriately.
- Compete.
- Make money.
- Have a career or expect to be a failure.
- Take tests.
- Follow leaders.
- Belong.
- Accept the truth of what is presented to you to learn (and only one truth exists).
- Learning is memorizing.
- Knowledge is a set of data that can be learned and repeated.
- Most of what is important in the world was accomplished by great (white) men, such as Christopher Columbus, Isaac Newton, George Washington, and Abraham Lincoln.
- I am accountable for my behavior.
- There is one "normal" lifestyle that is considered most desirable, and it can be measured in part by what I own and what services I can command.
- Society has problems, and these problems have to do with individual acts and with individuals doing the wrong thing.

- I am capable of having or causing these problems and must watch over myself.
- If I fail to control myself, society has forces that will capture and punish me.
- My culture, and everyone's culture, is Christian and "American" and based on the English language, involving allegiance to all three.
- Our nation is greater (more modern than, more progressive, more democratic, more free) than all others. We bring civilization and these other traits to the world.
- What is normal and desirable is that some groups of people have power over other groups of people.
- What is "abnormal" is usually tied to people who do not have power.
- What happens to me personally or in my family or relationships is not to be mentioned here.
- I will eventually have a family and a long-term male/female relationship.
- The useful knowledge of the world has to do with physics, chemistry, and math; "English" is only useful because it is a "tool of communication."
- We live in a melting-pot society where everyone just needs to learn to get along with everyone else.

This picture of what we learn in the hidden curriculum includes things we all may agree are horrible, things that may seem good to many of us, and things we can't decide about. Some items on the above list may not ring true to all of us, and many items could be added — twelve years is a long time to be in school, assuming we finished high school. What is more important to acknowledge is what young people experience simply by being in a room, one that you are about to enter.

Teaching Liberation

An alternative approach to teaching is crucial when the subject is sexism, racism, adultism, and the struggle for social justice. Young people have experienced all of these and know more or less perfectly well what injustice, inequality, and abuse are about. Our work here is to begin with their experiences, to draw these out, to examine them, and to uncover the underlying social realities that cause them as a first step to changing them. With this analysis in hand, the participants themselves can begin to take charge, figuring out with each other how to stop abuse and to make the peace; they are achieving what Freire referred to as *conscientization* — becoming "conscious," or politically and socially aware. And because this work is personal, about real lives, and involves analysis and group process, the room and the teachers have to look different.

Facilitation

As the facilitator, your purpose is to bring the group together, making room for everyone to participate in a beginning-to-end process. In this context, facilitators learn as well as teach. Moreover, two facilitators working together can watch out for each other, share the tasks, and model the cooperative relationships we want young people to develop. This cooperative example is particularly effective where there is a difference of age, ethnicity, race, sexual orientation, or gender between the facilitators and that difference (if it is safe) is acknowledged and valued.

The Room

Placing the chairs in a semicircle (see Figure 4.2) where everyone can make eye contact with everyone else brings the group itself into prominence and makes it much easier for young people to interact with each other — a crucial part of the teaching. It can also work to have youths sit on the floor or on top of their desks, or you can have them move their chairs around the room to make themselves comfortable. In fact, what they may do is move into clusters close to their friends, which can allow them to feel safer about participating. You can use these informal cliques to begin discussion. Beginning in such clusters may additionally help you and everyone else to hear from existing constituencies, as a prelude. As you move along and add in icebreakers and dyads to mix students up, you will build enough safety for individuals to speak outside their cliques. Changing the room adds to the informality of the group climate. It also de-centers the teacher somewhat so young people can learn from each other and the facilitator can learn from the young people as well as facilitate.

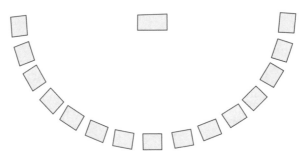

Figure 4.2. A semicircular layout

The Icebreaker

Icebreakers is our name for group games, warm-up exercises, and even songs or other music that further promote informality and a relaxed group climate. The usual classroom norms for youth are quite strict, if often unspoken: You have to be in a seat, sitting still, no laughing, no playing, no physical contact. This is, after all, how "serious" adults are supposed to behave. But often these guidelines can prohibit or inhibit us from listening to and learning from one another, and especially from seeing one another differently. In effect, they reflect the target/nontarget structure right in the human body! The topics we are gathered to talk about are serious enough without adding in heavy, adult-enforced behavior.

A single class period and a confined classroom setting may not provide enough time or space to do a group game. But in virtually all other workshop settings, icebreakers are important to use with young people and (even especially) with adults at the outset and periodically throughout the process. An icebreaker may be as minimal as everyone standing in place and stretching or as maximal as playing musical chairs. Consult any of the "new games" and "theater games" books for possibilities (see, for example, the Hunter House SmartFun series of game books as well as other resources in the Bibliography). Ask young people you work with what games they play.

The Agreements

The next step is to create agreements (see page 170) to promote group safety right from the outset. This process further alters the traditional setting by having the group take some charge of itself and enabling its members (including the facilitators) to make a commitment to respect one another and to participate. When a group makes and keeps agreements regarding confidentiality, "I" statements, and no put-downs, it is modeling the just and reciprocal relationships across lines of gender, race, and age that you are trying to build.

The Hand Signal

One final agreement to make with the group is the hand signal. At certain arranged points in the workshop (for example, during dyads), a number of people may be speaking at once. To restore silence and attention in the group without yelling "Quiet!" a facilitator will raise their hand; when participants see the raised hand, they (a) stop talking and (b) raise their hands. This signal is another way in which group members help each other take responsibility for the process.

The Dyad

A dyad is two people who talk to each other, one at a time, about what they are thinking or feeling. In a group process where emotional issues are up for discussion, moments will arise when everyone in the group will have things to say, even those who typically never talk. It is at those moments you can have everyone break into dyads, timing them so that each person in the dyads gets two to three minutes to talk to their partner about what is up. The talker uses "I" statements; the listener pays attention without indulging in cross talk or piggy-backing. Both agree not to break confidentiality later by telling someone else what was said. If the talker runs out of things to say, the listener is allowed to encourage them to talk some more, to repeat what they said, or just to stay silent and notice how they are feeling. These guidelines foster personal interaction in the group, allow every participant to get some attention, enable people who never speak with each other to do so, and make room for nontalkers to talk. (Facilitators can also use this time to think about what to do next in the group or to think about what they themselves are feeling.)

Of course, the dyad guidelines, by the typical social standards, are an unusual way to communicate. Few of us are trained to listen well to someone talk about what they are feeling without immediately interrupting to talk about how we are feeling, trying to give advice, or trying to solve the other's problems; next to none of us has the regular experience of having someone pay complete attention to us. So it is appropriate to have the facilitators demonstrate a dyad with each other at the outset, modeling for the group participants how to listen (and how not to listen). Here again, the time limit of a single class period may prohibit the positive use of the dyad, but it is an essential building block for longer workshops.

Role-Plays

Freire worked with his adult pupils by starting with the participants' real-life situations, making them the core of the work. What makes an experience a life situation is the way it captures or expresses a larger theme in the participants' lives. The life situations to explore involve conflicts people really face when power is being abused. Analysis shows that the conflict is based in a power imbalance kept in place in the society in which the participants live. You can construct a role-play to express this life situation. For example, you might use a father-son role-play in which a father berates his son for not being "man enough." The scene is a personal one that many sons experience; the theme is the abusive socialization of boys to be men.

In workshops you can role-play short dramatic scenes with which youth can identify, using facilitators or young people themselves to enact the parts. The process works somewhat as follows:

Stage 1: Present the role-play — the life situation — that workshop participants actually face. Part of this process may include facilitators' or participants' acknowledging their personal experiences of this life situation and how it has affected them.

Stage 2: Facilitate the group in unraveling the scene, identifying the conflict (the abuse), and thinking out loud about the possibilities for changing the outcome of the role-play.

Stage 3: Facilitate the group in discovering an underlying structure that sets the stage for the conflict to occur and the theme behind the structure.

Stage 4: Conduct a group discussion in which facilitators and participants collaborate to problem solve, to strategize, and to learn from each other how to change.

Stage 5: Facilitate participants' acknowledging and claiming the power they have to change situations of abuse and injustice, and make commitments of mutual support and empowerment to each other to stop the oppressive forms of power that have been passed on to them.

Some Final Guidelines for You as a Facilitator

1. Model strength, openness, respect, trust, love, and cooperation.

2. Encourage and support openness and growth.

3. Provide information about power and violence in society.

4. Respect the intelligence of everyone at all times.

5. Help each person identify personal issues and solutions to problems.

6. Provide a social justice framework for particular interpersonal situations.

7. Provide a variety of options and encourage the creation of new options for problem solving.

8. Do not try to force change on anyone.

9. Prevent people from trashing one another.

10. Emphasize that being rude, lecturing others, having an attitude of disrespect, or believing you have the most accurate information or the "correct" politics are all nonempowering attitudes.

11. Encourage and stress the importance of taking small steps toward effectively dealing with issues and participating in activities pertinent to those issues.

12. Acknowledge that people are already doing a lot of work to improve themselves and their communities.

13. As an outsider to any particular group, focus attention, facilitate discussions of people's experiences of power, share information, and focus on group self-consciousness.

14. Refer the group back to its own resources.

15. Emphasize that the group should obtain information and services through nonprofessional sources and networks that already exist.

16. In most general situations, and in some specific aspects of all situations, emphasize that there are some common issues.

17. Help break down the insularity of family and relationship concepts that prevent community intervention.

18. Model and practice community intervention — friends and family reaching out to each other.

19. Talk from the heart.

In Closing

Beyond the role-play; beyond the successful class, workshop, or in-depth training; and beyond your facilitation, this educational process pictures adults and young people — males and females of very different ages, sexual orientations, racial and economic backgrounds, and physical and mental abilities — finding common understanding, common language, and common cause to face up to the real conditions that limit us all. The solutions each group finds for its life conditions will be different. A process that works well will promote that group's making its own solution and making it work. A process that works brilliantly will empower that group to reach out to educate other groups — a picture of social justice–based liberation at work.

THE AGREEMENTS

Early on in classes or groups with young people, we help the group work out some group agreements. These are basically guidelines about communicating well: speaking for yourself, talking about how you feel, effectively listening to others, and so forth. These guidelines are important to make clear but sometimes hard to talk about without lapsing into jargon about "sharing feelings"; being "assertive," "aggressive," or "passive"; and the like. Speaking the language of "I" statements" and "talk about what's going on for you" can sometimes make it sound like all our problems, including violence, would be solved if we just knew how to talk — or, somehow, to talk better to each other. This interpretation misses the point that unequal power, institutional oppression, interpersonal violence, and internalized oppression make it dangerous for people to express themselves directly and to listen respectfully to others. The problem is not communication.

At the same time, the guidelines reflect a basic human fact about us: We have all been hurt in various ways and have had lots of experiences of not being listened to well, so we have developed a billion ways to protect ourselves from getting close to each other and becoming vulnerable to further hurt. Sometimes to break down these walls, we have to structure things a bit through the use of guidelines or agreements. It probably works best to get working consensus among the group, adults and youth together, to live by these guidelines for the duration of the group and to expect the entire group to do so.

1. Confidentiality

Each person agrees to keep confidential what comes up in the group, unless it is dangerous to do so—that is, unless a situation described in the group really requires us to get some outside help (for example, someone is being hurt, is hurting themselves, or is hurting someone else). This confidentiality means that I don't repeat what someone else says in the group outside the group without getting permission from that person. It also means that I don't talk to that person outside the group about what they said in the group without getting their permission. And if they say "No," it means no.

If you are a mandated reporter of abuse, you will have to explain to the group in advance that in any of the above situations you cannot completely honor confidentiality but will be working positively with youth dealing with abuse to get help.

2. Amnesty

As a companion to confidentiality, everyone agrees not to treat others differently, to blame them, or to hold or use what they say in the group against them after the group ends. This amnesty is particularly crucial where members have relationships outside the group, such as parent/child, boss/worker, teacher/student, or intimate friends.

3. Respect/Listening

Each person agrees to listen to others in the group and to expect that the group will listen to them. This agreement also means that one person talks at a time, and everyone agrees not to put down, to make fun of, to minimize, or to attack other people in the group or themselves. (Putting myself down happens, for example, when I begin my statements by saying things like, "Well, this probably isn't important, but…" or "This may sound stupid, but….")

4. Speak Up, and Share the Mic (*Microphone*) (Also Known as "No Divas!")

You agree to take a chance when you open up to others and help others take the same chance to open up to you. And if you find yourself talking a lot, think about stepping back and making room for someone else. If you find yourself being silent, think about stepping up and speaking.

5. Right to Pass

Each person has the right not to talk in the group when they don't want to.

6. Let It Stand

Each person has a chance to say what they want without having it debated, denied, or attacked, or without it being agreed to or supported. The statement gets to stand on its own, without being taken over by someone else.

7. Feelings

Everyone in the group will experience feelings of hurt, sadness, boredom, or anger at times. That expression of feeling is part of the healing process. Each person agrees to respect and to allow expression of those feelings, including their own.

8. "I" Statements

People agree to speak for themselves and their own experiences when talking and not to speak for others. This means using the word "I" in place of the words "you," "we," or "they." This is a very difficult agreement to keep but a crucial one. It helps us speak about what is true for us and keep close to how each of us feels. Much of what we have to unlearn, after all, is misinformation about "them," "you," or "us."

It can be good practice for those from privileged groups to learn to temper their opinions and generalizations by using "I" statements. At the same time, some young people may need support in speaking up and expressing their views, particularly if their previous experience has been marginalization or exclusion. Using "I" statements may also be difficult for young people from cultures in which putting forth one's individual views, especially as a young person or young woman, is discouraged. For this agreement in particular, facilitator modeling, ongoing practice, and gentle reminders will help.

9. Try on the Process

Everyone agrees to try on the process. No one is required to agree with it or to accept it — just to try it on.

10. Take Care of and Enjoy Yourself

Everyone agrees as much as possible to take charge of their own needs (taking stretch and bathroom breaks, making themselves physically comfortable, asking for help when they need it). This includes enjoying and having fun during the process.

We always finish with:

11. Other Agreements

Ask members of the group to add any other agreements they want the group to commit to for increased safety in the group.

Additional agreements can be made for particular groups; for example, about no drug or alcohol use, or the importance of punctuality. For extended workshops (over-

nights or weekends), we might add an agreement about no sexual contact between group members, both to build safety and to encourage participants (and facilitators) to notice what feelings might be behind the urge for sexual contact.

You may feel discouraged if the process of coming to agreement takes longer than expected. Young people may have never had a chance to explore how they want to create a healthy and respectful environment together. Because the agreements will be referred back to during the sessions, it is important that they get the time and attention they deserve. This process is crucial in establishing early on that young people are full participants and that you trust them to decide how to establish the group culture.

Sometimes when the agreements are established we will ask a group what it would be like if we lived by a set of agreements like these in our family, schools, and neighborhoods. What would be different? We might then say that to carry these agreements out into our lives, we each have some work to do. We might mention one specific agreement that is hard for us to carry out. We ask them to pick one of the agreements that is challenging for them and that they need to work at. We then ask a couple of people to share the agreements they have chosen. We end by acknowledging that we all have work to do to reduce abuse and to make our communities healthier.

THE FIRST TWO MINUTES: HOW CAN YOUTH INTERVENE IN IMMEDIATE VIOLENCE?

Youth are present in social and living situations at moments in which a young person may potentially be harmed, in a wide spectrum of incidents ranging from offensive name calling or jokes to physical or sexual injury. Many such incidents are related to prevailing climate and social norms in student life that ignore, permit, or support such incidents. They go unchallenged, because witnesses to such situations don't recognize them as harmful, feel prohibited by prevailing conventions from intervening, or expect or hope that others will intervene. Witnesses are bystanders. Over and over again, youth and adults ask in our workshops about what they can do in situations of actual or imminent violence. The questions come with an urgency that reflects the real presence of threats and outright violence in their lives and feelings of helplessness instilled in all of us by the twenty-four-hour news cycle and seemingly endless headlines about crime, disaster, and war. What can young people who have mastered the concepts of oppression, resistance, and alliance really do in "the first two minutes"?

In violence-prevention programs around the country, "bystander training" has become a watchword for promising strategies. It makes sense to equip young people with skills and practice to intervene — safely — in conflicts they witness as "bystanders." Enabling students to feel empowered to face, to handle, or to prevent some kinds of abuse also invites them to take responsibility for doing something when such conflicts arise without waiting for others to take over or leaving it to adults.

However, it takes longer-term training to keep it up, to become allies to challenge social norms that, for example, condone or minimize incidents involving racist, homophobic, or sexist actions. Ongoing bystander practice can be and often is a foundation for becoming an ally. But in fact, being an ally is a lifelong task to be renewed every day. Short-term interventions based on a "here's-what-you-do-when" program that ignore the oppressive conditions that generate immediate violence can't replace this work. So while young people are resisting oppression and building alliances, how can they come to practice resistance and alliances in the day-to-day incidents they encounter?

You can design a short-term training commensurate with the goal of alliance, focused on what students can (safely) do to support each other in intervening *while* they are learning to become better allies. Here are elements for a sample agenda, beginning with researching the climate in the school: What incidents might count as situations to intervene in?

1. The Climate

Climate stands for the overall conditions of safety *for all students* at your school or institution: the weather. What is the weather like for your students, and for you? The climate in any locale — how students feel about being there — is a quick background indicator for what kinds of hurtful situations might arise. Where the climate for some is unsafe, everyone is a little less safe, and incidents of putdowns and abuse are more likely to show up. A long-standing model for gauging climate is the "nature of prejudice" pyramid that Gordon Allport developed in 1954 (see Figure 4.3).[30]

A climate in which put-downs, jokes about difference, and even hate-speech acts are widespread can be the grounds for some groups of students to begin to *avoid* other groups of students, especially those targeted for their "otherness" — target groups. (Allport labeled these acts "antilocutions.") Left in place, avoidance can become outright *discrimination*, embedded in the practices and sometimes the regulations of any institution. Unless discrimination is interrupted, it becomes justification for physical (and/or sexual) *attacks* and finally *murder*. (Allport used the word "extermination" to refer to the genocides practiced during World War II.) On this model, such acts as the 2006 slaying of Gwen Araujo, a teenage trans-

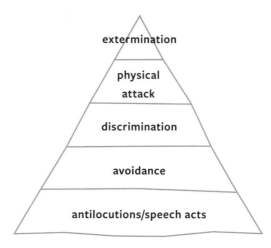

Figure 4.3. The "nature of prejudice" pyramid

sexual female in California, can be predicted, because the climate in Gwen's school and community was one in which (1) antigay jokes; (2) homophobic avoidance; (3) legitimized differential treatment, such as police harassment of queer youth; and (4) gay bashing prevailed. To the extent the model applies, students examining climate will be looking for the level of the pyramid that may fit their institution.

Climate questions to ask include the following:

▶ Do incidents of name calling, taunts, or teasing occur inside or outside the classroom?

▶ How often and how easily do students intermix by age, ethnic background, economic background, or other differences?

▶ How easily can students make jokes about those differences — or others related to body size, gender, or ability — that some would find offensive?

▶ Do such jokes show up in student publications, student media, or online comments or graffiti?

▶ Do all students feel seen and heard by you and other adults, or are there some who feel marginalized or excluded from classroom and school culture?

▶ If some incidents result in students' being suspended or expelled, are students from particular ethnic or racial backgrounds more likely to receive these penalties?

▶ What are the physical conditions of your facility — are the bathrooms and classrooms well kept and cleaned? Are doors, windows, and locks repaired quickly when broken?

▶ How safe does *every* student feel when speaking up in class? Walking through the hallways? Stepping off campus after school to go home? At events off campus or on weekends with other students, such as parties, games, dances, or concerts?

▸ Where does your immediate community of youth and adults fit on the pyramid above?

Your students can begin to gauge climate by researching it: developing a survey in the class or throughout the school. Such a survey, in bringing students' attention to climate issues, may actually improve the climate by raising not-so-hidden moments of conflict into public conversation. The "Climate Survey" in this section was developed by a parent and researcher, with student oversight, for a middle school in one of our Day of Respect programs. It can be administered anonymously via hard copy or online.

2. Mapping

Having determined levels of safety and respect, students can begin to map their campus, even diagramming it. Examining the facility and its environment, from classrooms all the way to where students live, what kinds of incidents are found that involve teasing, jokes, slurs, insults, unwanted physical or sexual touching, or fights? What incidents involve adults' behavior toward students? What conflicts based on race, gender, or other differences show up? When and where are incidents of various kinds more likely to occur? All this information can be voiced and charted to develop a picture of the climate.

3. Situations of Risk

Next, it may be time to consider actual situations of jest, insult, conflict, or violence in which students (and you) find it hard or dangerous emotionally or physically to intervene.

a. *Picturing a Situation*

Ask students to make themselves comfortable and to close their eyes or look at the floor. Give the following directions in a measured pace, allowing students time and silence to picture such a situation.

▸ Visualize a situation that made you uncomfortable — a situation in which someone or several people were making fun of, insulting, or hurting another person, you, or themselves.

▸ The situation might have involved a put-down or name calling, or a joke about race, mental ability, gender, or sexual orientation; it might have involved someone grabbing at or sexually pressuring another person; it might have involved someone you know who was hurting themselves or drinking or using drugs too much; or it might have involved someone beginning a physical fight...and you knew something was "off" or wrong, but you didn't know what to do or felt powerless or afraid to intervene.

▶ Take a few moments to look at what was happening in this scene: How might the person or people who are being teased, joked about, or hurt be feeling? What might be going on for the person or people who were instigating the abuse?

▶ Think about how it affected you or even affects you now.

▶ And finally, if you didn't intervene, what kept you from intervening?

At the close of the visualization, explain to students that you will have them talk and listen to each other for a few minutes to share what they visualized. Instruct them that a special condition of this discussion is that they agree not to use proper names or otherwise identify individuals as they report on the experiences they visualized.

b. Dyad/Triad

Have students form a dyad/triad in which they can take turns talking about the situations they visualized and what might have made it hard to intervene.

c. Report Back

Distribute slips of paper to students. Have them anonymously write down one or two sentences describing the kinds of risky situations they thought of. When they finish, collect the papers. Then take a few moments to read a sample of the writings out loud to the full class.

4. Barriers

Convene a group discussion on barriers based on the following scenario:

▶ Imagine you were a witness to any of the situations we read aloud from the slips of paper or go back to the situation you discussed in your dyad/triad, the situation you thought of. What gets in the way of your intervening? Talk about barriers to being an ally in this situation, such as fears, defying conventions, or becoming a target of violence.

▶ Define the "default position": What happens if no one does anything to stop the violence? What is the effect of not intervening? On anyone directly targeted? On everyone else? On you?

▶ What would it take for you to intervene? What kind of backup would you need from other students?

5. Taking a Stand: The Road Map

What kinds of actions can be taken to deal with a risky situation? The spectrum includes:

Figure 4.4. The spectrum of actions

Briefly review the following five-step guide for witnesses to take any of the actions, from being (visibly) present to doing something.

When you witness someone being hurt, put down, or targeted, in a situation showing up anywhere on the pyramid, from jokes to avoidance to discrimination to physical violence, what can you do? What can you do with the help of others? This is a *road map* (see Figure 4.5 below).

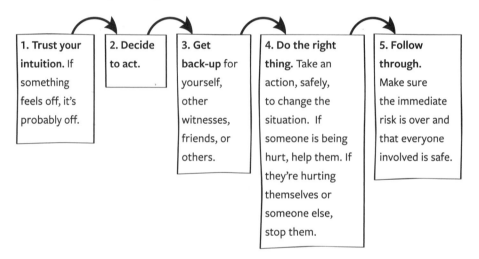

Figure 4.5. The road map

Take one of the risky situations that has been mentioned so far and have students brainstorm responses to this situation following each of the five steps above.

- ▶ How can you tell that something is "off" in this situation?
- ▶ What would it take for you to decide to act?
- ▶ What kind of backup could you quickly find, if any, to help intervene safely?
- ▶ What kinds of "right things" can be done safely to interrupt and to change the situation?
- ▶ Finally, what would be your next steps to make sure the situation won't recur or escalate?

6. "First-Two-Minutes" Role-Plays

Form six- to eight-member groups. The task of each group will be to imagine a risky situation and figure out how to intervene immediately to stop mistreatment. The group can pick a scene someone in the group has already visualized and written about or one of the following suggestions:

▸ a sexist, racist, ableist, or homophobic remark/joke is made in an all-men or all-women group

▸ a dangerous dare

▸ a possessive boyfriend

▸ urging alcohol on someone already drunk at a party

▸ hazing

▸ someone hurting themselves: over- or undereating, cutting, withdrawing, isolating

The group has the option of creating a role-play of an intervention or brainstorming a list of the top ten things a witness could do, following the road map.

For groups inventing role-plays, the following format is suggested:

▸ Each role-play is three to four minutes long.

▸ One of the actors introduces the role-play, briefly summarizing what is going to happen and identifying the actors and the characters they are playing.

▸ The role-play depicts a scenario of someone being hurt or put down. Each role-play includes at least four actors — two actors involved in the hurt at issue, one bystander who does nothing, and one bystander who does the intervention.

▸ The role-play develops the scene — goes on long enough so that the audience understands what is happening (what the hurt is) in the role-play — before the witness does the intervention.

▸ In preparing the role-play, actors agree among themselves ahead of time on a closing line or closing action — something that one of them says or does that signals the close of the role-play.

▸ At the close of the role-play, the actors involved in the hurtful action and the bystander who does nothing stay in character for a few moments on stage to enable audience members to talk to them or to ask questions. If time allows, the actors reenact the "intervention" part of the role-play with different audience members taking the part of the intervening witness.

For groups that are ready, have them take turns describing their scenarios and presenting their top-ten lists or performing their role-plays. For either presentation or performance, have other students respond with the following:

- ▸ Who is being hurt/targeted in the scene and who is performing the hurt?
- ▸ Where does this show up on the "nature of prejudice" pyramid on page 175 and what does it say about the overall climate?
- ▸ What actions do they agree with and what additional actions might they take?

7. Beyond Bystander to Ally

Review the definition of "ally": someone who takes a stand of solidarity with someone who is being targeted for oppression — a stand to dismantle the oppression and to support the targeted person's being 100 percent powerful. Review the actions of the "bystanders" who decided to intervene in the above scenarios:

- ▸ What did each of them do that put them in the role of being an ally?
- ▸ What else could each of them do, beyond the immediate situation — the "first two minutes" — to act as full allies? What changes in the larger environment could they work with others to achieve? What would be next steps in making this happen?

8. Commitments

- ▸ Distribute small pieces of paper or sticky notes. Have students anonymously write words of a pledge or commitment each will personally make as a next step to being a full ally. After a few moments, have them come up and tape or post commitments on a prepared poster.
- ▸ Group process: As a closing, have students volunteer to vocalize their commitments.

CLIMATE SURVEY[31]

The purpose of this survey is to get *your help to build respect and safety at school*. Please do NOT put your name of this survey. All information will remain confidential.

1. What grade are you in?
   ○ 6th   ○ 7th   ○ 8th   ○ 9th   ○ 10th   ○ 11th   ○ 12th

2. Do you feel a part of school life?
   ○ not at all   ○ some of the time   ○ most of the time   ○ all the time

3. How safe do you feel while at school?
   O very safe   O safe   O somewhat unsafe   O very unsafe

4. I feel comfortable walking through the halls.
   O not at all   O some of the time   O most of the time   O all the time

5. Is bullying and teasing a problem at school?
   O a very big problem   O a moderate problem   O a small problem
   O not a problem

6. What form does the teasing or bullying take? (check all that apply)
   O teasing   O name calling   O threats/intimidation   O sexual pressure
   O pushing and shoving   O physical aggression   O other

7. What do students at school get teased or bullied for? (check all that apply)
   O physical characteristics   O social skills   O cliques to which they belong
   O physical or mental or learning disability   O clothes they wear
   O economic status   O grades   O sexual orientation
   O gender ethnic group to which they belong   O immigrant status
   O their speech, language, or accent   O grade level   O other

	Not at all	Some of the time	Most of the time	All the time
8. In the last two months, how often have you been teased or bullied while at school?	O	O	O	O
9. In the last two months, how often have you teased or bullied someone at school?	O	O	O	O
10. Do students treat each other with respect at school?	O	O	O	O
11. Do students make jokes or use language that is disrespectful?	O	O	O	O
12. Do you make jokes or use language that is disrespectful?	O	O	O	O
13. Do students make comments about other students' body size or shape (such as too fat or skinny)?	O	O	O	O

(cont'd.)

	Not at all	Some of the time	Most of the time	All the time
14. Do students at school respect ethnic and racial differences?	O	O	O	O
15. Do students at school respect differences in citizenship status?	O	O	O	O
16. Do school teachers and administrators respect ethnic and racial differences?	O	O	O	O
17. Have *you personally* experienced ethnic, racial, religious, or gender discrimination at school?	O	O	O	O
18. Do students respect people's sexual orientation or the way they express their gender (lesbian, gay, bisexual, transgender) at school?	O	O	O	O
19. Do students respect people's economic backgrounds at school?	O	O	O	O
20. Are male and female students respectful of each other at school?	O	O	O	O
21. Do teachers and administrators respect female students at school?	O	O	O	O
22. Do teachers and administrators respect male students at school?	O	O	O	O
23. Do students respect people with disabilities at school?	O	O	O	O
24. Do students make jokes or use language that is hurtful?	O	O	O	O
25. Have you ever made jokes or used language that was hurtful?	O	O	O	O
26. Are some groups of students consistently tracked into lower or higher academic tracks than others?	O	O	O	O
27. Are some groups consistently disciplined more harshly than others?	O	O	O	O

(cont'd.)

	Not at all	Some of the time	Most of the time	All the time
28. Are any teachers or other staff members verbally, physically, or sexually abusive?	○	○	○	○
29. Do you think teachers and administrators respond appropriately when abuse occurs?	○	○	○	○
30. Is there an adult at school whom you would feel comfortable going to if you had a problem?	○	○	○	○

What do you think teachers and staff can do to intervene in abusive and unfair situations more effectively?

_____

_____

_____

_____

_____

_____

_____

_____

_____

If you have comments or more information about respect, teasing, or bullying, please feel comfortable to write them here (all surveys are anonymous):

_____

_____

_____

_____

_____

_____

_____

_____

USING THE MAKING THE PEACE PROGRAMS AND CURRICULA

Social-justice education can take place in multiple ways. Ideally it is woven into the entire curriculum, the pedagogy in the classroom, and the practices of the school — all aspects of the educational environment in which young people participate. This scenario is seldom the actuality, but it should be the goal.

Every academic subject is amenable to a social justice framework, including math and the sciences. We include resources in the Bibliography that reflect this approach. Social-justice education can also be woven throughout the English, literature, history, social-studies, biology, geography, political-science, art, and economics classes being taught at most high schools. You also have opportunities to promote this framework in health studies and social-living classes, in community-service projects, in school clubs, in after-school programs, and in nonschool youth environments, such as recreational and after-school programs, residential programs, and juvenile-justice settings. Each situation provides its own opportunities and challenges.

It is important to remember that social-justice education is more than a curriculum, a pedagogy, or an attitude. It is the active application of principles of safety, inclusion, justice, and community building to all aspects of one's life and educational experience. The focus is always on building community, developing critical thinking skills, and learning and practicing how to work with others to change the world for the better.

With these goals in mind we have written several different curricula and other books for you to use and have listed many others in the Bibliography section of this book. The following have been specifically developed from our work and the work of our colleagues over the last three decades.

Making the Peace: A Fifteen-Session Violence-Prevention Curriculum for Young People[32]

This high-school curriculum is also very useful for training adults to be more effective allies to young people in their teaching and youth work. It can be used in a training session or a series of classes, or it can be woven into a semester of literature or social studies. It has also worked well as an orientation series for ninth-graders, college freshmen, or other groups of youth entering new educational settings for the first time to begin to shift the culture at a school or other youth-focused institution. The curriculum contains a facilitator's guide, curriculum, reproducible handouts and information sheets, and an extensive resource list. Direct application of the model outlined in this book can be found in detailed lesson plans for class sessions on the following topics:

- what violence is
- the roots of violence
- becoming allies
- how violence is learned
- race
- class
- gender

The final sections of the curriculum teach youth to assess safety inside and outside the classroom and to make commitments to prevent violence. Lesson-plan topics include:

- guns and violence
- self-directed violence
- how to assess your campus
- how to become long-term allies
- what's next: beyond the classroom

Making Allies, Making Friends: A Curriculum for Making the Peace in Middle School[33]

This middle-school curriculum is designed to help young people develop social skills and to build cross-cultural relations, to see themselves as active members of a caring community, and to be able to work with others to transform the world around them. It works well as a stand-alone series of sessions or when it is woven into students' regular coursework. The exercises are easily adaptable to a wide variety of youth settings. As a companion to *Making the Peace*, this curriculum also has a facilitator's guide, handouts, detailed lesson plans, and resources geared toward middle-school youth.

Part One sets the foundations. It includes class sessions on:

- building respect, safety, and setting agreements
- my personal identity and the people I come from
- the heart exercise
- my family and my community
- roots of violence
- power and power over: the Power Chart and target and nontarget groups
- being an ally

Parts Two through Five are modules on dealing with particular oppressions and immediate violence.

Part Two, "Building Bridges across Race and Ethnicity," outlines the following class sessions:

▸ racism and the heart exercise

▸ racism on the Power Chart

▸ race and history

▸ how to analyze cultural bias

▸ researching truth in history: textbook and alternative accounts of US historical events and African American, Asian American, Latin American, and Native American groups

▸ critical media skills and positive cultural images

▸ resistance and alliance

Part Three, "Understanding and Alliances Across Gender Differences," presents sessions on these topics:

▸ introduction to gender

▸ act like a man/act like a lady box

▸ gender equity

▸ unlearning heterosexism

▸ understanding transgender

▸ building alliances across gender

Part Four, "Alliances Across Class Differences," offers five class sessions:

▸ introduction to class

▸ the American dream (The Class Race exercise)

▸ the economic pyramid

▸ getting by and getting together

▸ building alliances across class

Part Five, "Dealing with Violence Here and Now," contains six sessions:

▸ personal boundaries

▸ the bully

▸ dealing with physical abuse

- being a best friend and ally
- dealing with sexual abuse
- being safe and being free

Part Six returns to foundation sessions on taking the following actions:

- mapping schools
- analyzing our school
- research project on stopping violence at my school and in my community
- next steps in being allies
- the ally commitment
- evaluation and appreciation

Days of Respect[34]

This guidebook and curriculum outlines a full-day, full-school event conducted for all students by trained facilitator teams of students, parents, teachers, and administrators: a "day of respect" dedicated to producing a school-wide commitment to preventing violence. It includes a map and timeline, detailed agendas, tips for training facilitators, budget considerations, a student survey, and evaluation materials.

I Can Make My World a Safer Place: A Kid's Book about Stopping Violence[35]

Written for young people ages six to eleven, this interactive and illustrated book provides sensitive and simple information about physical, sexual, and emotional violence to help adults and children discuss and develop a plan of action for staying safe. It also engages young people in thinking about what they can do to encourage peace at home, in their neighborhood, and in the world.

Young Men's Work: Stopping Violence & Building Community and Young Women's Lives: Building Self-Awareness for Life[36]

These two gender-specific, multisession curricula help young men and young women (ages fourteen through thirty) come together and address issues of violence, personal development, healthy relationships, and community building, giving them the skills to become allies for themselves, each other, and the community. The facilitator's guides include guidelines for running the programs, the full curricula, and reproducible handouts and information sheets. Supplementary materials include a video and workbooks for each program.

Boys Will Be Men: Raising Our Sons for Courage, Caring, and Community[37]

The premise of this book is that the cycle of violence and injustice will not stop until boys are raised to become powerful and loving participants in the struggle to end violence and injustice. It provides practical tools for educators and parents to empower boys and young men to step out of the "Act Like a Man" box to become allies to themselves; each other; and all those excluded, marginalized, or abused.

Uprooting Racism: How White People Can Work for Racial Justice[38]

This book provides white teachers, youth workers, and students information about the dynamics of racism in our society, institutions, and daily lives along with stories, suggestions, advice, exercises, and approaches for working together to fight racism.

You Call This a Democracy? Who Benefits, Who Pays, and Who Really Decides[39]

This book for adults and high-school students demystifies the economic system and how class, wealth, and power work in the United States. It raises questions about what democracy means in our daily lives, communities, and institutions.

SECTION 5

Conclusion: Do You Have My Back?
Young People and Solidarity

Today, across the country, young people and their allies are fighting to reverse three decades of slashed education budgets; spearheading movements for immigration reform; protesting the ongoing wars on terror; battling the punitive trapping, treatment, and abuse of young people in the criminal justice system; taking stands against trafficking; and joining worldwide networks of people their age to confront global warming. Every one of these efforts is an emphatic refusal to accept hopelessness in the face of seemingly intractable social ills. In every one, young people are making commitments to have each other's back.

In this book we have outlined a model to use and short-term directions to take in preparing young people to prevent violence and to build just communities. But they have not waited on us to get involved. What has sometimes been slightly labeled as "youthful idealism" (or clueless optimism) on their parts is for many activist youth a clear-eyed recognition of the impacts of violence upon them.

At the same time, many other young people, beset by violence and attendant hopelessness, have also not waited on us, turning to gangs, interpersonal violence, criminal activity, drug abuse, or suicide to deal with their pain and anger.

In our model we have highlighted *resistance* and *alliance* as the principal tools for liberation of young people. But we understand that young people need practical skills and practice to use these strategies. What looks like resistance is always at risk of being turned by the society into another expression of oppressive power, as when girls learn they can rebel against parental and societal prescriptions for female passivity by consuming cosmetics and sexually provocative clothing. What looks like alliance is always at risk of conversion into the takeover or rescue of the oppressed, denying their agency yet again, as when adults unreflectively medicate or discipline young people they care about "for their own good."

What is at stake is the world we and they will live in — the one that *all of us* will inhabit. What will it take to make that "us" genuinely and globally inclusive? What will it take for large numbers of youth and adults to join to end systems of oppression and to reclaim our world from the corporate, political, and cultural elites that are doing their best to destroy it? To restate our goals in words we borrowed from Victor Lewis in the first edition of this book, what will it take to build communities based on safety, healing, liberation, and justice?

Young people's best strategy, the one combining the powers of genuine resistance and genuine alliance, is *solidarity* with each other and with us. This kind of strategy can be seen in play on every basketball court and in constant invention on the Internet (for example, Facebook and Twitter organizing, blogging, MoveOn .org, and more). For us to hold up solidarity as a real possibility for young people is only to catch up with what many young people already believe in, hope for, and practice as best they can. And to hold it up powerfully is to squarely face the war, exploitation, and violence that threaten it across the world. That is the work for young people and for all of us, together. The dignity, love, and sense of power with purpose that come with solidarity, with having each other's back, is also, of course, solidarity's great joy. Welcome to that work.

1. See, for example, Debra Van Ausdale and Joe R Feagin, *The First R: How Children Learn Race and Racism* (Lanham, MD: Rowman and Littlefield, 2001).

2. This article is adapted from Creighton and Vasquez, *Building Justice Facilitator Guide*, http://www.socialjusticeeducation.org, 2003. An earlier, shorter version can be found in the facilitator's guide to Myhand, Vasquez, and Creighton, *Making Allies, Making Friends*, (Alameda, CA: Hunter House, 2003).

3. The word was coined in the late nineteenth century by a German Christian writer as a faux-scientific term for the more explicit "Jew-hatred" in popular usage. He used the word to extol the (in his opinion) justifiable negative opinion of Jews that most Germans held.

4. Harrison Simms, Hugh Vasquez, and Erica Sherover-Marcuse.

5. We thank Ariel Luckey for suggesting this innovation.

6. We thank Ramesh Kathanadhi for suggesting this innovation.

7. You can start with some of or all the categories previously filled in if limited time is a factor.

8. Thanks to Ramesh Kathanadhi for this metaphor.

9. Adapted from Paul Kivel, *Uprooting Racism: How White People Can Work for Racial Justice,* rev. ed. (Gabriola Island, BC: New Society, 2011).

10. David Finkelhor, et al., "Violence, Abuse, and Crime Exposure in a National Sample of Children and Youth," Pediatrics 124, no. 5 (2009): 1411–23.

11. Copyright 1991, Paul Kivel, adapted from Martin Cano, with additions from Creighton, Amen, Myhand, Vasquez, and the TODOS Institute. In the many forms it has taken, picked up and adapted by programs across the country, it has also been titled Level Playing Field, American Dream, Privilege Walk, and Horatio Alger exercise, among other names.

12. *Net financial wealth* refers to all the wealth that a person owns excluding housing, minus their debts. It would include checking and savings accounts, stocks and bonds, commercial land and buildings, and so on.

13. For a history of these struggles and movements, see Howard Zinn, *A People's History of the United States: 1492–Present* (New York: Harper Perennial Classics, 2003).

14. Steven H. Woolf, et al., "The Health Impact of Resolving Racial Disparities: An Analysis of U.S. Mortality Data," *American Journal of Public Health* 94, no. 12 (Dec. 2004): 2078–81.

15. People from oppressed groups have long named the ways that those with power benefit from systems of oppression. We also, in particular, acknowledge with gratitude the pioneering work that Peggy McIntosh has done on white and male privilege. See McIntosh, Peggy. "White Privilege and Male Privilege: A Personal Account of Coming to See Correspondences Through Work in Women's Studies." (Wellesley, MA: Wellesley College, Center for Research on Women, 1988).

16. We thank Dana Kivel for this exercise.

17. This "working assumption" approach is adapted from Erica Sherover-Marcuse, "Towards a Perspective on Unlearning Racism," 1985, http://www.unlearningracism.org/writings.htm.

18. Exercises in the companion *Making the Peace* (Chapters 9 and 10) and *Making Allies, Making Friends* curricula (Chapters 2.9 to 2.13) as well as in the *Young Men's Work* and *Young Women's Lives* curricula continue these discussions. See the bibliography under Kivel, Creighton, Vasquez, and Myhand.

19. More specific material, including exercises on sexism and male privilege, is available in Paul Kivel, *Men's Work: How to Stop the Violence That Tears Our Lives Apart* rev. ed. (Center City, MN: Hazelden, 1998).

20. Copyright 1999, Paul Kivel.

21. Department of Justice statistics for 2000, http://bjs.ojp.usdoj.gov/content/pub/html/fjsst/2008/tables/fjs08st404.pdf.

22. Figure is from 2007 from "Recent Trends in Household Wealth in the United States: Rising Debt and Middle-Class Squeeze — an Update to 2007," by Edward N. Wolff, Jerome Levy Economics Institute, Working Paper #589, March 2010, available at http://www.levy.org/pubs/wp_589.pdf.

23. Although this concept is new, the actual oppression is not.

24. At the end of 2010 President Obama signed into law a bill that ended the military's "Don't Ask, Don't Tell" policy opening the way for gays and lesbians to participate fully and openly in the armed services.

25. Adapted from an exercise by Marsha Saxton.

26. Pew Forum on Religion and Public Life. *The U.S. Religious Landscape Survey Reveals a Fluid and Diverse Pattern of Faith.* February 25, 2008. Available at http://pewresearch.org/pubs/743/united-states-religion. (The 75 percent includes 51 percent Protestant and 24 percent Catholic. This means that at least one out of every four students is Muslim, Jewish, Hindu, of some other religion, agnostic, or atheist).

27. Rytina, Nancy. "Estimates of the Legal Permanent Resident U.S. Population in 2008" US Department of Homeland Security, February 2009. http://www.dhs.gov/xlibrary/assets/statistics/publications/ois_lpr_pe_2008.pdf. Hoefer, Michael, Nancy Rytina, and Bryan C. Baker. "Estimates of the Unauthorized Immigrant Population Residing in the United States: January, 2009." US Department of Homeland Security, February, 2009. http://www.dhs.gov/xlibrary/assets/statistics/publications/ois_ill_pe_2009.pdf.

28. US *Statistical Abstract*, 2010.

29. República del Ecuador, *Constituciones de 2008*, accessed August 6, 2009. Political Database of the Americas, Georgetown University.

30. Graphic by Sarah Gamble.

31. This survey was created by Susan Schoenrock, educator, researcher, and parent involved in creating a "Day of Respect" program at Stanley Middle School in Lafayette, California.

32. Paul Kivel and Allan Creighton (Alameda, CA: Hunter House, 1997).

33. Hugh Vasquez, M. Nell Myhand, and Allan Creighton (Alameda, CA: Hunter House, 2003).

34. Ralph Cantor (Alameda, CA: Hunter House, 1997).

35. Paul Kivel (Alameda, CA: Hunter House, 2001).
36. Allan Creighton and Paul Kivel, *Young Men's Work*, rev. and exp. ed. (Center City, MN: Hazelden, 2008); M. Nell Myhand and Paul Kivel, *Young Women's Lives*, (Center City, MN: Hazelden, 1998).
37. Paul Kivel (Gabriola Island, BC: New Society, 1999).
38. Paul Kivel, rev. ed. (Gabriola Island, BC: New Society, 2011).
39. Paul Kivel, rev. ed. (New York: Apex Press, 2006).

Glossary

ally: Someone from the nontarget group — or a different target group — who stands with others to challenge injustice; someone who will question and resist the institutionalized oppression a targeted group may experience by acting in solidarity with those treated unjustly.

colonialism: Domination and exploitation of the labor and resources of the people of a territory or state, a "colony," by another state or by a ruling culture within the territory or state.

conditioning: The physical, mental, and emotional training of members of a nontarget group to accept and to enact, consciously or not, oppression of the target group.

de-development/underdevelopment: Terms describing conditions in cultures, global locations, or states exploited, or kept in a client/worker status, by "overdeveloped" countries or multinational countries. De-development extends underdevelopment to include the process by which overdeveloped countries siphon off the wealth of formerly self-sufficient countries and literally force them into dependency.

guilt/resentment: Two feelings a nontarget can have when confronted with the target's experience of oppression. Either emotion can function to deny the target person's experience, once again highlighting the precedence of the nontarget over the target.

hegemony: A system of oppression that is so dominant that its worldview and key values are internalized and accepted as normal by those it benefits and even by some who are its targets.

homophobia: Irrational fear and hatred of homosexuality and anyone who identifies as anything other than heterosexual. Can also mean fear of being homosexual oneself or of even appearing to be so.

internalized oppression: The "internalizing," or believing, on the part of members of a targeted group, the lies and misinformation that the nontarget group disseminates. Internalized oppression is always an involuntary reaction to the experience of oppression on the part of the target group.

intersections: The combinations or "intersections" of multiple target and nontarget identities that actual people have and live within. Every person has a complex set of intertwined identities.

Islamophobia: Irrational fear and hatred of Islam and Muslims.

neocolonialism: The continuing domination and exploitation of the labor and resources of people from formerly colonized countries by people from overdeveloped countries or multinational corporations.

nontarget group: A group whose members, consciously or not, are conditioned to oppress members of the corresponding target group, to benefit from their oppression, and to collude with systems of oppression.

oppression: The systematic, institutionalized, pervasive, and routine degradation and exploitation of and violence against individuals because of their membership in groups identified as inferior by gender, race, socioeconomic status, sexual orientation, and other differences — groups on the "downside of power." Systems of oppression are established and then justified by ruling elites who gain power and wealth from their operation. Examples of oppression:

ableism: The systematic, institutionalized, routine day-to-day exploitation, violence, and marginalization directed at people living with physical, mental, emotional, or learning disabilities.

adultism: The systematic, institutionalized, routine day-to-day exploitation, violence, and marginalization directed at young people.

ageism: The systematic, institutionalized, routine day-to-day exploitation, violence, and marginalization directed at elders.

anti-immigrant oppression: The systematic, institutionalized, routine day-to-day discrimination, violence, and marginalization directed at those who are or are perceived to be immigrants or refugees to the United States.

anti-Jewish oppression: The systematic, institutionalized, routine, day-to-day discrimination, violence, and marginalization directed at Jews.

anti-Semitism: See **anti-Jewish oppression**

anti-Muslim oppression: The systematic, institutionalized, routine, day-to-day discrimination, violence, and marginalization directed at Muslims and people perceived to be Muslim.

Christian hegemony: The systematic, institutionalized, routine day-to-day discrimination, violence, and marginalization directed at Muslims, Jews, Hindus, Buddhists, atheists, agnostics, and other non-Christians.

classism: The systematic, institutionalized, routine day-to-day discrimination, violence, and marginalization directed at people with fewer or low financial resources.

heterosexism: The systematic, institutionalized, routine day-to-day discrimination, violence, and marginalization directed at lesbians, gays, bisexuals, and queer people. Also sometimes (mis)used to describe mistreatment of transgender and intersex people.

racism: The systematic, institutionalized, routine, day-to-day discrimination, violence, and marginalization directed at people of color (people of African, Arabic, Asian, Latina/o, Middle Eastern, Native American, or Pacific Islander descent) and multiracial people.

sexism: The systematic, institutionalized, routine, day-to-day discrimination, violence, and marginalization directed at girls and women.

transgender oppression: The systematic, institutionalized, routine day-to-day discrimination, violence, and marginalization directed at people who are transgender and people perceived to be outside the binary-gender system.

overdevelopment: A term describing conditions in affluent cultures and nations consuming an excessive and unequal share of world resources at the expense of "developing" or "underdeveloped" cultures or countries.

pansexual: Attraction to people not based on their sexual identification (that is, regardless of whether the object of attraction is male-, female-, or transgender-identified).

privilege: Unearned advantages or benefits that members of a nontarget group possess due to the oppression of target groups.

queer: People whose gender identities or expression is consciously not consistent with conventional standards for masculine or feminine behavior or appearance.

resistance: The challenging of systems of oppression by members of a target or nontarget group.

reverse racism/sexism: The claim by a member or members of a nontarget group (in these instances, by white people or men) of *systematic* victimization or oppression by a member or members of a target group (in these instances, by people of color or women), which is nonsensical under this definition of oppression.

sexual orientation: The specific gender(s) that a person is attracted to, including homosexual, bisexual, pansexual, heterosexual, and asexual sexualities. "Heterosexuality" is sexual attraction to or sexual activity between partners self-identified as male and female; "lesbian or gay sexuality" is sexual attraction to or sexual activity between two partners who both identify as male or as female; "bisexuality" is sexual attraction to or sexual activity with people who identify either as male or as female; "pansexuality" is a sexual orientation toward particular other people regardless of their sexuality or gender expression. The term "homosexual" is now widely discredited by lesbian and gay people, because it dates from earlier psychological classifications of same-sex orientation as a mental disorder. "Transsexual" is a term for people who identify as a gender different from that assigned to them at birth, in practice ranging from cross-dressing (although not all or even most cross-dressers are transsexual) to surgical and hormonal transformation. "Trans" or "transgender" includes transsexuals and anyone who identifies as neither male nor female, someone outside a gender-binary framework altogether. Some people are attracted only to people who are transgendered or "trans," and some are attracted to people who may be male, female, or transgender. In other words, multiple sexual orientations are possible. "Gender queer" and "gender neutral" are terms sometimes used by those who do not fall into traditional categories of sexual orientation, and "gender fluid" by those who move across (or outside) the spectrum. "Intersex" refers to people with sex chromosomes or anatomical attributes not considered exclusively female or exclusively male, whether manifested at birth or later in life. Some people may simply question what their identities are. And finally, people can be or can choose to be "asexual," whether simply living without practicing a sexuality or living entirely outside sexuality as such.

target group: A group whose members are vulnerable to exploitation, violence, and marginalization and are socialized to internalize their inferiority.

trans/transgender: An umbrella term for someone whose self-identification, anatomy, appearance, manner, expression, or behavior challenges traditional societal definitions of masculine and feminine, regardless of sexual identity.

transphobia: Irrational fear and hatred of people who are transgender and of anyone appearing to fall outside a traditional male/female gender binary.

xenophobia: Fear and hatred of people who are perceived to be not members of one's group or community.

Resources

The following resources are for adults doing social-justice education with young people.

Books

Adams, Maurianne, Lee Anne Bell, and Pat Griffin, eds. *Teaching for Diversity and Social Justice: A Source Book.* 2nd ed. New York: Routledge, 2007.

Adams, Maurianne, Warren J. Blumenfeld, Carmelita (Rosie) Castaneda, Heather W. Hackman, Madeline L. Peters, and Ximena Zuniga, eds. *Readings for Diversity and Social Justice.* 2nd ed. New York: Routledge, 2010.

Adler, Frances Payne, Debra Busman, and Diana Garcia. *Fire and Ink: An Anthology of Social Action Writing.* Tucson: University of Arizona Press, 2009.

Au, Wayne, ed. *Rethinking Multicultural Education: Teaching for Racial and Cultural Justice.* Milwaukee, WI: Rethinking Schools, 2010.

Au, Wayne, Bill Bigelow, and Stan Karp, eds. *Rethinking Our Classrooms.* Vol. I and II. Milwaukee, WI: Rethinking Schools, 1994.

Ayers, Rick, and Amy Crawford, eds. *Great Books for High School Kids: A Guide to Wonderful, Engrossing, Life-Changing Reading.* Boston, MA: Beacon, 2004.

Ayers, Rick, and William Ayers. *Teaching the Taboo: Courage and Imagination in the Classroom.* New York: Teachers College Press, 2011.

Barton, Angela Calabrese, Jason L. Ermer, Tanahia A. Burkett, and Margery D. Osborne. *Teaching Science for Social Justice.* New York: Teachers College Press, 2003.

Bass, Ellen, and Kate Kaufman. *Free Your Mind: The Book for Gay, Lesbian, and Bisexual Youth — and Their Allies.* New York: Harper Perennial, 1996.

Bigelow, Bill. *The Line Between Us: Teaching about the Border and Mexican Immigration.* Milwaukee, WI: Rethinking Schools, 2006.

Bigelow, Bill, and Norm Diamond. *The Power in Our Hands: A Curriculum on the History of Work and Workers in the United States.* New York: Monthly Review Press, 1988.

Bigelow, Bill, and Bob Peterson, eds. *Rethinking Columbus: The Next 500 Years.* Milwaukee, WI: Rethinking Schools, 1992.

———. *Rethinking Globalization: Teaching for Justice in an Unjust World.* Milwaukee, WI: Rethinking Schools, 2002.

Braus, Nancy, and Molly Geidel. *Everyone's Kids' Books: A Guide to Multicultural, Socially Conscious Books for Children.* Brattleboro, VT: Everyone's Books, 2000.

Calderon, JLove, and Marcella Runell Hall, eds. *Love, Race, and Liberation: 'Til the Whole Day Is Done.* New York: Love-N-Liberation Press, 2010.

Carlsson-Paige, Nancy. *Taking Back Childhood: Helping Your Kids Thrive in a Fast-Paced, Media-Saturated, Violence-Filled World*. New York: Hudson Street Press, 2008.

Cammarota, Julio, and Michelle Fine, eds. *Revolutionizing Education: Youth Participatory Action Research in Motion*. New York: Routledge, 2008.

Chapman, Thandeka, and Nikola Hobbel, eds. *Social Justice Pedagogy Across the Curriculum: The Practice of Freedom*. Hoboken, NJ: Routledge, 2010.

Chomsky, Aviva. *"They Take Our Jobs!" and 20 Other Myths about Immigration*. Boston, MA: Beacon, 2007.

Christensen, Linda. *Reading, Writing, and Rising Up: Teaching about Social Justice and the Power of the Written Word*. Milwaukee, WI: Rethinking Schools, 2000.

———. *Teaching for Joy and Justice: Re-imagining the Language Arts Classroom*. Milwaukee, WI: Rethinking Schools, 2009.

Cowhey, Mary. *Black Ants and Buddhists: Thinking Critically and Teaching Differently in the Primary Grades*. Portland, ME: Stenhouse, 2006.

Creighton, Allan, and Paul Kivel. *Helping Teens Stop Violence: A Practical Guide for Counselors, Educators, and Parents*. Alameda, CA: Hunter House, 1993.

———. *Young Men's Work: Stopping Violence and Building Community*. Rev. and exp. ed. Center City, MN: Hazelden, 1998.

Cushman, Kathleen, the Students of "What Kids Can Do," and Lisa Delpit. *Fires in the Bathroom: Advice for Teachers from High School Students*. New York: New Press, 2003.

Dalai Lama, The. *Worlds in Harmony: Compassionate Action for a Better World*. 2nd ed. Berkeley, CA: Parallax Press, 2008.

Darling-Hammond, Linda, Jennifer French, Silvia Paloma Garcia-Lopez, eds. *Learning to Teach for Social Justice*. New York: Teachers College Press, 2002.

Delgado, Melvin, and Lee Staples. *Youth-Led Community Organizing: Theory and Action*. New York: Oxford University Press, 2007.

Delpit, Lisa, and Joanne Kilgour Dowdy. *The Skin That We Speak: Thoughts on Language and Culture in the Classroom*. New York: New Press, 2008.

Derman-Sparks, Louise. *Anti-Bias Curriculum*. Rev. ed. Washington, DC: National Association for the Education of Young Children, 2010.

Derman-Sparks, Louise, and Patricia G. Ramsey. *What If All the Kids Are White: Anti-Bias Multicultural Education with Young Children and Families*. New York: Teachers College Press, 2006.

Dilg, Mary. *Our Worlds in Our Words: Exploring Race, Class, Gender, and Sexual Orientation in Multicultural Classrooms*. New York: Teachers College Press, 2010.

Giecek, Tamara Sober. *Teaching Economics as If People Mattered: A High School Curriculum Guide to the New Economy*. Boston, MA: United for a Fair Economy, 2000.

Gillmor, Dan. *We, the Media: Grassroots Journalism by the People, for the People*. Sebastopol, CA: O'Reilly Media, 2006.

Ginwright, Shawn, Pedro Noguera, and Julio Cammorota. *Beyond Resistance! Youth Activism and Community Change: New Democratic Possibilities for Practice and Policy for America's Youth*. New York: Routledge, 2006.

Grant, Tim, and Gail Littlejohn. *Teaching about Climate Change: Cool Schools Tackle Global Warming*. Gabriola Island, BC: New Society, 2001.

Gutstein, Eric. *Reading and Writing the World with Mathematics: Toward a Pedagogy for Social Justice.* New York: Routledge, 2005.

Gutstein, Eric, and Bob Peterson. *Rethinking Mathematics: Social Justice by the Numbers.* Milwaukee, WI: Rethinking Schools, 2005.

Hall, Marcella Runell. *Conscious Women Rock the Page: Using Hip-Hop Fiction to Incite Social Change.* New York: Sister Outsider Entertainment, 2008.

Highlander Center. *A Very Popular Economic Education Sampler.* New Market, TN: Highlander Center, 1997.

Hill, Marc Lamont. *Beats, Rhymes, and Classroom Life: Hip-Hop Pedagogy and the Politics of Identity.* New York: Teachers College Press, 2009.

Howard, Gary R., and Sonia Nieto. *We Can't Teach What We Don't Know: White Teachers, Multiracial Schools.* New York: Teachers College Press, 2006.

Kick, Russ. *You Are Still Being Lied To: The Remixed Disinformation Guide to Media Distortion, Historical Whitewashes and Cultural Myths.* New York: Disinformation Company, 2009.

Kivel, Paul. *Boys Will Be Men: Raising Our Sons for Courage, Caring, and Community.* Gabriola Island, BC: New Society, 1999.

———. *I Can Make My World a Safer Place.* Alameda, CA: Hunter House, 2001.

———. *Men's Work: How to Stop the Violence That Tears Our Lives Apart.* Rev. ed. Center City, MN: Hazelden, 1998.

———. *Uprooting Racism: How White People Can Work for Racial Justice.* Rev. ed. Gabriola Island, BC: New Society, 2011.

Kivel, Paul, and Allan Creighton. *Making the Peace: A 15-Session Violence Prevention Curriculum for Young People.* Alameda, CA: Hunter House, 1997.

Kohn, Alfie. *Beyond Discipline: From Compliance to Community.* Alexandria, VA: Association for Supervision and Curriculum Development, 1996.

Ladson-Billings, Gloria. *The Dreamkeepers: Successful Teachers of African American Children.* Brattleboro, VT: Everyone's Books, 2000.

Lee, Enid, Deborah Menkart, and Margo Okazawa-Rey. *Beyond Heroes and Holidays: A Practical Guide to K–12 Anti-Racist, Multicultural Education and Staff Development.* Rev. ed. Washington, DC: Teaching for Change, 2007.

Levin, Diane E. *Teaching Young Children in Violent Times: Building a Peaceable Classroom.* Gabriola Island, BC: New Society, 1994.

Lewis, Barbara A. *The Kids' Guide to Social Action: How to Solve the Social Problems You Choose and Turn Creative Thinking into Positive Action.* Minneapolis, MN: Free Spirit, 1998.

Loewen, James W. *Lies My Teacher Told Me: Everything Your American History Textbook Got Wrong.* New York: New Press, 2008.

———. *Teaching What Really Happened: How to Avoid the Tyranny of Textbooks and Get Students Excited about Doing History.* New York: Teachers College Press, 2009.

Louie, Miriam Ching, and Linda Burnham. *Women's Education in the Global Economy: A Workbook of Activities, Games, Skits and Strategies for Activists, Organizers, Rebels, and Hell Raisers.* Oakland, CA: Women of Color Resource Center, 2000.

Luckey, Ariel, *Free Land: A Hip Hop Journey from the Streets of Oakland to the Wild West.* DVD and curriculum guide. Oakland, CA: SpeakOut, 2010.

Marshall, Elizabeth, and Ozlem Sensoy, eds. *Rethinking Popular Culture and Media.* Milwaukee, WI: Rethinking Schools, 2011.

Martinez, Elizabeth (Betita). *500 Years of Chicana Women's History/500 Años de La Mujer Chicana.* Piscataway, NJ: Rutgers University Press, 2008.

———. *500 Years of Chicano History/500 Años de La Historia Chicano.* Albuquerque, NM: Southwest Organizing Project, 1991.

Meyer, Elizabeth J. *Gender, Bullying, and Harassment: Strategies to End Sexism and Homophobia in Schools.* New York: Teachers College Press, 2009.

Mogel, Lize. *An Atlas of Radical Cartography.* Los Angeles, CA: Journal of Aesthetics & Protest Press, 2008.

Moses, Robert P., and Charles E. Cobb. *Radical Equations: Civil Rights from Mississippi to the Algebra Project.* Boston, MA: Beacon, 2002.

Muse, Daphne, ed. *The New Press Guide to Multicultural Resources for Young Readers.* New York: New Press, 1997.

Myhand, M. Nell, and Paul Kivel. *Young Women's Lives: Building Self-Awareness for Life.* Center City, MN: Hazelden, 1998.

Nam, Vickie. *Yell-Oh Girls! Emerging Voices Explore Culture, Identity, and Growing Up Asian American.* New York: Harper, 2001.

National Center for Immigrant and Refugee Rights. *BRIDGE: Building a Race and Immigration Dialogue in the Global Economy.* Oakland, CA: National Center for Immigrant and Refugee Rights, 2004.

Nieto, Sonia. *The Light in Their Eyes: Creating Multicultural Learning Communities.* New York: Teachers College Press, 2009.

Olsen, Laurie. *Made in America: Immigrant Students in Our Public Schools.* New York: New Press, 2008.

Orner, Peter. *Underground America: Narratives of Undocumented Lives.* http://www.mcsweeneys.net: McSweeney's, 2008.

Orr, David W. *Ecological Literacy: Educating Our Children for a Sustainable World.* San Francisco, CA: Sierra Club Books, 2005.

Pelo, Ann, ed. *Rethinking Early Childhood Education.* Milwaukee, WI: Rethinking Schools, 2008.

Pelo, Ann, and Fran Davidson. *That's Not Fair! A Teacher's Guide to Activism with Young Children.* St. Paul, MN: Redleaf Press, 2002.

Perry, Mark. *Walking the Color Line: The Art and Practice of Anti-Racist Teaching.* New York: Teachers College Press, 2000.

Pollock, Mica, ed. *Everyday Anti-Racism: Getting Real about Race in School.* New York: New Press, 2008.

Praxis/Economic Justice Project. *Economics Education: Building a Movement for Global Economic Justice.* Philadelphia, PA: American Friends Service Committee, 2001.

Rethinking Schools, Ltd., ed. *New Teacher Book: Finding Purpose, Balance, and Hope During Your First Years in the Classroom.* Milwaukee, WI: Rethinking Schools, 2004.

Rose, Stephan J. *Social Stratification in the United States: The American Profile Poster.* 2nd ed. New York: New Press, 2007.

Sapon-Shevin, Mara. *Because We Can Change the World: A Practical Guide to Building Cooperative, Inclusive Classroom Communities.* Upper Saddle River, NJ: Pearson, 1998.

Schneidewind, Nancy, and Ellen Davidson. *Open Minds to Equality: A Sourcebook of Learning Activities to Promote Race, Sex, Class, and Age Equity.* 2nd ed. Englewood Cliffs, NJ: Prentice Hall, 1997.

Struyker, Susan. *Transgender History.* Berkeley, CA: Seal Press, 2008.

Szakos, Kristin Layng, and Joe Szakos. *We Make Change: Community Organizers Talk about What They Do — And Why.* Nashville, TN: Vanderbilt University Press, 2007.

Taft, Jessica K. *Rebel Girls: Youth Activism and Social Change Across the Americas.* New York: New York University Press, 2010.

Takaki, Ronald. *A Different Mirror: A History of Multicultural America.* Boston, MA: Little, Brown and Company, 1993.

Tatum, Beverly Daniel. *Can We Talk about Race? And Other Conversations in an Era of School Resegregation.* Boston, MA: Beacon, 2008.

———. *"Why Are All the Black Kids Sitting Together in the Cafeteria?" A Psychologist Explains the Development of Racial Identity.* New York: Basic Books, 2003.

Teller-Elsberg, Jonathan, Nancy Folbre, James Heintz, and the Center for Popular Economics. *Field Guide to the U.S. Economy: A Compact and Irreverent Guide to Economic Life in America.* Rev. ed. New York: New Press, 2006.

Ulrich, Laurel Thatcher. *Well-Behaved Women Seldom Make History.* New York: Vintage, 2008.

Van Ausdale, Debra, and Joe R. Feagin. *The First R: How Children Learn Race and Racism.* Lanham, MD: Rowman and Littlefield, 2001.

Vasquez, Hugh, M. Nell Myhand, and Allan Creighton, with TODOS Institute. *Making Allies, Making Friends: A Curriculum for Making the Peace in Middle School.* Alameda, CA: Hunter House, 2003.

View, Jenice, Alana D. Murrey, and Deborah Menkart, eds. *Putting the Movement Back into Civil Rights Teaching.* Washington, DC: Teaching for Change, 2004.

Wade, Rahima C. *Social Studies for Social Justice: Teaching Strategies for the Elementary Classroom.* New York: Teachers College Press, 2007.

Zinn, Howard. *A People's History of the United States: 1492–Present.* New York: Harper Perennial Classics, rep. 2003.

Zinn, Howard, and Anthony Arnove. *Voices of a People's History of the United States.* New York: Harper Colophon, 2004.

Zirin, Dave. *A People's History of Sports in the United States: 250 Years of Politics, Protest, People, and Play.* New York: New Press, 2009.

Publishers and Distributors

Redleaf Press — www.redleafpress.org

Rethinking Schools — www.rethinkingschools.org

Teachers College Press — www.teacherscollegepress.com

Teaching for Change — www.teachingforchange.org

Film Distributors
Bullfrog Films — www.bullfrogfilms.com
California Newsreel — www.newsreel.org
GroundSpark (formerly Women's Educational Media) — www.groundspark.org
Media Education Foundation — www.mediaed.org
New Day Films — www.newday.com
Women Make Movies — www.wmm.com

Web Resources on Adultism
The FreeChild Project advocates, informs, and celebrates social change led by and with
young people around the world, especially those who have been historically denied
the right to participate. Facilitates training and workshops and offers excellent on-line
database. www.freechild.org/SNAYR/adultism.htm.
The National Youth Rights Association (NYRA) is a youth-led national nonprofit organization dedicated to fighting for the civil rights and liberties of young people through
educating people about youth rights, working with public officials, and empowering
young people to work on their own behalf. www.youthrights.org.
Survey of North American Youth Rights is the premier Internet information source about
current youth rights, advancement of youth rights, youth suffrage, youth liberation,
and youth-rights issues. http://freechild.org/SNAYR.
Youth on Board supports young people to be an active force for change in all aspects of
their lives and ensures that policies, practices, and laws reflect young people's roles as
full and valued members of their communities. www.youthonboard.org.
Youth Wisdom Project. *Making Space, Making Change: Profiles of Youth-Led and Youth-
Driven Organizations*. Oakland, CA: Movement Strategy Center, 2004.

Articles
"Adultism" — An edition of *The School Mediator by School Mediation Associates*. Vol III
1/04 Includes definitions and quotes. http://www.schoolmediation.com/newsletters
/2004/01_04.html.
Bell, John. *Understanding Adultism: A Key to Developing Positive Youth–Adult Relationships*. Identifies ageism at all levels of society with examples and analysis. http://www
.freechild.org/bell.htm.
Checkoway, B. *Adults as Allies*. WK Kellogg Foundation, 1998. http://www.wkkf.org
/knowledge-center/resources/2001/12/Adults-As-Allies.aspx.
Males, Mike. Hard-hitting, fact-filled books and articles that break down adultist, anti-
youth media stereotypes. http://home.earthlink.net/~mmales.
Sazama, J., and the Resource Center for Youth and Their Allies. *Get the Word Out!* Youth
on Board, 2004. http://www.youthbuild.org/site/apps/nlnet/content3.aspx?c=ht
IRI3PIKoG&b=4807771&ct=6875811.
YouthLib.com. Tools for Youth Liberation Activists articles and blogs on youth
liberation.

Magazines

ColorLines — www.colorlines.com

Dollars & Sense — www.dollarsandsense.org

In Motion Magazine (online only) — www.inmotionmagazine.com

Left Turn — www.leftturn.org

Mother Jones — www.motherjones.com

Ms. — www.msmagazine.com

The Nation — www.thenation.com

Rethinking Schools — www.rethinkingschools.org

Teaching Tolerance — www.tolerance.org

Tikkun — www.tikkun.org

YES! — www.yesmagazine.org

ZCommunications — www.zcommunications.org

Organizations Providing Further Social Justice Education/Training and Other Resources for Youth and Adults

Anne Braden Anti-Racist Organizing Training Program at the Catalyst Center — www.collectiveliberation.org

Center for Popular Economics — www.populareconomics.org

Educators for Social Responsibility — www.esrnational.org

Highlander Research and Education Center — www.highlandercenter.org

Midwest Academy — www.midwestacademy.com

National Coalition Building Institute — www.ncbi.org

The People's Institute for Survival and Beyond — www.pisab.org

Project South — www.projectsouth.org

SOUL (The School of Unity & Liberation) — www.schoolofunityandliberation.org

Southwest Organizing Project — www.swop.net

United for a Fair Economy — www.faireconomy.org

University of Massachusetts Amherst, Department of Social Justice, Social Justice Education Concentration — www.umass.edu/sje

Western States Center — www.westernstatescenter.org

Conferences

National Association of Multicultural Education (NAME)

National Conference on Race and Ethnicity in Higher Education (NCORE)

National Organizers Alliance

Teachers 4 Social Justice (T4SJ)

White Privilege Conference (WPC)

Websites Offering Information and Resources for Social Justice Education

AlterNet — www.alternet.org

The Black Commentator — www.blackcommentator.com

Center for Economic and Policy Research — www.cepr.net

Center for Popular Economics — www.populareconomics.org
Color of Change — www.colorofchange.org
Columbia Journalism Review — www.cjr.org
Common Cause — www.commoncause.org
Common Dreams — www.commondreams.org
Counterpunch — www.counterpunch.org
DataCenter — www.datacenter.org
Democracy Now! — www.democracynow.org
FAIR (Fairness & Accuracy in Reporting) — www.fair.org
Independent Media Center — www.indymedia.org
IPS (Institute for Policy Studies) — www.ips-dc.org
MoveOn.org — www.moveon.org
Pacifica Radio — www.pacifica.org
Project Censored — www.projectcensored.org
SONG (Southerners on New Ground) — www.southernersonnewground.org
TomPaine.com — www.tompaine.com
Truthout — www.truth-out.org
Working Group on Extreme Inequality — www.inequality.org
ZCommunications — www.zcommunications.org

More Violence-Prevention Resources for Schools
The **Making the Peace** Program

MAKING THE PEACE: A 15-Session Violence Prevention Curriculum for Young People ... *Paul Kivel and Allan Creighton, with Oakland Men's Project*

Making the Peace is written to help young people break away from violence, develop self-esteem, and regain a sense of community. It provides exercises, role-plays, handouts, homework sheets, and discussion guidelines to explore issues such as dating violence, gangs, interracial tension, suicide, sexual harassment, and the social roots of violence.

The program is in three units. **Part One** explains basic concepts and establishes a framework of safety and respect. **Part Two** looks at the forms that violence takes. **Part Three** introduces individual and group activities that can help to make the peace. The opening chapter offers guidelines to teachers for using the curriculum in a classroom, and there are practical suggestions throughout. All handouts and homework exercises are ready to use and are designed for easy reproduction.

192 pages ... 15 photos, 35 handouts ... Paperback $29.95

MAKING ALLIES, MAKING FRIENDS: A Curriculum for Making the Peace in Middle School ... *Hugh Vasquez, M. Nell Myhand, and Allan Creighton with the Todos Institute*

This curriculum offers more than thirty innovative classroom sessions addressing diversity and violence issues that middle-schoolers face. The flexible design includes foundation sessions and four follow-up tracks of elective sessions. Each session includes a warm-up, theme information, and an experience or activity. Art and culture are a key part of the activities, which include journal writing, role-plays, murals, storytelling, and more.

224 pages ... 11 photos, 29 illus., 37 handouts ... Paperback $29.95

DAYS OF RESPECT: Organizing a School-Wide Violence Prevention Program ... *Ralph Cantor, with Paul Kivel, Allan Creighton, and Oakland Men's Project*

This manual is a step-by-step guide for designing and staging a unique, collaborative, schoolwide event that brings young people, teachers, parents, and the community together to create a climate of respect and tolerance in their school. The program, developed by an experienced teacher and the Oakland Men's Project, emphasizes hands-on practice in building nonviolent relationships and includes planning outlines and checklists, timetables, permission slips, training exercises on gender and race, and evaluations.

64 pages ... 6 photos, 21 handouts ... Paperback $17.95

To order call (800) 266-5592 or visit www.hunterhouse.com
Visit our website for details on Making the Peace posters and specials;
more violence-prevention resources, including the GROW and STARS
workbooks, and nonviolent activity books (the SmartFun series).
Prices subject to change without notice.